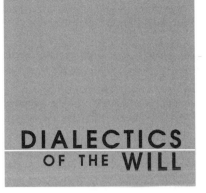

DIALECTICS
OF THE WILL

DIALECTICS
OF THE WILL

Freedom, Power, and
Understanding in
Modern French and
German Thought

John H. Smith

 WAYNE STATE UNIVERSITY PRESS
DETROIT

Kritik: German Literary Theory and Cultural Studies

Liliane Weissberg, Editor

A complete listing of the books in this series can be found at the back of this volume.

Copyright © 2000 by Wayne State University Press, Detroit, Michigan 48201.
All rights are reserved.
No part of this book may be reproduced without formal permission.
Manufactured in the United States of America.

04   03   02   01   00   5   4   3   2   1

Library of Congress Cataloging-in-Publication Data
Smith, John H., 1954–
    Dialectics of the will : freedom, power, and understanding in modern French and German thought / John H. Smith.
      p. cm.—(Kritik, German literary theory and cultural studies)
    Includes bibliographical references and index.
    ISBN 0-8143-2856-3 (alk. paper)
    1. Will.   I. Title.   II. Kritik (Detroit, Mich.)
BJ1461 .S55 2000
128'.3—dc21

99-047069

For my mother and father

Contents

Preface   9

Introduction: Dialectics and the Will   11

1   Historical Dialectics of the Will's Contradictory
    Determinations   29

2   The Free Will and the Cause of Desire: Kant, Sade,
    Adorno, Lacan   49

3   Will, Power, Will to Power: Nietzsche, Foucault,
    Habermas   91

4   The Will to Interpretation: Gadamer, Derrida,
    Heidegger's Nietzsche   125

Conclusion: A Dialectical Model of Agency and
the Will of Theory
(Feminism, Queer Theory, Nationalism)   167

    Abbreviations   179
    Notes   181
    Bibliography   223
    Index   233

Preface

This book began as a side project of another study and then took on a life of its own. I had been researching the phenomenon of abulia or pathological crises of the will, the male counterpart of hysteria, a phenomenon that cut across a wide variety of discursive fields (medicine, psychology, sexology, forensics, philosophy) in the late nineteenth and early twentieth centuries. As part of that research, I had to look into both the philosophical background of the concept of the will and some contemporary theories, foremost Foucault's and Lacan's, which interrelate the will, representation (discourse), and desire. I was struck in the philosophical literature by the dialectical knots formed around the concept of the will, the tensions and contradictions pulling it throughout its history in opposing directions, e.g., toward reason and impulse, toward freedom and determinism, toward metaphysics and empiricism, toward law and transgression. And I was struck by the number of contemporary theories in which the will, otherwise a term seemingly relegated to the past, plays a significant role. My interest then shifted temporarily from the study of *weakness* of the will to its *centrality* in discussions of such fundamental concepts as freedom, power, and understanding.

The argumentative logic of the following study is thus legitimated by the different levels on which it operates. The overarching concern is to sketch out a dialectical model of the will or, more precisely, the activity of willing. The contradictions that go into this dialectic are derived from the historical tradition of philosophical discussions of the will (introduction and chapter 1) and from three structurally parallel arguments. Each of the three main chapters focuses on one of the master concepts associated with the will—freedom, power, and understanding—and engages two contemporary thinkers, one French and one German, in a dialogue mediated through a common German philosopher. Hence, Adorno and Lacan are read together on freedom, desire, and the will against the background of Kant (and Sade); Foucault and Habermas are read together on power and the will against the background of Nietzsche; and Gadamer and Derrida are read together on understanding and the will against the background of Heidegger. The goal is not to show that one or the other of these thinkers is right or wrong or better or worse but, rather, to reveal how productive and fruitful they all are when the tensions between them are read as positive contributions to a dialectical model of the will. Such a model would maintain the freedom of individual agency to interpret and change the world even as that agent is recognized as embedded within structures of causality, power, and meaning. The will is that dialectical concept that unites the co-originality (*Gleichursprünglichkeit*) of the individual's transcendence of a situation that in turn, paradoxically, transcends the individual. The conclusion plays out some productive consequences of this dialectic for some contemporary theories of gender, sexuality, and nationalism.

Numerous organizations and individuals have supported the endeavor to write this book. For their generous financial support, I wish to thank the Alexander von Humboldt-Stiftung (Bonn), the University of California, Irvine (UCI) Research Committee, the UCI School and dean of Humanities, the Focused Research Project on "Women and the Image," and the Critical Theory Institute. For their words (and letters) of encouragement and recommendation, I wish to thank Professors Stanley Corngold, Sander Gilman, Walter Hinderer, and Robert Holub. Professors Manfred Frank and Jochen Hörisch offered their time and intellectual stimulation both before and during my research year in Tübingen. I also express my appreciation to my supportive friends and colleagues at UCI, especially the graduate students who sat through early versions of this project, and the Lacan reading group (particularly Professors Julia Lupton, Ken Reinhard, and Bruce Fink). Finally, as always, my loving gratitude to Professor Newman, Jane, for her willing and unwilling participation in this project.

Introduction

Dialectics and the Will

The concept of the will is certainly one of the major concepts of Western thought.[1] Although the Greek philosophers had no single term to cover what we would today consider the will, the discussions of Plato and especially Aristotle on the soul and the faculties that move us to action influenced subsequent theories of the will.[2] Christian thought on freedom of the will, from St. Paul, through the Church fathers and the Reformation, to the present day, has probably been the most fertile ground for conceptions of willing, with a particular focus on whether the individual or God is capable of determining actions (and ultimately salvation).[3] The dominant philosophical schools of the modern era—Empiricism and Idealism—faced off beginning in the seventeenth century (and continue to face off) over the role of the will, even its existence, in their views of human beings and ethics. In the nineteenth century, the will opposed *Geist* in the parallel traditions emanating from Fichte, Schelling, and Schopenhauer on the one hand and from Hegel on the other. And in our own times, philosophical movements as varied as analytic theories of action, phenomenological hermeneutics, structuralism, and poststructuralism return again and again to the will and critiques of the will.[4]

In all of these discussions, the will occupies a central position because of its association with other key concepts of the Western tradition. To have a view of a human being's place in the world is to have a conception, implicit or explicit, of the will, and vice versa. It seems difficult "to bracket the notion of willing out of modern political philosophy."[5] Whether we are free to act or must follow some laws and powers beyond ourselves, whether we are capable of innovations or are constrained by the events that precede any action, whether or not we have some core self, whether that core is knowable or not, and whether our understanding of the world is organized (unified) by that core or fragmented by shifting constellations of desires and sensations—these kinds of issues are inevitably, and with varying degrees of explicitness, at stake in discussions of the will. And these kinds of issues, conversely, generally presume some stake in, or against, a particular conception of willing.

Granted, it might seem to some readers interested in contemporary theory that the will is an outmoded concept. For some, it carries the bad aftertaste of nineteenth-century attempts to develop what could be called "irrationalist Idealisms" in a Schopenhauerian vein. In many discussions of Nietzsche, for example, the question is raised whether he "freed himself" from the historical burden of past views on the will or remained trapped in the "metaphysics of subjectivity" so often associated with voluntaristic philosophies.[6] For others, consciously or not under the influence of Ryle's critique, the will is the "ghost in the machine" par excellence, a faculty of mind or a special autonomous "stuff" with an untenable metaphysical status.[7] For those working in the wake of feminism, the will might appear to be a masculinist concept, universalized falsely to the "human" condition in order to justify a male mode of acting and relating.[8] And for yet others, the fascist atrocities committed in the name of its "triumph" have tainted the will so negatively with justifications for domination that it is in principle a suspect concept. Indeed, we could measure the gap that separates us from the beginning of this century by the fact that in the decades surrounding 1900, the will enjoyed a boom in philosophical and psychological attention, whereas now it has been displaced by focus on desire, politics, language.[9]

But the concept of the will (or its displacement in the analytical tradition into what could receive the predicate "voluntary") is by no means absent from contemporary thought. Obviously, theories of ethics and action would address the issue of the will. What forms the focus of this study, however, is the way the will appears where one would not necessarily expect it in modern and postmodern thought—indeed, one may be surprised to find it there at all.[10] There are specific and central points in the work of diverse contemporary thinkers—I shall focus on three odd couples, Adorno and Lacan, Habermas and Foucault, Gadamer and Derrida—where the will appears as an object of investigation and/or where a conceptual space for a theory of the will is opened up in their work, even if (generally to their disadvantage) the thinkers do not develop the implied theory. The mapping out of that space of the will takes us through these thinkers' central concerns, even where the will is not explicitly thematized. In other words, there is a place in contemporary thought for discussions of the will, and where this place is not appropriately illuminated, the lacunae left generate aporias that lead us to a richer conceptualization.[11]

My thesis, then, is that reflections on the will and the history of its conceptualization are crucial for working out positions in contemporary thought on such issues as freedom, agency, desire, power, intersubjectivity, and understanding. But these reflections, I shall argue, need to be dialectical in the sense that they incorporate contradictions. The reason is threefold.

First, a model that would account for human agency, for our sense of being able to direct our activity in innovative ways, for the ability to say "I want," remains inadequate if it tries to define these phenomena in terms of partial determinations that exclude their opposites. Indeed, the inadequacy is revealed by aporias that arise from one-sided, nondialectical (metaphysical) definitions. For example, to say that willing gains its strength by arising spontaneously, independently from, or even opposed to either mental representations or natural causality isolates willing from action in a way that makes it literally ineffectual; i.e., an approach that would grant the will absolute independence/power renders it empty. Hence, the most effective model of the will must be open to the fusion of contradictory properties.

To illustrate what kinds of properties are involved in willing, it is useful, second, to turn to the history of the concept of the will. The thinking of Western philosophers on willing has been marked through and through by contradictory interpretations and so no position can be developed that settles the dispute for "one side"; rather, this history shows us that only a thinking through of both sides of the contradictions together can be fruitful. That is, by turning to the many historical conceptualizations of willing, we can see that the kinds of determinations and properties associated with this central human activity consistently break down into binarisms and attempted resolutions.

And third, the contemporary positions from philosophy and theory I shall examine will themselves square off in dialectical pairs where one depends on the other even as they might be polemically locked in wheel-spinning opposition. Precisely Kant's, Nietzsche's, and Heidegger's historical positions on the will in association with freedom, power, and understanding offer the possibility of a dialectical explanation and thus can productively contribute to the debates in contemporary thought. Kant, Nietzsche, and Heidegger can open up new avenues for argument in contemporary theories by introducing into them richer conceptions of the will. Moreover, it should be clear that I am not interested in a "return" to the past philosophers since their conceptions of the will gain significance only in the light of their contemporary receptions. The goal is a model of the will that accounts for the opposing positions that are our unavoidable legacy (the "last will and testament" of modernity).

I have decided to focus on the concept of will because other fundamental concepts of contemporary theoretical discourses—subject, meaning, history, reason, language—have not been able to bring together the conflicting strands of modern/postmodern thought in productive ways. Thus, for example, the debate over the status of reason as a concept inherited from the Enlightenment has tended to split even the "postmetaphysical" thinkers into "rationalist" and "irrationalist" camps.[12] Furthermore, those alternatives have not been able to account for key features of experience that are at the heart of our academic and nonacademic debates. Hence, the focus on the subject and its "death" (e.g., at the hands of "language") has left the question of agency largely unaddressed. Perhaps this is because many modernist and postmodernist discussions revolve around epistemological issues rather than explicitly ethical and political ones. By placing a complex, dialectical, "decentered" concept of the will in the "center," I hope to provide not a new foundationalism but a different ground or meeting place for these discussions to occur.

Dialectic

In highlighting dialectic and in arguing for a dialectical understanding of the will, I am employing the term in a sense that borrows from many traditions. It is my conviction that the will, and the fundamental concepts associated with it, are most productively grasped by seeing how opposing determinations are continually thrust upon each other. This conviction is not intended to have the force of a prescription based on some presumed metaphysical identity of logos and being, as if there were some intimate connection "out there" between the dialectical determination of concepts and the unfolding of reality.[13] But it does seem to me that in order to avoid precisely the trap of developing a "metaphysical" theory of the will (in the bad sense of abstracted from reality, derived from pure concepts), it is necessary both to provide descriptions and, as is my focus in this text, to turn to historical discussions that can be analyzed for their opposing categories. That is, I hope to show that dialectical theory is most fruitful to the extent that it takes into account the *kinds of arguments* that *historically* have been proposed concerning the will. Although concepts like dialectic and will have roots in metaphysical traditions, I would hope to use them more "pragmatically" to "tell a richer story" about a concept with a tradition of complex and contradictory arguments.[14]

The original understanding of the term "dialectic" in Greek thought stressed the notion of a mode of presenting arguments.[15] Beginning with the Sophists, and culminating in Plato, dialectic meant a dialogical principle of countering one plausible argument or assertion with an equally plausible yet opposite one. Indeed, it is hard, if not impossible, to imagine a cognitive endeavor that is not fundamentally dialectical, since any argument moves from a position (A) to an at least partial negation (−A) in order to state a different one. This would be true, of course, even for a critique of this very view. For this reason, although dialectic is related to polemical argumentation, its inherent negativity need not unfold in a "warlike" but, rather, in a discursive fashion.[16]

For the Sophists, such argumentation made possible the constant movement, a partially destructive yet necessary argumentative force that prevented concepts from hardening into false certainties. Their form of education (*Bildung*), as Hegel said, made "that which is hard and fast (*das Feste*) . . . begin to vacillate and lose its hold."[17] To a considerable extent, their ethics and politics arose from that critical stance. Recent attempts to resuscitate the Sophists for our postmodern discursive formation tend to stress not their reputed arbitrariness and lack of commitment but, on the contrary, their insistence on the validity of pragmatic dialectical argumentation for social interactions.[18]

In Plato, this possibility of a potentially endless chain of assertions and counterassertions exists alongside a different notion, according to which the dialectical exchange leads the partners to the recognition of the futility of representing truths in terms of simple assertions. The result in this latter case would be either the knowledge of lack of knowledge or the attempt to formulate truths in a form other than straightforward assertions. Dialectic, both in its argumentative and propositional form, is thus intimately related to irony.[19]

It was Hegel who more than any other philosopher strove for a mode of representation that would both grow out of the argumentative exchange of counterpositions and not be just one more in the series of exchanges. Dialectic became a logical method. Indeed, this mode or method unfolds even at the level of the sentence. The dialectical (or speculative) sentence, according to Hegel, has within itself the movement between contradictory stances. In his example from the *Phänomenologie des Geistes* [*Phenomenology of Spirit*], "God is Being," we go from the subject to the predicate and back, since neither one is meaningful without the other.[20] Because this movement cannot be "contained" within a single sentence, however, i.e., because the tension leads the reader to consider wider "syntheses," Hegel was forced to ever larger dialectical contextualizations. For that reason, he had to define the truth as totality, "das Ganze" (or, as he says, it only exists in a *System*), because each particular conflict of opposites, even if temporarily contained in a concept, sentence, or argument, presses beyond itself. "Absolute Knowledge," on this reading, is not some quasi-religious insight that puts questioning to rest but the recollection back on the many oppositions that had been proceeded through and the formulation of the necessity of that very process. Therefore, the notion of Hegelian *Aufhebung* as a permanent stabilizing of opposites— a view rightly rejected by much post-Hegelian thought from Kierkegaard and Feuerbach to Adorno and Derrida—is in fact a caricature of dialectical thinking.[21]

Schelling, in the introduction to his *Philosophische Untersuchungen über das Wesen der menschlichen Freiheit und die damit zusammenhängenden Gegenstände* (*Philosophical Inquiries into the Nature of Human Freedom*), written two years after Hegel's *Phänomenologie des Geistes*, likewise gives a brief (and somewhat more graspable) explanation of dialectical thinking. In criticizing the "dialectical immaturity (*Unmündigkeit*)"[22] of his own time (especially in comparison to the Greeks), he decries the typical misunderstandings that arise in the dialectical use of the copula.[23] He offers a series of examples of dialectical propositions—"the Perfect is the Imperfect" ("das Vollkommene ist das Unvollkommene"), "the Good is the Evil" ("das Gute ist das Böse"), or "necessity and freedom are one" ("Notwendiges und Freies [sind] eins") and "that the soul and body are one ("daß die Seele mit dem Leib eins ist")[24]—and argues that they are not to be so construed that the opposing terms simply are "identical" *in every way* (e.g., there is simply no difference between good and evil *as* good and evil). Rather, one must find which aspects of the subject are contained in the predicate and vice versa. Thus, for example, "evil is good" insofar as evil, as a negative, depends essentially for its *being* on the positive, the good; i.e., to the extent that there is evil, it owes its existence to the good. It is not by chance that these thoughts precede his essay on freedom, an essay that revolves at crucial points around the will, since the concepts of freedom, humanity, and willing are defined dialectically.

The connection between dialectic and the will, implicit in Schelling, can be traced back to Socrates. In his *Xenophon* he links explicitly the ethical act of preferring the good, i.e., the fundamental action of human choice—*proairesis,* the closest the Greeks came to a theory of volition—and the act of selecting out (*dialegein*) among alternative possibilities. This last act is of course related to the discerning discourse that we associate with dialectic as a basic mode of thought.[25] As Gadamer points out, this connection can be found as well in Aristotle: "After all, dialectic, as the art of differentiating rightly, is really not some kind of secret art reserved for philosophers. . . . To be a human being means always to be confronted with choices. As Aristotle puts it, human beings 'have' *proairesis* (choice)."[26] Hence, the dialectical method that I shall employ in analyzing the will is justified on historical grounds given both the contradictory ways in which the will has been defined and the associations between dialectics and human agency. The conundrums and dilemmas we face when trying to account for willing and agency, in other words, not only make a dialectical approach to these phenomena necessary but have historically brought out a range of contradictory approaches. My goal will be to consider how to understand the contradictory determinations that are united in the activities of willing; then I will reflect on the way these contradictory determinations unfolded in the history of Western thinking on the will; and finally, in the bulk of my argument, I will show that a dialectical understanding of willing can give us a different way to deal with arguments in contemporary thought.

One of the more negative associations that persists in contemporary thought about dialectics ties it as a mode of thinking to a metaphysics that has been criticized now for at least a century. Dialectic, the argument runs in any number of forms, is made possible by the unfolding of *Geist* or Logos in a basically Christian tripartite movement (unity-disunity-reunification; Father-Son-Holy Spirit; Eden-Earth-Second Coming; etc.).[27] With the abandonment of both the ground and the direction of the movement as a *grand récit,* dialectic would seem to have no basis. My use of dialectical argumentation would try to take this critique into account in three ways.

First, a rejection of metaphysics (the suspected presence of which has almost become the standard charge in ad hominem arguments in contemporary debates, enough to dismiss an opponent out of hand) should entail not a rejection of dialectic but its support. That is, if we see metaphysics as the hypostatization of one form of being as, literally, absolute, without mediation, without relation to some other, then a critique of metaphysics involves precisely dialectical argumentation that would reveal the dependence of the absolute on its opposite (i.e., the *Bedingtheit* of the so-called *unbedingt,* the mediation of the unmediated). The advantage of not throwing out the dialectical baby with the bath water of metaphysics is that dialectics also allows us at any time to show the dependence of the conditional on something always beyond itself.[28]

Second, I would follow Hannah Arendt in rejecting a metaphysics of absolute Spirit and relate dialectic instead to the will. Her argument focuses on the force of negation.[29] Dialectical thinking, as Hegel says and the Sophists always showed, proceeds thanks to a constant negation. And although the ability to perform that negation rests in general in the mind (*Geist*), it is more precisely to be associated with the will. The reason is, according to Arendt following Koyré, that in temporal terms negation is associated with the future, the constant overcoming of the present; and the human being turned toward such a negating future is the willing I, as opposed to the reflective, thinking I (which is turned toward the past or the *nunc stans* of contemplation).[30] Although Arendt (and others) might in turn see the will as a separate faculty of mind (with metaphysical assumptions), this is not necessary if we say that the same negative force of dialectics is at work whenever we say "I want"—thereby negating a present state that also is itself negative ("wanting").[31] Although we will see more of these arguments below, the point to be made here is that one can make a case for an intimate relationship between dialectic and will that rejects a metaphysics of *Geist.*[32] This move is one way I would legitimate the linkage of terms in my title.[33]

Finally, to counter the association of ("bad") metaphysics and dialectic, I would emphasize the level of *argumentation.* As the organization of my study implies, dialectics does not exist in the abstract interaction of Ideal Forms but in the confrontation of specific historical positions. Because our understanding of major phenomena carries within itself the traces of past approaches, and because those approaches in the case of willing can be cast in terms of an ongoing dialectic, the study of that history is crucial for a rich analysis of the phenomenon. Although I would claim that willing is inherently dialectical, that assertion does not occur in a vacuum but is also, and essentially, a result of a history of reflections on the will that unfold dialectically. Through this attention to the exchange of positions, I hope to contribute not just to a better understanding of terms that we, for better or worse, have not been able to do without but also to a praxis of argumentation that engages opposing positions in a nonpolemical way in order to illuminate possibilities in both. By avoiding the negative *inhering* in any position, including one's own, too much criticism takes the form *of* a negation of another position, and hence antagonism and rejection. I would like to work *with* various positions, showing only how each attempted totalization does not work because of an inherent movement that thrusts it onto another. In this sense, the negativity is a positive force.

Thus, the thinkers I deal with are engaged (*nolens volens*) in a dialectic about the will. Although some of the pairs pursue an active confrontation, I see the dialectic in each case as arising from a third thinker from the German tradition. By returning to the dialectical possibilities contained but not always exploited in those grounding thinkers, we can work out a more fruitful relationship between the contemporary pairs. Concretely, the polemical battle lines often drawn between Frankfurt School Critical Theory and "poststructuralism"—Adorno vs. Lacan, Habermas vs. Foucault—or between hermeneutics and deconstruction—Gadamer vs. Derrida—can be demilitarized by rereading each side as a totalization of a partial position taken from an older German philosophical theory of the will—Kant's, Nietzsche's, or Heidegger's. In engaging these thinkers' theories of the will in a constructive dialectic, I am not seeking a metaphysical foundation for any future ethics, but, rather, am striving to develop a more dialogical and less agonistic form of polemic than typically dominates contemporary discussions.

What emerges from these dialectical interactions is a rich conceptualization of the will that can be used in dealing with key issues (freedom, power, understanding) because it accounts for opposing determinations. This conceptualization is grounded in arguments from the history of philosophy. By bringing that potential to the surface, I can contribute to the ongoing history of this concept and to a positive exchange between contemporary positions otherwise locked in unfruitful oppositions.[34]

A Dialectical Model of the Will

The model of willing that emerges from an examination of multiple historical positions can be approached by developing the activity of willing out of the phenomenon that underlies philosophies as diverse as Leibniz's, Hegel's, and Nietzsche's, namely "life." Where Leibniz stressed the teleological organization of living organisms in contrast to the nonpurposive and deterministic relations that exist between inanimate objects, and therefore called for a philosophical organic understanding of the world that departed from a mechanistic model, Hegel was one of the first thinkers to take the activity of the living organism as a serious model for philosophy. To understand life, Hegel argued, one must think dialectically, for life itself is a process of self-differentiation and gathering into unities, of encounter with and appropriation of otherness, of individuation and the insignificance of the individual vis-à-vis the species, of systematic development and unpredictable innovation. These apparently abstract characterizations apply across all life forms, from the splitting and recombination of single-cell organisms to the complex unfolding of evolutionary processes. Of course, Hegel used this organic model to comprehend the development of Spirit.[35] It was Nietzsche, however, who, having worked through Schopenhauer's metaphysics of the will, saw the activity of willing in terms of the dialectics of life.

Willing, according to this vitalist view, unfolds in a multifaceted dialectic. It is the self-reflexivity of some of the facets, born of the complexity of willing organisms, that differentiates willing from life. That is, structurally, to will is to live. Just as there is no life without the engagement of an individual with some Other in both a resistant and an appropriating way, so too willing never occurs in the abstract but only in relation to some object or activity. I always "want (to do) something." Just as the life of any individual organism floats, we might say, on the sea of life that supersedes it, so too the willing individual emerges (as will be strikingly evident in Lacan's theory) out of the context of a willing Other. Just as new life forms emerge in unpredictable ways out of a given constellation of forces, such that evolution has a necessity only in retrospect, so too willing is capable of innovative acts that initiate new chains of events.[36] Just as life forms constitute themselves in an interplay of self-differentiation and unification, so too my willing fragments me into myriad acts of will that are nonetheless "mine"—not because there is a self independent of them that "owns" them but because I *am* the willing itself.

And yet willing contains a self-reflexive aspect that, though present in a sense in all organized systems, can attain high degrees of self-awareness in us.[37] Thus, there is a simultaneous knowing and not knowing to my willing. Insofar as it is connected to most of my biological functions, my willing occurs in a radical sense unconsciously; radical because I can neither direct these functions nor could I function as a whole if my attention were focused on the plethora of wants that my mind and body attend to at any given time. But this is not to say that I cannot knowingly direct portions of my physical energies for periods of time. One might even develop a kind of calculus of the will and argue that those periods of time could be infinitesimally small, and yet so long as they are not zero they can initiate changes in my behavior or the world that are tremendously magnified from the "initial conditions." In this way my rational autonomy can be guaranteed not as an independence from the realm of the empirical but as my self-defining, self-determining location within the infinitesimal interstices of the empirical. As the guarantor of autonomy, these acts of willing both give the self its law and guarantee the transgressive possibilities of the self vis-à-vis any Law.

The model of willing I am outlining here does not depend on any specific version of philosophical vitalism. Indeed, one might get a sense of the unique status of willing by expanding upon the concept of the infinitesimal just mentioned, especially as it relates to energy in general. One of the most recent and ingenious attempts to rethink human agency, the "thought experiment" proposed by Hans Jonas, takes this approach and leads to a reconciliation between the mental and physical, even as it maintains their difference.[38] Beginning with the aporias of the metaphysical and positivist positions, he provides a model that at least should show the possibility of the influence of the mental on the physical. Such a model would show the possibility of a nondualist (antimetaphysical) and nonpositivist (antireductionist) understanding of human behavior. (Jonas says the particular form of the model is less relevant than its use in dismissing the claim of the impossibility of such a connection.) Imagine, he says, a cone balanced on its point in ideal space. It would take an infinitesimally small amount of energy to push it over.[39] At the point of interaction between the mental and the physical, such a limit could be posited, a gap bridged by acts of will, a space infinitesimally small yet never eradicated completely. The mental receives its energy from the input into the organism (e.g., the end of a chain from physical sensation to mental image must leave some "rest" of energy "submerged" and transformed in the mental sphere if the law of conservation of energy is to be maintained); it merely "returns" it in infinitesimal amounts in initiating actions. Jonas says:

> The brief formula of psychic behavior is therefore: Generated from an infinitesimal amount of energy, it is capable of generating yet another infinitesimal amount of energy. In this "in-between" (*Inzwischen*), the infinitesimal amounts have "submerged" beneath the physical surface. And yet, just as an underground stream has not disappeared into nothingness, so too these energy impulses don't emerge out of nothingness when consciousness acts. This "in-between" or mediating process (*Inzwischen*) is itself the sphere of subjectivity and its freedom.[40]

Precisely this concept of an "Inzwischen," of a place and temporality mediating the oppositions, would be the location of a dialectically determined will. What we see there is the effort to maintain the key elements of a "meta-physical" position against the reductionism of the positivists—especially the "power" of the subject to introduce change, to transcend—without implying the need for a separate entity behind the willing.

This dialectical model of willing is essentially dynamic given the internal split that constitutes it. A crucial consequence of adopting such a model, then, is that it becomes impossible to reduce acts of the will to one of its aspects; i.e., to do so, in principle, leads to limited understandings and aporias. This is not to say that in practice we do not at any given time need to establish a priority in the play of forces active in willing. For example, there are times when we stress its conscious, rationally controlled vs. its driven aspect, or its innovative vs. its empirically determined side, or vice versa. But we cannot generalize that priority into an abstract and quasi-predictive statement. For example, when attempting to resolve issues of individual accountability vis-à-vis social forces (as in court cases), each case must be weighed separately. Although this undoubtedly places great strain on a legal system, all efforts to generalize on one of the possible poles—individuals are "free" or individuals are "determined" by the social pressures—in fact undermine themselves. (The idea of a free agent independent of social forces defeats the social system that would argue for the necessary responsibility of individuals toward society, and the notion of the individual at the mercy of social forces is belied by the attempt of the individual not to be at the mercy of the legal system judging the case.) The "free will" thus becomes an issue in such cases insofar as the dialectics of willing involves an interplay of forces, the outcome of whose interaction cannot be determined even though there is no freestanding agent, hovering as it were outside that interplay of forces. Such a model is from one point of view weak since it cannot offer general answers to questions like: "Should the courts treat individuals as freely willing and hence able to choose their own actions?" But it is strong in its capacity to offer reasons why free will must be maintained dynamically and hence neither guaranteed by some fixed metaphysical agency nor rejected by some reductive empiricism.

One way of formulating these issues is in terms of a binarism at the heart of willing, namely activity and passivity. In his discussion of the "psychophysisches Problem," which analyzes subjectivity at that in-between place of the will, Jonas furthermore refers to the doubleness of our mental life. We can extend his argument to see the inherent dialectic in willing in general. He lists a number of dualities that characterize human agency, culminating in that of activity vs. passivity: "that our being-subjects has this double aspect, consisting of receptivity and spontaneity, sensuality and understanding, feeling and willing, suffering and acting, in short that we are at once active and passive."[41] The will as simultaneously active and passive is an insight that runs throughout the Western tradition, generally in the form of aporias that arise when the one side is thought independently of the other.[42] For example, from Hobbes's view that the will is only the last effect in a causal chain, one arrives at its absolute passivity.[43] Opposed to this, the pure activity of willing would make it radically arbitrary, transforming it into the problematic notion of *Willkür*.[44]

Modern psychology has been most preoccupied with this duality of the will. In some ways we can consider this fascination a reformulation of the problem of *akrasia* raised first by Aristotle. If the will is a fundamentally active force, how can one explain its failure at given times? And if it is a merely passive phenomenon (vis-à-vis drives or reason), how can one explain its ability at times to supersede these forces?[45] Eisler defines the parameters in his *Wörterbuch der philosophischen Begriffe:*

> If the will flows immediately out of individual feelings, which are "bound" to sensations and images (*Vorstellungen*), then it is *instinctual and reactive* . . . if it is preceded, however, by a struggle of motives, a process of contemplation, then we have an act of willfulness (*Willkür*) or choice. This latter act, what we consider willing in the narrow sense, is an active engagement of the ego, often accompanied with the sensation of "effort"; it has its nucleus in the will itself.[46] (my emphasis)

Both characteristics belong to the will, but their relationship is open to vicissitudes.

Consider some of the following schematic possibilities that have been at the center of debates between empiricists and those who would posit a separate will as free.[47] If the active-passive distinction is unimportant, then the will is usually seen as (like) a passion (it determines action but is itself fully determined by other causes). If the active-passive distinction is important, then there are two possibilities: (a) the passions influence the will and the will determines action (the problem here being that although the will is made active, it responds to the passions), or (b) a dualist position allows some actions to be determined by the passions and some to be determined directly by the will. The first position summarizes the status of the will for most Enlightenment thinkers.[48] What we will consider below in Kant is a complex structure that essentially splits the will: One will serves as a primal "cause" of desire, and another will (associated with the law) responds (repressively) to those desires. To the extent that Kant collapsed the two, giving priority to the latter, he had a highly problematic model; but to the extent that he saw the need for a will "beyond" desire and the (will of the) law, he developed a fruitfully dialectical will that is *both* active and passive.[49] It is a model that we can use to understand issues of psychopathology.

A debate raged around 1900 over the difference between the will as the force behind action and the forces behind the will to act.[50] But these two positions are not unrelated, and dynamic models of the will demonstrate how the will's activity must be but the flip side of its passivity. Psychopathology has come to play a central role in this issue because it focuses on the deregulation of the fine tuning between activity and passivity in the will. The opening of the entry on "Will (disorders of)" from James Baldwin's influential 1902 *Dictionary of Philosophy and Psychology* gives one the sense of how an interpretation of excess can easily be turned into an interpretation of deficiency, and vice versa:

> Disorders of the will, like those of other functions, seem divisible into those of excess and defect; but the former term requires a special interpretation. An excessively vigorous will is not a disorder; but the term hyperboulia, which is literally equivalent to this, indicates an abnormal tendency to action. The tendency of an impulse, under the suggestion of a thought or motive, to engender execution, is excessive or abnormal. But this in turn may properly be regarded as a deficiency of inhibition, i.e., of the restraining power of a higher over a lower will-mechanism.[51]

The will in the narrower sense of active inhibition could be excessive, leading to a dampening of all impulses to execute action; or the active, inhibiting will may be too weak, calling forth the "reactive" impulses, which then become overly active.[52]

From a different ethical perspective, Levinas offers an alternative positioning of the will between activity and passivity. He begins from the existential status of passivity vis-à-vis death, the ultimate annihilation of my willing. And yet, my death, insofar as I am experiencing its inevitable coming, is not immediate. Rather, between me and my death is the opening up of what Levinas calls the "time for the Other," a spacing that awakens in me a "desire" that is beyond both egoism and need (since it, by definition, can never be fulfilled—either in life or death). The phenomenological and existential description of this in-between state, my temporality in the face of future death, is that of the human being "suffering in patience": "This situation where the consciousness deprived of all freedom of movement maintains a minimal distance from the present, this ultimate passivity which nonetheless desperately turns into action and into hope, is *patience*—the passivity of undergoing, and yet master itself." This duality is, for Levinas, the "truth of the will."[53]

What we have here, if we recall Jonas's image of the "Inzwischen," is the will located not just between drives and practical reason, but between forces that at any time exert an active influence, making the will, from the other perspective, appear passive. That is, the position of the will makes it possible for it to be both active and passive. If we imagine the self as an active force motivating behavior and the self as passive effect of other forces, the will, in the middle, becomes the site of dual determinations, the condition of possibility of the self.

To make this model more concrete, I shall play it out through a reading of two of the more influential texts of the last few years that deal with widely diverging cultural phenomena. I take the first example from Bill Readings's influential and wide-ranging study, *The University in Ruins*. There the debates around the canon in the United States play a significant role in "literary culture" precisely because the peculiar "will" of the nation is at stake. He states: "The point is that, as a republican immigrant democracy, the United States is founded not in tradition but in the will of the people, is more like France than Germany."[54] This fact has the immediate consequence that there are decisions to be made, since tradition does not automatically rule. Hence we see that the one function of willing as decision making is operative in Readings's account. That is, "the tradition is, in effect, what the will of the American people decides it is" (85). The act of willing here is innovative and creative as opposed to the blind or merely repetitive following of traditional dictates. ("The autonomous *choice* of a canon, rather than submission to the blind weight of tradition, parallels the choice of a government rather than submission to hereditary monarchy" [16].) Readings stresses the claim "that in establishing the canon the American people chose their own historical ethnicity in a free exercise of rational will" (85).

And yet, Readings goes on to undermine the notion of a singular, totalizing (national) will. The debate about the canon is, he argues, a "salutary one" because the questioning of the very "*function*" of the canon reveals the impossibility of "authoritatively integrat[ing] popular will and an ethnic function under the rubric of culture" (85). The will of the people, like all willing, is by no means uniform but is split, plural, evolving, and unpredictable. Such a will does indeed exist—Readings never seems to want to give up the term—and the canon could still be seen in a way to "reflect" it. But we must now be sure to see the canon as *essentially* in crisis, in dispute, because the "will of the people" can not be reduced to a single entity. In fact, for Readings the attempt to use the canon to establish a unified will of a "nation-state" is directly related to the exclusionary mentality and practices of racism: "The nation-state's unification of the field of political life as the representation of a *self-identical* popular will is structurally complicit with such injustice" (104; my emphasis). Opposed to this falsely unifying will, i.e., opposed to the attempt to impose a unity, Readings would see an inherently diverse will of radical (true) democracy, a "republican will," in other words, that generates "canon wars" precisely because it is not some singular thing but a non-thing whose definition exists, dialectically and self-referentially, in its search for a definition. Readings's stimulating argument rests on an implicit conception of the nature of willing in general.

The second example I take from the introduction to Judith Butler's *Bodies That Matter*. Here, too, we see the way a contemporary theorist already works with the problematics of willing. But she consistently shies away from developing, or even using, the will to explain her interesting model of agency. Butler points to the need for a dialectical approach to agency, but she excludes the possibility of willing. Or conversely, she simultaneously reduces the will to inadequate oppositional categories even as she calls for their rethinking.

The context of her opening arguments to *Bodies That Matter* can be viewed from two perspectives. First, Butler is responding to those critics who accused her of either destroying agency (since she appears to see the gendered/sexed self as a mere effect of other forces) or, on the contrary, of reintroducing an abstract agent that can choose its mode of "performing" gender. And second, she is addressing the broader conflict in gender and sexuality studies between constructivism and essentialism. Faced with both issues, Butler strives to distance herself from these options, showing that she would not ally herself with either since both sides collapse. In short, although she might balk at the term, Butler could be seen as pursuing a basically dialectical mode of argumentation.

She presents a model of agency that arises out of a process of "citationality," enforced yet incomplete repetitions of codes and norms. The subject is, for Butler, neither the independent creator of its own possibilities (which are prescripted for it), nor the product of naturalistic forces (since the processes unfold in the realm of semiosis, where interpretive acts are necessary). It is both active and passive. Agency responds to, indeed emerges out of, a network of practices and reacts innovatively to them.

The problem is that Butler does not take advantage of the dialectics of the will that are in fact present in her discussion. Whereas these very possibilities for interaction between human beings and their world, interactions that in fact define both the individual human being (as a male or female, for example) and the world for him or her, *are* human willing, Butler time and again displaces the concept of the will, thereby leaving herself open to the very criticisms she wanted to address. That is, it becomes clear that Butler can only think of the will in one of its reductivist forms, as willful and fantasmatically autonomous. She writes, for example: "According to the biblical renditions of the performative, i.e., 'Let there be light!,' it appears that it is by virtue of *the power of a subject or its will* that a phenomenon is named into being. In a critical reformulation of the performative, Derrida makes clear that this power is not the function of an originating will, but is always derivative" (13). And again, she rejects the version of constructivism that might presuppose a "voluntarist subject who makes its gender through an instrumental action," an "agent who precedes and performs that activity" by an act of "willful appropriation" (7). These passages reveal a perfectly valid rejection of an inadequate concept of willing, but they unfortunately also signal Butler's own problematic distrust of a broader notion of willing that could support her argument. Hence, when she writes of the networks of codes around gender and sex that form "the matrix through which all willing first becomes possible, its enabling cultural condition" (7), willing itself becomes inappropriately derivative.

Butler's Nietzschean warning that we need to be wary of the conceptual schemes imposed by our subject-verb-object grammar can help us develop a better model of willing. We should not think of a "will" (subject) that "wants/wills" (verb) some "thing/activity" (object) since an agent or will that is separate from the activity of willing itself, and an activity of willing that is devoid of content (a representational goal or movement), would make no sense as a "willing." It would be some bizarre kind of unwilling or static will. Rather, we need to see human willing as a process that both individuates agents, i.e., is crystallized around a self or subject, and thereby at the same time thrusts that subject toward a realms of objects (context). We can interpret willing as a bidirectional process:

$$s \longleftarrow w \longrightarrow o$$
$$\text{subject} \quad \text{willing} \quad \text{objects}$$

Willing unfolds from a point that is a kind of "zero degree" (the "limit" at the intersection of the mental and physical) and consists only in the dual directionality of the willing. The willing is directed on the one hand "back" to *create* a sense of a subject or agent and on the other "forward" to objects and activities that come to be seen as the "goals" of the subject. Note that this model would prevent us from falling into the error that Butler rightly criticizes, namely considering the will as a property of the subject, connecting it to the world. That model would look like:

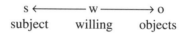

$$s = w \longrightarrow o, \text{ or } s \longrightarrow w \longrightarrow o$$

The nonfixed essence of willing produces both the need to go in both directions and the possibility for change that is not "voluntaristic." In terms of Butler's example, "I" (as some being with a little willing agent inside) do not choose or "will" my sex/gender; the willing "I" is neither a fixed essence nor a determined effect. Given my willing, however, an "I" emerges in a particular relation to objects and the discursive context. At the same time, that "I" and the arrangement of objects are sustained by an irreducible willing that disrupts my ego and possible connections to objects.[55] The instability inhering in the system is not a "systematic" feature of the system itself (as

Butler seems to imply) but the result of its status as a product of human willing. Similarly, the identity of the willing subject is equally unstable.

Hence, Butler critiques the view that we stand in front of the closet and "pick" our identity the way we choose our clothes. And I would agree that the subject emerges out of the storehouse of representations and carries their traces. But that "emergence" is not merely a product of the representations, but, rather, a consequence of our conscious and unconscious willing. Hence, the will exists at the intersection, making our agency fundamentally heteronomous, able to choose and implicated in the choices. The act of "choosing" (or forming) an identity is, then, like the act of choosing the clothes, only what is deceptive in the latter case is that the picture mistakenly places the agent fully outside the closet. (In the case of identity-choice, the picture sees us—an independent agency—standing "outside" of ourselves.) In fact, as in all cases of willing, the "engendering" of the subject arises from the simultaneous production of a self with a sense of autonomy and the relations that self must have to objects, actions, and effects. My independent (subversive) and dependent stances toward the codifications of gender norms emerge from my essence as a willing agent, thrust upon the world, thrusting myself upon the world, and thrust back upon myself from a paradoxical position of wanting. Here, too, as in the example above with the courts, the actual freedom arises not from such autonomous positioning but from a movement we make that is never fully predictable. There is a self-reflexive or recursive structure between my sense of self and the images, identities, and representations I receive, and the freedom of my willing consists in the gap that both separates and connects them. I am willing/wanting because these two aspects of my self— my "active" directedness and my "passive" receptivity—neither coincide completely with nor isolate themselves from each other. Willing captures this dialectic at the heart of human freedom, power, and understanding.

1

Historical Dialectics of the Will's Contradictory Determinations

If willing is an inherently dialectical activity that is made up of irreducibly contradictory components, then one would expect conceptualizations of this activity to reflect this structure. Efforts to capture the nature of willing conceptually have throughout two thousand years of Western thought generated a movement of partial determinations ("will is x," or "will is y," or "will is non-x," or "will is non-y," etc.) that arises because each such determination is revealed to be inadequate. Taken as a whole, however, this movement can allow us to develop ways to combine the contradictory determinations into a richer, dialectical understanding of the will.

Since the concept of the will involves, whenever it is used, the traces of past contradictory determinations, the history of the definitions of willing makes up the structure and the background of the efforts at modern and postmodern reformulation by the thinkers I shall analyze. To investigate this structure, I shall not attempt a linear *Begriffsgeschichte* of the will; that would amount in fact to a summary of the history of Western philosophy.[1] Rather, I shall organize the historical discussion around a series of issues that run through the two millennia of the will's conceptualization, issues that have consistently generated contradictory views of the will.[2] My point is that different debates locate the will in fields of tension around particular issues and those tensions can be isolated so that (1) we can understand better tensions existing in contemporary views of agency and (2) we can see what categories the dialectics of the will must entail. The history of the concept can thus be mapped out in terms of opposing positions, each of which captures partial aspects of the act of willing. By looking at some particular philosophical arguments that grapple with basic oppositions, I argue that the dialectics of willing can be grasped by seeing how such positions are played out over time.

Let us consider some basic questions that have emerged in debates concerning human agency:

> Granted that we act with some kind of independence (and even this might be disputed by strict determinists—see below), can we speak of *one* identity motivating or coordinating our actions? Or rather should we understand our actions as collections of competing motivations (bodily, mental, emotional, desiring, etc.), fragmentary "coalitions" of forces commanding behavior in different ways depending on the different strengths at a given time?

> Even though our willed motivations might be the most intimate aspects of our selves, can we really pretend to *know* them? After all, do we not often oppose the will—closely associated with desires and drives—to reason? Or rather, should we not consider our willing as that which is (or ought to be) most known to us since we consider our actions most ethical (even "human") when they are at the behest of our rational faculties? As an example of this deep ambiguity, consider how we speak of our innermost *un*conscious will as well as the imposition of our will as *rational* (conscious) control.

> At one extreme, does it even make sense to speak of a will or willing at all since humans seem thoroughly determined in their actions by laws—either "natural" ones or the "law of reason" (which have even been equated)? Or do we need to adopt a kind of voluntarism, that is, the view that willing is precisely that feature of human behavior that transcends or transgresses the rule of law?

> Does not the individual will unfold only in relation to others, i.e., in relation to some collective will, be it divine, sociopolitical, or linguistic? Does that relationship lead to the dissolution or emergence of individual agency?

Out of these questions we can formulate four sets of rudimentary binarisms that capture the way willing is defined, time and again, by contradictory determinations:

1. The will as simple (unified, fixed character); the will as complex (fragmenting, innovative)
2. The will subjected to or superseding intellect/reason; the will as knowable or unknowable (with what kind of knowledge?)

3. Determinism versus indeterminism; empiricism versus metaphysics; will as real versus the will as transcendental "thing"
4. The individual versus the universal (will); the will as giving versus following laws.

My point is to show that in relation to these issues we encounter a history of conflicting interpretations of "the will as x" and "the will as non-x." Forming a consistent pattern, these contradictory determinations of the will are inescapable *as contradictions* in thinking through a theory of the will because willing itself unfolds in a contradictory fashion. In the history of its conceptualizations, the will occupies a kind of empty middle space that gets defined in a back-and-forth motion as either one side or another of a debate. Rather than reject the concept as hopelessly locked in fruitless conflict,[3] we can turn these tensions to our advantage. The goal will be not to see the will in terms of one side or the other but to use the contradictory determinations as the parameters to understand the space in the middle that it must occupy. In the later chapters, we shall encounter the opposing characteristics of will in various formulations by modern and contemporary thinkers. Looking at these thinkers from the perspective of this historically unfolding dialectic illuminates their relation to the tradition and opens up a dialectical reading that focuses on human agency in terms of a will both split and formed by a contradictory nature.

To clarify what I mean, let me introduce a simple diagram that plays a role in later chapters, especially in the discussion of Lacan. It consists of two interlocking circles, a Venn diagram. Each circle represents a pole in a binary opposition that defines the will:

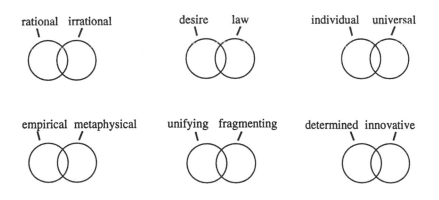

The image is intended to illuminate the dialectical interplay that has characterized the historical conceptualizations of the will.[4] The tendency to see the will as this or that (empirical or transcendental, free or unfree, rational or irrational, individual or universal, etc.), the tendency that makes up the centuries of ongoing debate about the will, is depicted by the function of exclusive disjunction[5]:

nature	reason
desire	law
unchanging	innovative
empirical	metaphysical
unifying	fragmenting
individual	supraindividual

nature	reason
desire	law
unchanging	innovative
empirical	metaphysical
unifying	fragmenting
individual	supraindividual

Indeed, from the perspectives of the opposing poles, this in-between space will often have the status of a void or might not even exist. The exclusion of this space and the refusal to take the other position into account would thus look like a partial or incomplete circle:

But if we see the will as occupying the center (inclusive conjunction), then we can understand how it takes part of positions that, *from their own perspectives* (i.e., undialectically), are contradictory and exclusive. The contested space of willing is best conceived, then, as the site of intersection, the place where both sets of determinations apply (even though, again, from each particular perspective the other determination seems to be impossible).

Contested space of willing

The middle ground is thus not a compromise that ends tension but the very site of that tension of partial determinations, a non-place or nonentity that can nonetheless account for the generation of the oppositions.

Needless to say, although this model represents graphically the simultaneity of opposites that makes up the will, its explanatory power remains limited insofar as it remains static. That is, as we saw in the introduction, willing is best conceived of as a *process,* not as a thing (faculty) in a particular location or, as this model implies, as itself a location. Willing is the activity that opens a space in the subject, a gap that at the same time connects the subject qua subject to the world qua world. Were it not for the opening (as process, *spacing,* not just space) that occurs between the two circles, they would not have this peculiar status of being both separated and connected—instead they would be either completely disconnected or collapsed into one. The interlocking circles, joined around an in-between space that helps to constitute them in their relationality, illustrates that through my willing I am able, for example, both to distinguish myself from natural chains in a causal network and to engage necessarily with that network, both to rely on representations as goals of my actions and to respond to them innovatively, both to preconsciously motivate my intellect and to knowingly direct my actions. The overlapping and contested space—or perhaps more dynamically conceived as spacing—between the opposing conceptions, reminds us that willing needs to be grasped as a complex "both-and/neither-nor."

The German philosophers explored in the body of the book—Kant, Nietzsche, Heidegger—have mapped out a fully dialectical determination of the will. That is, they have indicated the variable contours of a conception of will that, as an in-between spacing, relates the oppositions associated with it in a dialectical structure. But their interpretations also laid the seeds for another round of opposing positions. These three philosophers did not lay the matter to rest once and for all since their attempted dialectic of the will led in turn to modern and postmodern oppositions. In particular, their reception shows that despite the potential for a dialectical model of willing inhering in their thought, these philosophers formulated their arguments such that they invited (and received) one-sided readings as well. By looking at those founding positions through the tensions raised by the pairs of contemporary thinkers, in particular with an eye toward recovering the dialectic from the mere (polemical) opposition, we can work out a new model of the will as a fruitful *coincidentia oppositorum.*

Now to the four sets of historically based oppositions. The development of the concept of the will in the Western tradition has been typically summed up as a linear process, for example:

> It can be said that (1) there is little reliance on will in most of ancient moral and political philosophy, though this is less true of Aristotle than of Plato; (2) will is confined mainly to questions of sin and good acts—that is, to private acts—in the Christian philosophy that succeeded Platonism and Aristotelianism; (3) will is raised to a central but not exclusive, social and political place in the great age of social contract theory [Enlightenment through Idealism]; and

(4) will is made supreme, and actual creator of moral value, in existentialism, though even its adherents fall back on idealism when confronted with the problem of commitment to inhuman or antihuman "leaps toward existence"[6]

But I shall organize my discussion differently, namely in terms of the basic issues about which thinkers have taken constantly overlapping and conflicting positions, i.e., offered contradictory determinations over time. I shall highlight how Greek, Christian, and modern (especially Idealist) conceptions of the will played out dialectical positions on key questions of human agency in such a way as to point to the necessity of defining the will so that it incorporates both positions. These historical positions are not intended to be complete in any systematic sense (either in number or in exposition). In fact, I will occasionally circle back in my presentation to a number of major thinkers (Plato, Aristotle, Augustine, Kant, Schelling, Schopenhauer, et al.) to show how features of their analyses of willing respond in dialectical fashion to problems in understanding agency. I hope thereby to make plausible the claim that contradictions in philosophical interpretations of willing traverse a wide variety of movements, periods, and thinkers dealing with the will and to present the terms that reappear in contemporary debates. I present in schematic form the way significant positions have conflicted and intersected in order to lay the dialectical groundwork (the "partial determinations") for the detailed analyses in the following chapters.[7]

Will as the Unifying, Unchanging vs. Fragmenting, Innovative Force of Selfhood

The first two definitions in the neo-Kantian Rudolf Eisler's truly encyclopedic article on *Wille* in *Wörterbuch der philosophischen Begriffe* set up a polarity between a unified/unifying and fragmented/fragmenting understanding of will: "Will is 1. the general term for all kinds of instinctive and active volitional processes, 2. the unifying force, the disposition wants, the constant faculty of willing, either as a psychological or metaphysical agency."[8] On the one hand, the human organism consists of a variety of often conflicting drives, desires, motivations, volitions, that move the person in any number of ways. The will and the act(s) of willing are associated with this shifting basis of the self. On the other, the will represents the "core self," the constant force that responds to the world by organizing it in a consistent fashion. In the former view, there is a potential for an endless and uncontrollable series of volitions; in the latter, the individual is formed uniquely, and his/her "personhood" is characterized by the same will behind all acts.[9]

If according to Kant, the "I think" (*cogito, Ich denke*) forms the "unity of apperception" by "having to be able to accompany all my thoughts" (*Kritik der reinen Vernunft [Critique of Pure Reason]*), the "I will" (*volo, Ich will*) is more complex insofar as it is both more unified and more split. We can see why it should offer the self an even more fundamental unity than apperception since an act of will must even precede the decision to think (a problem we will discuss below in the relation between willing and reason). But willing also occurs thanks only to a largely indistinct collection of motivations. The abstract simplicity of the one conception conflicts with the irreducible plurality and complexity of the other. The will is either transcendentally indivisible or experientially composed of diverging elements.

We can understand the consequences and reverberations of these definitions of will if we consider the aporias and contradictions that arise when we introduce other concepts connoting unity or fragmentation. Consider, for example, the following set of binarisms that Schiller derives from Kant: person or character vs. condition, being vs. becoming, duration or constancy vs. temporality or change (*Person* vs. *Zustand, Sein* vs. *Werden, Beharren* vs. *Zeit* or *Veränderung*).[10] Given these oppositions, it would seem as if will would certainly come down on the left side while something like inclination (*Neigung*) would be associated with the concepts on the right. Idealist (and not just Idealist) thought would see a clear hierarchical priority of the permanency and consistency of voluntary actions as opposed to the changeableness of desires and inclinations. Indeed, beginning with Aristotle, the ethically good man is not distracted by desires or aversions; he can make a decision and stick to it.[11] When we speak of someone with an iron will, after all, or when a character like Gustav von Aschenbach in Thomas Mann's *Death in Venice* has the will to "persevere" (*durchhalten*), we associate will with constancy and stability of inner being.

And yet, the will has been associated just as clearly with the principle of change. The very "spontaneity" of the "I will," which should be the solid *foundation* of our character, opens up the possibility of *undermining* fixed categories and behaviors. Even Aristotle attributes to the will, i.e., to the activity of wanting/willing (*boulesis*), the ability to have an impossible object; reasonable choice or rational desire (*proaisesis*), however, limits itself to the possible.[12] This distinction makes of the will a kind of radicalized desire that (potentially) transcends not only the existing but also the possible. In this radical mode it can therefore not have the existing possibilities as its ground, and it takes on an independence from its own conditions and introduces potential arbitrariness that undermines the organization of the self.[13] In German, this ambivalently powerful aspect of free willing is captured in the word *Willkür*. As Eisler defines it in *Wörterbuch der philosophischen*

Begriffe, it is "1. the independent will, the ability to choose, in contrast to drive (*Trieb*), 2. lawless, individual, unprincipled, unmethodical wanting and acting."[14] Hence, the independent (*selbständige*) will located behind all our choices and giving them their consistent and uniform meaning contains at the same time the potential for flipping over into its fickle, fragmenting, and arbitrary other—and vice versa.

We can reformulate this debate in phenomenological and hermeneutic terms by considering the creation and interpretation of meaning.[15] "Meaning" here is not limited to just linguistic signs but includes also the organizing principle of an individual's life, i.e., how our lives have meaning and how within the context of a life individual activities (also linguistic) attain meaning. At stake is the notion of a continuous or unified sense (and sense of self). Two issues help us approach this problem of the will's ambivalent role in signification. First, the will, at least since the Idealists, has been associated with the notion of "self-determination" (*Selbstbestimmung*). But this notion itself has two different interpretations. On the one hand, it allows for the continuity of selfhood. On the other, it is the very possibility of change. I. H. Fichte, the nineteenth-century post-Kantian, summarizes both aspects in his definition: Will is "the ability of the spirit to change its given condition or to stand firm against some emerging change."[16] Will both maintains selfhood and is the condition for its change. If hermeneutics deals with the fundamental role of the phenomenon of understanding (*Verstehen*) in determining my place in the world, then the will, as the stable or unstable source of my (self)determining projections, is central.

The second way of seeing the will's connection to hermeneutics is to interpret it as that which grants meaning. Although it may not seem so obvious today to link the will and the production of meaning, the tradition offers clear and useful associations once we recognize how both activities provide *direction* (orientation) for the mind.[17] Gadamer has argued that all meaning implies a "sense of direction"; in his words from *Wahrheit und Methode:* "Aller Sinn ist Richtungssinn."[18] By this he means that the important thing about the way human beings construct meaning is not that they discover meanings existing ideally "out there" (either in a strictly Platonic sense or the way one could interpret *Sinn* in Frege) but, rather, that meaning grows out of the movement of interrogation and is identical with the directedness of consciousness. This phrase is ambiguous and Gadamer would encourage the different connotations: all consciousness (à la Husserlian phenomenology) is intentional, i.e., directed at something and meaning gives us that "sense of direction"; also, conversely, for there to be meaning, consciousness must be focused, directed. It is via these two senses of meaning as *Richtungssinn* that we arrive at a connection to the will, for this is precisely how the will has been defined by diverse thinkers.[19]

We therefore see developing out of the concept of the will two different hermeneutics of the self in the sense of any individual's ability to interpret the world, his/her own behavior, or the products of another person as a unified or fragmented entity. Moreover, given the interrelation of these views, we are compelled to look for ways to conceive of the two sides of the will as mutually interdependent. Out of the tension of these two positions we shall seek definitions of power and understanding.[20]

The Will and/versus Reason

The relationship between the will and reason, which generally raises the twin questions of whether the will's motivations are knowable and whether the will is secondary to the intellect, forms one of the deepest fault lines in the history of Western thought.[21] It runs through basic philosophical issues from the Greeks to the present and generates some of the most perplexing aporias. Much can be gained for contemporary discussions by looking at the tensions between reason and the will in history because what is often at stake in today's debates is the limits or abandonment of rationality. And yet these debates could be arbitrated differently by emphasizing the relationship between the will and reason. For example, the interaction between Habermas and poststructuralism can be illuminated (and reinterpreted) by shifting the focus of analysis to the role the will plays in both, since this concept itself contains a dialectical relationship between rationality and irrationality.

Because the Greeks had no separate theory of the will, a theory that would see the will as a unique substance, mental agency, or faculty, there would have been no essential challenge to the reign of reason.[22] Their intellectualism left no room for voluntarism.[23] For Plato and Aristotle, despite their other differences, and for much of the medieval tradition based on them, the will itself was not an issue; rather, they were interested in certain kinds of actions that we would call "voluntary."[24] These would on the whole have been considered subsets of the class of rational actions. For Socrates and Plato, the concern focused on the class of actions associated with *techne,* in which knowledge and ability are united; that is, ethical behavior was a matter of knowing what is right and how to do it.[25] There was no separate "mode" of the mind called "willing" that could have opposed reason "voluntarily." One does something intentionally that seems (i.e., is known to one) to be best. To be sure, one could act out of the immediate force of desires or passions, and one could act badly (evilly). But all these cases were interpreted in general as actions out of ignorance (of the Good) or loss of emotional control.[26] No one, in this view, could act knowingly and willingly in an evil fashion. Freedom comes "from knowledge" in the sense that it is derived from it, rather than opposed to it.[27] Reason and knowledge make the human being free, and his or her actions "voluntary," by liberating the agent from the grip of the appetites.[28]

The clearest opposition between reason and the will among the Christian scholastics is that between Aquinas and Duns Scotus. For Aquinas, *voluntas* would fall under the category of *rationalis appetitus* and, in a strict sense, then, the will was subordinated to the force of reason.[29] Thomas Aquinas says: "If Intellect and Will be compared with one another according to the universality of their respective objects then . . . the Intellect is absolutely higher and nobler than the Will . . . [because] every movement of the will [is] . . . preceded by apprehension whereas . . . apprehension is not preceded by an act of the will."[30] And yet, the fact that *appetitus* underlies *both* shows that the will, or the activity of willing in a broader sense, has the potential of transgressing its rationalist boundaries to become part and whole. Indeed, this is the ground for a more radical voluntarist position.[31]

In part derived from the notion of love or desire for God in Augustine, this alternative tradition introduces a conception of an "appetitive drive" in man and creation that is more powerful and fundamental than knowledge since the latter is useless unless man is "turned" to God by some other force of will.[32] (Whether that will is individual or divine is still a matter for debate within this tradition, as we shall see below.) Duns Scotus, who represented a stronger form of "voluntarism" against the intellectualist tradition of the scholastics, stressed precisely the primacy of the will.[33] In his view, nothing other than the will is the total efficient cause of volition. Although Aquinas sees such qualities as courage and temperance related to intellect, Scotus attributes all virtues to the will. The intellect is certainly needed (since we need to know the object of our willing to be virtuous), but only as a secondary cause. "The will," Scotus writes, "by commanding the intellect is a superior cause in respect to its act. But the intellect, if it is the cause of volition (i.e., as a partial cause by supplying the knowledge of the object), is subservient to the will."[34]

To shift to a more modern formulation of this debate over the status of knowledge and/of the will, let us consider German Idealism.[35] The intellectual landscape in late eighteenth-century Germany was in large part shaped by the tension between reason and the (freedom of the) will. In particular, the tension arose because of the reception of Spinoza, whose panlogistic thought was made popular by Friedrich Jacobi. In his study on G. Fichte, Neuhouser summarizes Jacobi's position: "The most important aspect of Jacobi's interpretation of Spinoza was his formulation and defense of the claim that the belief in human freedom is incompatible with the view of reality that reason seems to require us to accept."[36] If reason, namely, leads us to view the world as a gapless succession of cause and effect (or at least, every event has a "sufficient reason" explaining it), there seems to be no room for freedom or the will.[37] That is, much of later Enlightenment thought in Germany, especially the most important formulations of Idealism, can be seen in the context of a debate over the status of reason and the determinations of the will. The controversy over Spinoza established the task for philosophers either to choose (or to mediate) between a free will that is fundamentally irrational and a fully knowable reality that integrates the will into a network of rational (causal or at least sufficient) determinations.[38]

The will as defined by the major Idealists is marked by this inherent doubleness.[39] Fichte calls the activity of willing a "Tathandlung" and takes the knowledge of it as the basis of his *Wissenschaftslehre*, i.e., he interprets Kant as offering a fundamental kind of knowledge (of willing) and then uses this as the foundation of a system of philosophy. He is thus able to ground a Cartesian certainty (knowledge) not in the *cogito* but in the *volo*. This attempted unity of thought and volition in the form of their immediacy to consciousness points in two directions. Schelling, beginning in the early years of the nineteenth century and culminating in the *Freiheitsschrift* (1809), sees the will increasingly as the "Urgrund" of being.[40] As such, it is removed further from the sphere of knowledge and closer to that of "feeling" (*Gefühl*) or "premonition" (*Ahnung*). Schopenhauer merely stretches these two poles—namely a primally antirational will (*Wille*) and a superficially knowable world (*Vorstellung*)—to their metaphysical limits.[41] Like Schelling, he stresses the radical unknowability of the will even though we have a direct access to the will as that which is most intimately "familiar" to us beyond the knowledge offered by reason (the "Satz vom Grund").[42] Hegel takes the Idealist unity of reason and volition in the other direction, highlighting the function of thought. As Arendt says, his assumed unity works only "on the assumption of the existence of *one* World Mind ruling over the plurality of human wills and directing them toward a 'meaningfulness' arising out of reason's need."[43] The radical nature of willing is thus grounded in *knowledge* of the Absolute Spirit (in the sense of both the individual's knowledge of its meaning and the World Spirit's self-knowledge).[44]

If the historical concepts of willing relate it to knowledge in such consistently contradictory ways—determined by reason or beyond reason, most known or most unconscious—we can suspect that the will is best conceived of dialectically. Wanting occurs in the sphere of knowledge, but at the same time introduces into that sphere an element of the unknowable.

The (Empirical) Will as Determined or the (Metaphysical) Will as Indetermined

In most accounts of the history of the concept of the will, the debate between determinism and indeterminism takes a central position.[45] In this debate, the will either suffers from a positivist reductionism (it becomes "nothing but" the interaction of other forces) or is raised to the status of a transcendent metaphysical entity. What is at stake is the will as it occurs in the formulation of "freedom of the will," for if human beings are determined, what place would the will and freedom have? Furthermore, the question arises what kind of freedom would we have if the will were fully "indetermined"? And both questions have serious consequences for our concept of law, either as a given (of nature, God) determining us or as man-made (the undetermined ground of autonomy). The tensions between the will as determined and the will as determining depend largely on *what* it is related to and what one takes to be a "cause."[46] The back and forth between these two fundamental positions indicates the need for a dialectical determination.

Empiricism and positivism are the most important deterministic theories that, viewing behavior from the perspective of the body and natural laws, would eclipse the role of (free) will.[47] With the rise of the natural sciences in the seventeenth century, thinkers like Hobbes and Locke attempted to explain the will strictly in terms of the functions of the human organism.[48] Hobbes's critique especially dominates subsequent determinisms. His argument in *On Liberty* interprets behavior in terms of the appetites (impulses, passions), which he sees as having a cause in something other than themselves, whereby "it follows that voluntary actions have all of them necessary causes, and therefore are necessitated."[49] Because they unfold in a series of alternates, the stronger of the impulses wins out over the weaker. The final impulse before some action is actually taken comes to be attributed *after the fact* with the quality of "willed" or voluntary. As Oberdiek says: "Now deliberation for Hobbes amounts to nothing more than a tiny war of desires and aversions, a war that continues until one side gains the upper hand. This would seem to eliminate will altogether, and in an important sense it does. Will, Hobbes declares, is simply the last appetite in deliberating, that desire or aversion finally nudging us to act in this way or that."[50] Thus, for example, a number of unconscious sensations may finally lead up to the impulse for me to get up from the chair and get a drink of water. That final impulse, in fact only the last effect in a causal chain, gets *interpreted* as having been "willed." Similarly, for Locke (or at least one side of Locke, see below for another), the will is determined by either "the most pressing uneasiness" or the strength of "present satisfaction."[51] In this view, of course, there is ultimately no need to posit such a thing as will at all, a conclusion drawn by Ryle and the logical positivists, who abandoned the concept as a false reification.[52] The concept of freedom, which had otherwise for centuries been linked to the will, becomes itself suspect or is interpreted only in terms of the lack of constraint from other individuals or social institutions.[53]

The extreme empiricists and positivists in the nineteenth and early twentieth centuries were determined to reduce the will to physical processes in the brain.[54] Ernst Mach represents the culmination of such efforts. The will is merely the precondition of a movement of the body. The sensation of voluntary action is caused by the possibility of the influence of our own representations and associations (which are again merely physiological and chemical) on the mechanisms of the body. The human being is no different from the physical realm of mechanics. He claims "that our hunger is not so essentially different as it might now seem from the attraction of sulphuric acid and zinc, and our will is not so different from the pressure a stone exerts on its underlying support."[55] Willing is thus absorbed fully into the causal chains or networks of natural phenomena.

Opposed to the Empiricists, but equally deterministic, are variations of rationalist arguments that see reason dictating to the will (or to the body via the will). More precisely, what we see over the development of Western thought growing out of the Enlightenment is a strand that would reduce the will to practical reason itself.[56] In order to save the will and freedom from the reduction to *physically* based impulses, inclinations, laws, and appetites, Kant, or at least one aspect of his thought, would interpret the will in terms of the ability to follow the dictates of the self-given laws of practical reason.[57] Ironically, this interpretation is itself deterministic. Kant writes: "Through its practical laws, Reason immediately determines the will."[58] Since Kant wants to maintain the freedom of the will, however, he must then define freedom precisely as such a determination by laws of reason. This one-sided argument contains, as we shall see in chapter 2, an obvious paradox between freedom and determination and hence the seeds of a more fruitful dialectic between freedom and causality (determination).

The indeterminist position contrasts with both empirical and rational determinism by positing will as *Willkür*, the power of radical freedom of choice. If Aristotle, in attempting to bridge reason and desire, laid the groundwork for conflicting traditions that focused on one or the other, he also opened up a different direction for conceptualizing the will by pushing back his analysis to a point before either reason and desire, namely to the human capacity for choice.[59] *Proairesis,* choice, he says in Book VI of *Nicomachean Ethics,* is the starting point of any action. As an action unfolds, clearly reasons contribute to the motivation and physical desires are involved in a causal chain. But at least logically prior to these is the agency of choosing itself, or, to avoid the notion of a separate faculty, we could still see the human being in a *state* of potentiality ultimately "free" to choose.

In Christianity, the question of the *liberum arbitrium indifferentiae* was whether or not man could, on his own, make the fundamental choice between good and evil. This tradition is marked precisely by the shifting positions between determinism and indeterminism.[60] The earliest church fathers tended toward a stronger form of indeterminism. The patristic writers

Justinus, Nemesius, Gregory of Nyssa, Origines, and Pelagius argued for the ability to choose between two things ("unum ex duobus eligere"). And although reason often had to play a role, the deciding factor was the *liberum arbitrium* itself, which, given man's position between the spiritual and the corporeal, good and evil, could choose one or the other.[61]

Schopenhauer did the will the questionable service of raising it to the center of his philosophy by granting it the status of a being behind all beings. His metaphysics universalizes from this transcendental status of the will in radical form that makes it inaccessible for contemporary readings.[62] His analysis of the will in *Die Welt als Wille und Vorstellung* moves from a highly plausible phenomenology of the body, via a *metaphorical* extension, to a metaphysical entity. That is, he begins from the perspective of our self-experience and experience of the world through our body: "[The individual's] knowledge, which is the conditioning bearer of the world as representation, is . . . thoroughly mediated through a body."[63] Because our body is *known* to us in a way different from other experience, because I must be aware *of* my body as mine before I can experience anything *through* it, Schopenhauer posits its "substrate" as something even more fundamental, namely as will (142–53). This awareness is then "carried over" to all of nature: "whoever, I say, has come to this conviction [of the relation between will and body] will immediately see it as the key to knowledge of the essence of the totality of nature—one need only *transfer (übertragen)* it to all phenomena" (154; my emphasis). This notion of "übertragen" (he writes also of "hinüberführen" [154]) is a metaphorical extension of individual experience onto a metaphysical plane.[64] It is just one small step then for him to argue that "it is *one and the same will* that reveals itself" in all of nature (193). The will becomes, through a literalization of metaphor, *the* metaphysical substance "behind" the veil of physical entities.[65]

But this metaphysical isolation of the will leads to serious problems since the notion of a radically "indifferent" will raises Buridan's famous image of a donkey that starved standing exactly in the middle between two identical haystacks because it lacked anything determining a decision.[66] Moreover, any indeterminist position that focuses on the human ability *arbitrarily* to make a decision is open to Hegel's critique of the "morality" of the Romantics, namely that such voluntarism amounts to an apparent "freedom" that is in fact less a matter of choice than an impulse pushing the individual to one action or another without grounds. In other words, grounding freedom in radically arbitrary choice leads either to the inability to choose or to unfree reasons for choosing.

Given these dialectical turns, it is no wonder that Schelling argued in his essay on the nature of human freedom for the need to think both positions, which he associated with necessity and freedom, together: "It is time that the higher, indeed the only proper opposition emerge, that between necessity and freedom, so that in this way the innermost concern (*der innerste Mittelpunkt*) of philosophy will come into view."[67] That *Mittelpunkt* is a theory of the will. As Schöpf writes succinctly in *Handbuch philosophischer Grundbegriffe*, the alternative *Willkür* versus *Determination* "dissolves in favor of a mutual interpenetration of initiative and pregivenness, choice and dependence, self-determination and being-determined."[68]

The Individual and the Supraindividual Will

Implicit in many of the arguments we have seen thus far is a perspective that reads the history of debates in the Western tradition as a tension between the individual and a supraindividual will, or between the will and the world of active forces into which it is thrust. For the interpretations by Christian writers, this meant the relationship between the individual and the divine will and the possibilities for salvation inhering in the one or the other. But that argument has left its mark as well on modern secular theories that are torn between defining the highest expression of freedom in the individual will and integrating the individual within a universal/social order that offers the source of all moral concepts (including freedom). The will is at the center of the debate over the position of the individual's free play vis-à-vis a greater order. Although this debate unfolded originally in religious terms, its modern formulations have consequences for issues of politics and language.

The arguments of Spinoza and Leibniz were crucial for shifting this debate into secular terms.[69] Although abstract, their formulations set the terms for discussions of the ultimate power or powerlessness of the individual will. Spinoza can be interpreted as subsuming the individual will under the universal because he sees only the one Being and all else in the world is but a *modus* or attribute of that Being (God, Nature, substance). All things (finite modes, not the infinite) can thus be traced back to some cause or reason.[70] He does not see any separate faculty or force of the will, just concrete volitions explainable by the principle of sufficient reason. Objectively all our actions are necessitated by the universality of God, but because we are not aware of the causes we have the *illusion* that a particular, individual act is free.[71] Leibniz's monadology and theodicy, on the other hand, although equally in the grip of the principle of sufficient reason, posit the possibility of a force that acts in the individual entities or monads. Each monad is driven by a force, *conatus,* but because of the self-contained nature of each monad, the will is exercised in an individualized striving for the good.[72] Of course, given the universal nature of the good, Leibniz argues for a harmony of these strivings, but he never denies their individual nature. He avoids determinism by claiming that "the motive of the good inclines the

will without necessitating it."[73] Thus, despite charges that he encourages
a determinism of the universal reason, he guarantees the freedom of the
individual.[74]

Schelling's essay on human freedom likewise stands at the cusp
between religiously and secularly grounded discussions of the relationship
between the individual and the absolute. It reads like a curious mixture of
Christian mysticism and Enlightenment rationalism. Moreover, he stands
out for attempting to reconcile these different levels—the individual and the
supraindividual, the secular and the religious—dialectically. The opening
section of the essay, in which he clarifies the terms of the debate about the
freedom of the will, revolves around an attempt to argue for *both* the freedom
of the individual will and the necessity of locating that individual within a
"system" (divine, natural, and rational). He wants to show "that the denial of
formal freedom is not necessarily associated with the charge of pantheism"
(43).[75] His solution is to posit the will as the universal ground; but because
of the unknowable and self-determining and uncontrollable aspects of will
we have seen, it takes the form of primal or preoriginary being, "Ursein," so
that it itself is groundless, containing all things but not determining them:
"There is, in the final and highest instance, no other being besides willing.
Willing is originary being (*Ursein*), and all predicates of the one fit the other:
groundlessness, eternity, independence from temporality, self-affirmation.
All of philosophy strives only to give this its highest expression" (46). He
can therefore argue for both a totalizing universal (Nature, will, God) and the
freedom of the individual from determination since the former, precisely in
its groundless totality as *will,* leaves the individual will indetermined. As he
says, individuals stand out vis-à-vis the universal as points of light against
an indeterminate background of darkness.[76]

But the individual will stands in a tension-filled relation to a "universal" will not just in a religious and abstract philosophical sense but also
socially and politically. Consider, for example, what we mean when we speak
of the development of a "political will" (in the German texts this will appear
as *politische Willensbildung*). Since it does not refer to merely a collection
of individual wills, we need to look at its status and that of individual wills
in relationship to it. Rousseau gives this issue its modern formulation.[77]
Since according to Rousseau man is free in nature, the question is what kind
of social contract must be made so that he can live freely in society. The
answer is that each individual will contracts to follow the general, legal will.
In that way one gains a "second" freedom. The *volonté générale* is not the
same as the *volonté de tous* but, rather, the difference "left over" after all
the individual wills cancel each other out, or, in other words, the uniform
and homogeneous form of a community whose members substitute general
interests for their own particular ones. If the individual will goes against

the general, then the general will "forces him" to comply, i.e., forces him to be free. The individual will must *freely* subject itself to the general. In Cassirer's words:

> This submission, however, is no longer that of an individual will or of an individual person to other individuals. It means rather that the particular will as such ceases to be, that it no longer demands and desires for itself, but that it exists and wills only within the framework of the "general will" . . . now for the first time they have become individuals in the higher sense; they have become subjects governed by the will, whereas heretofore they had been motivated by their appetites and sense passions. The autonomous personality comes into being only as a result of being bound by the "general will."[78]

Rousseau is not rejecting or suppressing the existence of individual will but attacking the notion of a particular will *outside* the political community.[79]

Hegel likewise rejects the notion of the subjective grounding of morality in the individual will (indeed, since he tends to associate the will with the individual, he rejects the will as a basis of ethical behavior).[80] To define morality (as he says Kant does) by beginning with the individual perspective and universalizing it leads, for Hegel, to the ultimate immorality of individuals who think they can justify anything (he associates this with romantic irony). That is, the "formalism" of the Kantian ethic, which one achieves by abstracting from all *individual* interests to attain a "pure will" determined only by the law, leads to a law that is so devoid of content (it must only avoid contradiction) that it gives individuals free rein.[81] This recognition leads to the attempt to ground ethics and freedom again in the concept of *Sittlichkeit*, where "objektiver Geist" carries the determinations of individual behavior.[82] That is, this theory of the will grants the individual validity only insofar as it recognizes, and is recognized by, the universal and rational will as embodied in institutions.[83] For Hegel, in other words, the false universalism of Kant's "pure will" led to a more dangerous individualism of Romantic "willfulness," such that both positions could only be countered by a different conception of the general.[84]

All these debates play out the essential tension between the individual and his/her embeddedness in a predefined order. The inability of either position to account for key aspects of agency without appealing to the other, counter position reveals the need for a dialectical approach. Because ethics and politics place the will at the center of any attempt to interpret the extent of the freedom of individual actions we therefore need a dialectic that explains how willing partakes of both the individual and universal.

Having reviewed these different contradictions and attempted resolutions that have been played out in historical conceptualizations of the will, a "definition" could only take the impossible form of a condensation of these binarisms. The will is unifying (simple) and fragmenting (complex), is knowable and unknowable, is determined and indetermined, is innovative and limited by the empirically existing, is individual and supraindividual, is metaphysical and antimetaphysical, dependent on and creative of representations, is active and passive, is free of and ruled by the law. Such a statement clearly stretches the possibility of the copula to its extreme. What "thing" could ever unite these contradictions? Does this statement not boil down to the general form: a is x and non-x?

We need to follow two dialectical guidelines for the arguments of the following chapters. First, we can recall Schelling's thoughts on the dialectical sentence and the role of the verb "to be" in a proposition (judgment) of identity. To say, as he points out, that "this object is blue" does not posit a total identity or sameness (*Einerlei*), i.e., it does not say that in the way that this thing is an "object" it is also "blue," but, rather, states that *in some way* it is blue. Thus, to say that something is x and non-x means that one must look *for the ways* in which it is these two things. The difference between such an analysis and the majority of the historical treatments we have seen is that the thinkers dealt with in the following chapters lead us, if we focus on their dialectical potential and not their one-sidedness, to the search for the ways in which the will is double and to the embracing of those ways.

Second, given the significance of *activity* in the notion of the will, it would be better to use the possible ill ease that the statement above of the form "a is x and non-x" generates to our advantage. We can take those same contradictions and view them, and their odd identities, as undermining the hypostatization of the will as a "thing." We should thus reinterpret the statement with the formulation "willing involves." That is, human beings "will" to the extent that are involved in activities that unify their stimuli or actions and that challenge their unity; they "will" to the extent that they are involved in activities that reveal a spontaneous sense of self-awareness and that lead them to the limits of their knowledge; they "will" to the extent that they are involved in activities that are integrated into all kinds of larger causal or meaningful chains (structures) of events and that transform those chains in unpredictable ways; they "will" to the extent that they can both passively receive "input" and actively generate "output" of a different kind; and finally, they "will" to the extent that they ambiguously define themselves in terms of the law—to this extent, i.e., dialectically, human beings "will."

The analyses that follow work toward clarifying both the need for defining and ways to conceptualize central phenomena—freedom, power, understanding—in terms of the dialectical arguments surrounding the will. The arguments accomplish this by working through some problems and polemics in contemporary thought as rooted in various theories of the will from the history of German philosophy. Three levels of argumentation are therefore constantly interwoven: the historical (reception), the contemporary (polemics), and the conceptual. The goal is to see how a diverse and often conflicting assortment of modern and postmodern thinkers show the necessity of analyzing the will in dialectical terms and give us at least the tools of such an analysis. In so doing I hope to show how freedom, power, and understanding themselves are most fruitfully conceived in terms of an irreducible dialectic between individual and structure, the empirical and the transcendental, the arbitrary and the determined, fixed being and fluctuating becoming.

2

The Free Will and the Cause of Desire: Kant, Sade, Adorno, Lacan

But what would good will mean in psychoanalysis?
DERRIDA'S RESPONSE TO GADAMER, in *Dialogue and Deconstruction,* 1989.

Fundamental to the conceptualization of the will, agency, and freedom in Western thought is a contradiction seen in human nature between impulse and control, the individual's appetites and a higher (social) order, desire and the law. The will points in the opposing directions of a wish (for the possible or impossible) and denial of wish. It is viewed as pursuing some object or representation out of a psychophysical, causal need or as renouncing it "for a cause." One pole in traditional definitions of the will rests on the side of urges, instinct, drive, and irresistible passion against all reason; the other rests on the side of the rational repression of precisely those urges. The "wanting" contained in "willing" contains the ambiguity of both "being directed at getting something" and "going without." Willing, the basic "I want," therefore, is both the spontaneity of self-directed activity (*Selbstbestimmung*) and a lack in the subject motivating action. And since freedom is generally defined in terms of willing, i.e., to be free is in some way to be able to say "I will" (and to act on that volition), we need to look at these contradictory features of willing to gain a better understanding of freedom. This chapter discusses modern and postmodern attempts both to confront this contradiction and to work through it to what we might consider a dialectical model of a "heterogeneous free will."

The way to proceed toward such a model is to show how each opposing position, taken in isolation, leads to an aporia. On the one hand, the insistence on pure autonomy and spontaneity that is grounded in some rational presence in the subject, out of a core "agent within the agent," so that the subject prescribes the law to itself, will be shown to lead to its opposite—not freedom but a violent oppression of both the self and the Other (also within the self). But on the other hand, nature alone is insufficient for explaining human behavior since we are separated from nature and natural needs by language and the law—indeed, attempts to be human "before the law" bring down its full weight.[1] To move beyond these positions we can ask: How does the separation from nature create a gap in the subject that *as absence* fulfills the function of spontaneity that had been filled by an (untenable) assumption of a self-presence? That is, how can that lack (wanting) in the self between nature and the law be the cause of active volition (wanting)? To answer these questions is to develop a model of the free will that dialectically mediates the poles of willing. I shall address these questions by examining how Adorno and Lacan work out aporias in Kant and develop their own theories of subjectivity so that I can use them to expand dialectical possibilities inherent in Kantian ethics.

Kant's formulation of an ethics in the *Kritik der praktischen Vernunft* (1788) remains to this day the most influential attempt at a nonempiricist theory of the free will since both followers and critics must take the grounding of ethics in "practical reason" as a starting point.[2] Driven by the need to guarantee human freedom in a world governed by natural laws (causality, necessity), Kant appealed to the principles of pure practical reason that transcend any material cause as motivations of human action. At the heart of this dualistic account is the will, the faculty that allows human beings to participate in the spheres of both nature and the law. Thus, the value of Kant's ethics lies mostly in his ability to develop a truly dialectical analysis of the will. Without such a dialectic, either the two spheres exist merely side by side (whereby freedom and ethically grounded behavior have no justification) or the one is granted arbitrary priority over the other (which has equally violent consequences be it established as law over nature or nature over law).

Adorno and Lacan, two twentieth-century thinkers who would otherwise seem to have little in common besides their notoriously difficult styles, meet precisely at the point of intersection where the Kantian concepts clash, namely the will as transcendental mediator between nature and the law.[3] It is not that the will appears often in their writing, but it does occupy a key place that allows us to connect their thought to the logic of contradictory positions we have examined thus far. Traditional arguments concerning the will and these thinkers' theories of subjectivity are mutually illuminating.

From the opposing directions of neo-Marxist Critical Theory and neo-Freudian psychoanalysis, Adorno and Lacan approach Kant dialectically. The determinism of their own points of departure, Marx's and Freud's embedding of the will in either socioeconomic or natural, biological forces, could never accept a concept of freedom grounded in a self-governing, autonomous subjectivity. And yet, they see in Kant a valuable appeal to a nondeterminist position grounded in the self's contradictory nature that needs to be grasped *as such* (in a way Kant could not do) if the notion of a "free will" is to have meaning. That is, while they reject the obvious, traditional reading of Kantian ethics (according to which he calls for freedom as autonomy of Reason), they do not flip into determinism. Rather, they open up for us the possibility of a *dialectical* reading of Kant, according to which the will functions as a nonsubstantialized (lost) cause of our freedom.

My argument will pursue three modes of interaction between Adorno/Lacan and Kant that are moments in the development of a dialectical model of willing and freedom. First, Adorno and Lacan reject Kant for what they see as his "totalitarian" imposition of a rational will and a violent law that links him, ironically, to Sade. Their arguments involve one-sided readings that reject as dangerous Kant's own one-sided rationalist determination of will. Second, I trace out their internal critique of Kant, which, in a Kantian spirit, points to the insufficiencies and limitations of Kant's ethics so as to circumscribe the problem *with* Kant. They show how Kant pushes his own intellectualist position to its limit and points beyond himself in the direction of a more complex solution that he could formulate. And third, I offer a positive reformulation, which can allow us to reread Kant's theory of the will in dialectical terms. Through this reading we see: (1) that neither was Kant "superseded" by later theories nor does he represent a position to which we can "return," but that critiques like Adorno's and Lacan's can point us to a more promising interpretation of Kant that even supersedes them; and (2) that such an interpretation gives an account of the free will that "dialecticizes" its contradictory determinations by defining it as a quasi-transcendental site (hence not a hypostatized object) where the subject and Other interact.

The notion of freedom that can be gained from this synthetic reading of these three authors manages to maintain the individual's fundamental connection to the two spheres that define our humanity, nature and the law. Kant's paradoxical and problematic idea of a "causality through freedom" gains, in my interpretation, new meaning. It is not a cause in the sense of nature (i.e., not an object, need, inclination, impulse, instinct, etc.); nor is it the law self-reflexively imposed by the subject. Rather, we shall see how the "cause of freedom" is a will "dialectically determined" (Adorno) as the "cause of desire" (Lacan), a transcendental absence in the subject, generated by the interactions of nature and the law between which the subject must make an impossible choice, thrusting him/her necessarily, yet with the possibility of free action, onto both. In this reading, the cause of freedom, that which opens a space for us to act independently of psychophysical causation, needs to be accepted as a "lost cause"—it gives us an identity without itself being a self-identical object.

The Will as Reason's Domination

The conjunction of Adorno, Lacan, and Kant occurs, initially, thanks to a fourth figure: Sade. It is a historical fact inviting interpretation that Adorno, together with Horkheimer in the 1940s and Lacan in the 1960s, wrote essays evidently completely independent of one another in which Kant and Sade are read in terms not only of their temporal contiguity but, more important, of their conceptual linkage.[4] For Adorno/Horkheimer, Sade both makes clear and lives out the ideals of Kantian Enlightenment: "The work of the Marquis de Sade shows the 'understanding without the guidance of some other,' that is, the bourgeois subject liberated from tutelage" (*DA*, 93); and for Lacan, Sade's *Philosophie dans le boudoir* (1796) "completes" and "gives the truth of the *Critique* [*of Practical Reason*]" (KS, 55). Both of these formulations are clearly intended to shock the reader out of a preconceived understanding of Kant and to raise questions about the validity of Enlightenment ethics, in particular notions of freedom based on an autonomous, law-giving will.[5] How could Sade, who in the name of Nature chronicles "perversions" and brutally inhuman sexual relations, be the logical fulfillment of Kant, who in the name of duty and the law would rely solely on a self-directing Reason? Or more to the point: What hidden (sexual) dangers could possibly lurk in Kant's theory of Reason? Both Adorno/Horkheimer and Lacan show that a narrow definition of the will as the unifying force of practical reason not only pays the price of a loss of its other determinations but also, more important, suffers from the return of the repressed elements. The will limited to a form of dominating reason experiences a painful aporia in the revenge of a nature that comes to dominate it in turn.

Adorno/Horkheimer's argument appears straightforward, especially given the context of its writing in the 1940s: Kant's concept of Reason, defined as that which imposes order onto the world of phenomena, is only one step away from science in general as "calculating thought" ("kalkulierendes Denken") and "totalitarian order" ("totalitäre Ordnung"; *DA*, 93) and from Sade's systematic, indeed mechanistic organization of sexual pleasures in particular. To make this argument, Adorno/Horkheimer make a series of conceptual and semantic short circuits. Most important, they read Kant's *transcendental* arguments on the position of reason in *functional* terms. In this reading, they pursue a possible though ultimately limited interpretation of Kant rather than develop the richer dialectical potential of his work (that we shall explore below).

Adorno/Horkheimer begin their reductive reading by pointing out that Kant defines reason in terms of a fundamental unity. Perceptions could not be compared, thought could not occur, general and specific categories could not be related or hierarchized were there not a single principle or "collective unity" (*DA*, 88) that underlies the multifarious experiences of the subject. Kant called this the "unity of apperception" ("Einheit der Apperzeption") or the "I think" ("Ich denke") that must be able to accompany all internal and external sensations. For example, if there were not some sense, at some level, that it is "I" who saw the red ball yesterday and the red car today, "I" could never compare the two experiences and form the concept red; or if it there were not some sense, at some level, that it is "I" who thought one thing yesterday and something else today, "I" could not even say that I changed my mind. All perceptions would be discrete occurrences without any basis for comparison or contrast. The necessary, underlying form of unifying subjectivity is for Kant a transcendental given, an a priori condition of knowledge in principle.

The particular angle that Adorno/Horkheimer introduce through their reading of Kant is at first sight subtle, but it has significant consequences. They define the process of thinking as follows: "Thinking, in the Enlightenment sense, is the production of uniform, scientific order and the deduction of factual knowledge out of principles" (*DA*, 88). The key word here, I would argue, is "production" ("Herstellung"), which shifts the focus from a logical priority that interested Kant (namely, the experience of perceptions and thoughts in the *same* subject *presumes* an identity) to a temporal or functional relation (namely thought *manufactures* the unity). There is little doubt that the economic relations of bourgeois manufacture are indeed intended to echo in the above definition of thought itself. A little further along Adorno/Horkheimer refer to the notion of the "schematism of pure understanding," which for Kant is again a necessary precondition to knowledge,[6] as "the unconscious *working* ("Wirken") of the intellectual *mechanism*" (*DA*, 89; my emphasis). A priori conditions of unity have thereby been reformulated in terms of reified and reifying structures that enforce uniformity.[7] Having functionalized Kant in this way, Adorno/Horkheimer see in the Kantian subject and concept of reason "the instance of calculating thought, which the world organizes for the purpose of self-preservation and which knows no other functions besides those that prepare the merely material object as material of subjection" (*DA*, 90).[8] The proximity of *this* Kant to Sade, to instrumentalized science, to capitalist industry, and to fascism is not at all so surprising. The will that is defined parallel to this unity of thought, the *volo* corresponding to this *cogito,* is a domineering machine; the autonomous will of this subject is more like an automaton that subjects the difference of the Other to its uniform functioning. The will, in this reading, is turned into a "transcendental presence" that renounces its Other. Such a reading of Kant is in part accurate, yet nondialectical. It draws out the full implications of one (significant) side, or partial determination, of Kant's ethics, thereby making it possible to link him to an inhumane position.

The title and opening of Adorno's fragment argue for an intimate connection between this conception of Enlightenment morality and Sade. Sade's Juliette is merely the empirical expression of a Reason that imposes itself upon the other of itself, nature: "Reason is the organ of calculation, planning; neutral vis-à-vis goals, its element is coordination. What Kant founded transcendentally, the affinity of knowledge and planning, impresses the character of unavoidable purposiveness onto all details of the rationalized bourgeois existence; Sade had already developed this empirically a hundred years ago before the development of sports" (*DA*, 95). Sade, and his characters, live out the Kantian, one-sided determination of freedom as a "sadomasochistic" paradox: In the name of the will (as the freedom to determine behavior absolutely) the will (as a part of human beings tied to nature) is undermined. "It is my will," Sade's characters could be seen as saying, "to be free to experience whatever I want"; but in applying this principle in each and every experience, all they ever experience is their own willing. Over the course of a page, for example, Sade argues in *Philosophy in the Bedroom* that we should listen to the voice of nature to seek pleasure, then that we actually need to provide careful structure and order to experience pleasure, ending with the claim that he will "employ the same logic from beginning to end" (*PB*, 316f). The fact that their antinatural willing occurs in the name of nature only increases the force of their ironic bind.[9] Their insistence on feeling and pleasure leads to a rational "formalization" of experience that ends out "freeing" them from feeling (*DA*, 98, 99). The infamous state of "apathy" that Sade holds up as the ideal for his heroes demonstrates that they are driven by a will not to connect with others but to use others in order to "complete" themselves, become self-contained. Or, more pointedly, the Sadian hero *wants* desperately to put an end to all *wanting* (as potential lack). The self-Other combinations in Sade's writings lead not to mutual interpenetration but in fact to fantasmatic instances of bodies closed to the outside world. For Adorno, the following summary characterizes both Kant and Sade: "Since reason posits no goals with content, all affects are equidistant from it. They are merely natural" (*DA*, 96). Sade (or Juliette), merely draws the consequences that Kant, like the bourgeois order of "freedom" he would found, denies (*DA*, 101).

Here we see the first level of affinity to Lacan insofar as he, too, would seem to read in Kant (and then reject) a notion of Reason as domination over pleasure—a Reason active especially in the case of Sade where pleasure is proposed as the goal of rational activity. The goal-oriented processes of the rational activity in fact take precedence over the experience of pleasure. Thus Lacan stresses the inherent contradiction in the Sadian "imperative" that we have the "right to *jouissance*" since the "right," like the Kantian "ought," would seem to locate the motivation behind human agency in a willing so totalizing as to rule out the individual's pleasures. That is, when we read in Sade the justification that our right to enjoyment of any other person follows from the right to be free, i.e., not *possessed* by another (*PB,* 318f), it is one small step to the conclusion: "once you concede me the proprietary right of enjoyment, that right is independent of the effects enjoyment produces; from this moment on, it becomes one, whether this enjoyment be beneficial or damaging to the object which must submit itself to me" (*PB,* 320). For this right, anchored in an absolute will (dictated by Nature, *PB,* 323), dictates an "indestructible" (*PB,* 338) law that fixes our formal duties, not our particular likes and dislikes. Both Lacan and Adorno stress precisely this Sadian/Kantian structure of a will "beyond the pleasure principle."

The affinity of thought between Lacan and Adorno/Horkheimer expresses itself even at the level of phrases. Adorno/Horkheimer see parallel developments in the formalistic demands of Kant's systematic philosophy, the ritualization of sex in Sade, and the scientistic organization of bourgeois life: "The unique architectonic structure of the Kantian system announces an organization of all life according to goals without content. It does this like the acrobatic pyramids of Sadian orgies or the sets of principles guiding the early bourgeois loges" (*DA,* 95). And Lacan wonders, in a considerably more cryptic formulation with the same images: "For these human pyramids, fabulously demonstrating *jouissance* in its cascading nature, these tiered fountains built for *jouissance* to cast upon the d'Este gardens the iridescence of a baroque voluptuousness, the higher they make it gush into the sky, the closer we are drawn by the question of what is dripping there" (*KS,* 72). What Lacan seems to be addressing here is the development in Kant, Sade, and the revolution of the bourgeois order (especially the theory and practice of the French Revolution) whereby "happiness" in politics has become an "improper proposition" (*KS,* 71). It has been replaced by the "right to *jouissance*" and the "will" to the "freedom of desire" (*KS,* 71). Because the "revolution wills that its struggle be for the freedom of desire . . . the result is that it also wills that the law be free, so free that it must be a widow, the Widow par excellence [pun on French colloquialism for guillotine],[10] the one who sends your head into the basket however little it faltered in the affair" (*KS,* 71). That is, pleasure has been replaced by the *right* to pleasure, *jouissance* has been replaced by the *will* to *jouissance*. The two interconnected sides of will—nature and the law, drive and control—have been radically separated and the one allowed to eclipse the other. As a result, what flows is no longer desire but the blood released by the brutal imposition of the law.[11] Despite differences in orientation, the similarity of this initial criticism of Kant to Adorno's is striking. In the name of freedom, a kind of will is given rational autonomy over its Other, thereby destroying the dialectical bond that would have made a true freedom of the will possible.

Lacan's most critical formulations against Kant occur in the opening pages of his essay "Kant with Sade." Although Kant is given a unique status as a fundamental precursor of Freud for analyzing a realm "beyond the pleasure principle"—a status that, given Lacan's relation to Freud, has special weight and to which we shall return later—the tone of the first pages reduces Kantian ethics to the position of being merely antipleasure. Lacan focuses on the distinction Kant draws on at the opening of the *Kritik der praktischen Vernunft* between the notions of "gut" and "wohl," which in English could be rendered as the difference between the colloquialisms "doing well" and "doing good," as in the phrases "I'm doing well today" versus "Boy Scouts are always doing good." The first is a state of well-being or pleasure; the second is a mode of ethical behavior that may—in the case of Kant, *should*—oppose the former. Kant's argument is simple and powerful: Since the reasons for, and feelings of, well-being (*wohl*) change, they can never be the ground for consistent ethical laws (given the major assumption that ethical laws must be consistent). In Lacan's terms: "Thus, no law of such a good [*wohl*] can be enunciated which would define as will the subject who would introduce it into his practice" (*KS*, 56). In other words, will in the sense of ethics as self-determination leads to the exclusion of will as pleasure, as *das Gute* excludes the sense of "feeling *wohl*."[12]

At the core of his critical remarks on Kant, Lacan makes a series of semantic short circuits that parallel those of Adorno/Horkheimer. In Lacan's case, there is not so much a shift from a transcendental to a functional reading (he strictly maintains the sense of the categorical imperative as "unconditional"; *KS*, 56) but, rather, a slippage that moves from a necessarily *proposed* (pre*supposed*) distinction, to an *opposition* that is called an *imposition*. These largely rhetorical moves are his way of showing how a dangerously one-sided ethical will can emerge from Kant. For example, Lacan writes of the way one aspect of a good will ("doing good") gets raised to an exclusionary absolute (*the* Good):

> Let us note that this good is only *supposed* as the Good by *proposing* itself, as has just been said, over and against any object which would set a condition to it, by *opposing* itself to whatever uncertain good these objects might provide, in an a priori equivalence, in order to *impose* itself as superior by virtue of its universal value. Thus, its weight only appears by excluding anything—drive

or sentiment—which the subject might suffer in his interest for an object, what Kant therefore qualifies as "pathological." (*KS*, 56; my emphasis)

Lacan, at this point, would leave us where Adorno/Horkheimer have led us, namely at an interpretation and critique of Kant as a merely negative moralist, for whom independence (the "self-proposing good") is domination. On this reading, the difference between Kantian ethics and that of the Ancients is telling (Lacan stresses it in a way remarkably similar to Foucault): The latter strive for a Good that balances pleasures and responsibilities, whereas Kant's Good removes pleasure from the realm of the good.[13] Or, as he says in the *Seminar VII*, both Kant and Sade remove from ethics all appeal to sentiment: "If one eliminates from morality every element of sentiment, if one removes or invalidates all guidance to be found in sentiments, then in the final analysis the Sadian world is conceivable—even if it is its inversion, its caricature—as one of the possible forms of the world governed by a radical ethics, by the Kantian ethics as elaborated in 1788" (79). We have, to use the terms from chapter 1, not a dialectic but partial determinations of the good that have assumed totalizing (totalitarian) proportions.

Kant's fundamental move in ethics—the establishment of an "order of a purely practical reason or of a will" precisely "at the moment when the subject is no longer faced with an object" (*KS*, 56)—is left (at least in the beginning) for Lacan as a "paradox." The will as merely *opposed* to objects undermines its necessary relation to the Other and hence its own determination as *double*. Such a will is problematically autonomous, since it gains its autonomy by closing in on itself. In this way, we see that the rational will that would divorce itself from its bond to its Other does violence to itself. In striving for a state of pure activity, Kant would have to isolate volition from its objects and representations that, in their now oppositional state, threaten to cast the will into a position of passivity.[14]

Lacan argues that this violence of a one sided will against the self amounts to the individual's total subsumption under the signifying law. To argue this, he shows that the categorical imperative, to which one must submit all maxims for action, is an "analytical tautology" that works because of a kind of violent nominalism.[15] It would go something like this: In order to test an action against the categorical imperative, I have to be able to universalize the statement of my own action in terms of some kind of self-description, like "I, as x, do y," to see if a contradiction arises. For example, if I want to see if cheating is ethically permissible, I don't just say "I cheat" and generalize it to everyone but, rather, "I, as a banker, cheat." This procedure makes ethical statements "analytical" to the extent that contradictions can be rooted out merely at the level of the concepts involved (i.e., since bankers are defined as having the trust over people's money, it would indeed be a contradiction to have bankers cheat). But this presumes, Lacan's argument seems to imply, that the signifiers x and y have an absolutely defining, performative effect on the subject. Hence his "irreverent" variation from *Père Ubu* to the effect that it is Poland that defines the Poles.[16] The end result would be that the individual is completely subsumed under the signifier of the law, i.e., is viewed as if *nothing but* "x." The "I" disappears, often tragically, under its signifier as, say, "banker," "Pole," etc.

This argument is important because Lacan, in rejecting such an "analytical" approach to justifying behavior, must move toward "a more synthetic foundation" (*KS,* 57). Such a "synthetic" approach would bridge the gap between the universal and the particular, the signifier and the individual, the law and desire (nature)—a gap that was opened even in Kant, precisely where he then went on to deny and "fill" it. A synthetic solution would see that the self-determination of will relies at the same time on its Other, and the (empty) "place" of their interaction, the source of true freedom, lies only in a more dialectical and interactive account of willing, desiring, and the law. Adorno and, as we shall see, Kant himself, are likewise searching for such a synthetic or dialectical determination of the will. For this reason, we cannot stop at this one-sided reading of Kant but must look at how it points beyond itself.

Kant and Sade at the Limit of a Dialectic

Adorno: Kant's Negative Dialectical Model

It would be a mistake to read Adorno/Horkheimer's and Lacan's strong criticisms of Kant (via their associating him with Sade) as a rejection of the attempt to ground freedom in willing. Clearly they, like so many thinkers before them, reject a radical "autonomy view."[17] But they do not ultimately reject it for the sake of a determinism or "antiwill" empiricism. On the contrary, they reject autonomy because it leads, with tragic and painful irony, to determinism. We need to see how Adorno and Lacan, beyond their critiques, in fact proceed to use Kant and Sade to point them in the direction of a richer conception of will. They do so by making clear that the falsely totalized partial determination of will as Reason (Law) is indeed *partial,* that the danger lies not in the will but in its nondialectical interpretation. By taking Kant's argument to its limit and "putting Kant back in his place," so to speak, they also reveal how such a "limited" Kant can be connected anew to what he falsely excluded. As Lacan writes in the *Seminar VII:*

> [The categorical imperative], the central formula of Kant's ethics, is pursued by him to the limit of its consequences. His radicalism even leads to the paradox that in the last analysis the *gute Wille,* good will, is posited as distinct

from any beneficial action. In truth, I believe that the achievement of a form of subjectivity that deserves the name of contemporary, that belongs to a man of our time, who is lucky enough to be born now, cannot ignore this text. (77)

For Adorno, this move toward a dialectical model occurs in two stages: In the *Dialektik der Aufklärung* he and Horkheimer take Kant and Sade to the limits of the dialectic between science and myth (nature), while in *Negative Dialektik* he works out the two poles that he claims Kant was unable to synthesize. Adorno thus uses Kant to illuminate the missed chance for a fully dialectical determination of the will and freedom. For Lacan, it is Sade who brings us to the limit beyond which we might glimpse what Sade himself missed and what Kant only formulated abstractly: a unique kind of object, the "thing in itself," as "*cause* of desire" and new "ground" for our freedom. Sade, for Lacan, gives us the structure within which the consequences of choosing between a dialectical or nondialectical model of will become clear. Only after passing through these "critiques" of Kant and Sade—critiques in the Kantian sense of demonstrating their limits—can we return to Kant to see the full potential for a synthetic conceptualization of freedom and the will. Thanks to Adorno's and Lacan's critical readings we can see that the will, in order to guarantee its own existence, must be the paradoxically impossible, absent, and powerful point of intersection between Reason and Nature, Law and desire, universal structure and individual subject.[18]

Sade, for Adorno/Horkheimer, is more than just a bogey man, more than the sadistic realization of an inherent violence in Kant. Adorno uses Sade to unfold the dialectic of science and myth, Reason and Nature. We can not only learn from him the dangers of that dialectic but can (must) follow him through it to a point of liberation

If above we looked at how Adorno/Horkheimer and Lacan initially seem to use Sade to show what is wrong and dangerous in Kant's conception of the autonomous, self-determining will of practical reason, here I am more interested in how Adorno/Horkheimer see in Sade a powerful formulation of the dialectic of Enlightenment from which we can learn about the intimate connection between Reason and domination over nature. Sade is "truer" than Kant only because he shows this more plainly. Precisely Sade's *insistence* on "Ratio," write Adorno/Horkheimer, "has the secret significance that it liberated a utopian thought from its false mantle, namely the thought that is contained in Kant's concept of reason as well as in all great philosophy: the utopia of a humanity, itself no longer deformed, no longer requiring deformation of its world. By voicing the merciless moral of the identity of domination and reason, they show more mercy than the moral blither of the bourgeoisie" (*DA,* 127). The fact that these statements come at the *conclusion* of the "fragment," shows that Adorno/Horkheimer did or could or would not themselves portray the "utopia without its mantle"; but we need to pursue how his reading of Sade shows what it would be like to remove it to get to the "true" core of Kant.

Adorno/Horkheimer take Kant and Sade to their limits by setting their categories into dialectical motion. Consider, for example, the relation between strength and weakness, activity and passivity. If Reason is defined as "strength of character," or "strong will," then the "strong," dominant, "sadistic" in Sade is the epitome of Enlightenment, the ultimate rational man. He reveals in his relation to the "weak"—in particular, he reveals in the desire and pleasure he attains from his relation to those he controls—his own misery and anxiety, since they represent that which he must always repress in himself. Adorno/Horkheimer formulate the dialectic as follows:

> [The weak][19] live, even though they could be disposed of, and their anxiety and weakness, their greater affinity to nature because of their constant pressures— these are their life's element. That incites the strong to blind fury, for he pays for his strength with the tense distance from nature and must always deny his own anxiety. He identifies with nature by repeatedly producing the scream in others that he can never express. (*DA,* 120)

This model has remarkable similarities to the structure of the Sadian fantasy in Lacan, to which we will presently turn. But note how Adorno/Horkheimer use the Sadist's dialectic of desire to reveal what is lost in the "Distanzierung zur Natur." The "strong subject," in order to constitute itself as such, must undergo a process of splitting that, furthermore, it is not allowed to experience as such, since its "strength" resides precisely in its putative unity. In order to experience both the split and the "nature" from which it was split, the subject must impose (sadistically, in torture) a split onto another subject, identifying with it (erotically). In other terms, the interdependence of activity and passivity in willing is repressed for the sake of activity, whereby the active will must remain unconscious of its dependence on and suppression of its own passivity. Since, however, that passivity is also a source of pleasure, the active subject can only experience it when projected onto another. Likewise, the inherent dichotomy, which is lived simultaneously, between the will as unified/unifying and fragmented/fragmenting would be "resolved" by the Sadian subject in favor of an imposed unity; but precisely the repetitive pleasure procured through the fragmenting/ed Other reveals the impossibility of such a violently nondialectical "resolution."

What we have in the prototypical Sadian relationship, then, is the unmasked formulation of the dialectic of Reason as outlined in Kant. For Kant, human freedom and subjectivity is attained only through a rational will that is radically divorced from its desirous and drive-ridden other, a will whose only pleasure (and Kant always hesitates to use that word, although he does), is a "moral feeling" that arises not *in* doing something pleasurable but, on the contrary, exists only *after* rejecting immediate pleasure thanks to the correspondence with an "ought" that exists prior to any experience. Adorno/Horkheimer see Sade's (and Nietzsche's) contribution in the way he makes this dialectic conceptually clear and brutally explicit: "The Roman proverb, according to which being strict [*die strenge Sache*] is the true pleasure, is no exaggeration. It expresses the unresolvable contradiction of an order that transforms fortune into parody (where such fortune is even permitted) and creates only where it curses. Sade and Nietzsche eternalized that contradiction and thus raised it to the level of conceptual clarity" (*DA*, 121–22). It is probably more accurate to say that it was Kant who gave this dialectic between Nature and the order of the Law its conceptual form, showing how the subject is constituted as a will within its tensions, whereas Sade (and Nietzsche) painted out its consequences for an "enlightened" will that would deny its inherent contradiction. Kant and Sade thus take us, according to Adorno/Horkheimer, to the point where we need to make explicit the link between desire and the law, nature and reason. They bring us, in other words, thanks to their limited conceptions, to the need for a dialectical definition of willing. Adorno offers the outline of such an interpretation in his Kant chapter of *Negative Dialektik*.

Later in his oeuvre, Adorno explicitly looks to Kant for a "model" of the "negative dialectics" of modernity. By model, he means an example of thinkers who pointed to a fundamental ambivalence in dominant Western conceptualizations (like freedom) but who were incapable of thinking through the ambivalence to its "cause." The point of contact between Adorno and Lacan is Kant/Sade because the latter offered a conceptualization of the "will" that is "almost right," i.e., both Kant and Sade (especially when brought together) point to the "knotting" of desire and the Law. The will, after all, is the concept that has always in some form united both. But, as Adorno shows, at least one part of Kant does not maintain a dialectic in the will. Kant delineates the surfaces of contact between desire and the Law, nature and reason without exploring their interaction. Adorno's summarizing criticism of Heidegger applies to Kant as well: "He thinks right past the knot of the subject" ("Er denkt am Knoten des Subjekts vorbei"; *ND*, 276). Kant reveals for us, stumbling over them, the contradictory knots at the heart of the ethics of a philosophy of consciousness (*Bewußtseinsphilosophie*) but fails to pursue the ways in which the strands of desire and Law are interwoven. Thus, says Adorno, in a formulation recalling Lacan's at the end of "Kant with Sade," "Kant's speculation grows silent precisely where it would have to begin" (*ND*, 284).

For Adorno, the analysis of the concept of freedom involves the question of the freedom of the will. And that question leads to contradictions that are to be thought through rather than avoided or reductively resolved, since the issue of the will cannot be addressed in nondialectical terms: "The question of whether the will is free is certainly relevant; but at the same time these terms resist the need to express what they mean clearly" ("Ob der Wille frei sei, ist so relevant, wie die Termini spröde sind gegen das Desiderat, klipp und klar anzugeben, was sie meinen"; *ND,* 211). He therefore writes further: "We would have to reflect on the objects under consideration not to pass judgment on them as something that is or is not (*Seiendes oder ein Nichtseiendes*) but to see in them both the impossibility of their reification and the necessity of being 'objects' of thought (*die Unmöglichkeit, sie dingfest zu machen, ebenso wie die Nötigung, sie zu denken*)" (*ND,* 211– 12). As in Lacan, we are in the realm of peculiar "objects" that are neither substances nor nothings. The conceptualization of freedom and will is part Adorno's enterprise of a "negative dialectic" because they all need to be approached paradoxically via an alternative mode of addressing what seems like "an either/or that is as binding as it is questionable" (*ND,* 212). Since, as we have seen, the concept of the will has precisely this structure, it serves as a crucial "model" for thinking through nonidentity as the point of contact between opposites. Although, according to Adorno, Kant fails in his attempts to bring together the incompatible ("Inkompatibles verkoppeln"), he at least points to "what for him shatters the very realm of the calculable" (*ND,* 225). The "truth" of Kant lies then in the contradictions that he was honest enough to present even though he was not able to resolve them.

The basic contradiction that Adorno sees in Kant revolves around nature and freedom, a dualism that appears absolute and at the same time demands mediation. This tension makes for the uniqueness of Kant: "While Kant announces the dichotomy of what is and what ought to be (*den Chorismos von Seiendem und Seinsollendem*) in his practical philosophy, he is nonetheless forced to find points of mediation" (*ND,* 230). This impossible problem at the heart of Kant's reflection on the will and freedom explains both the "inversion" (or "perversion"; *Verkehrung*) and "its proximity to the truth of the matter" (*ND,* 230). Adorno shows how the tensions in Kant are contained in the concept of the will, which is marked by a dialectic between pure consciousness and its "supplement" (*das Hinzutretende*), the real.

Adorno's criticism of Kant, one that moves toward a positive for-mulation, rests on a reading that links the guarantees of freedom to the unity of consciousness (knowledge)—only then to show that in Kant we see the failure and dangers of this approach. Kant's failure points the way— negatively, dialectically. We saw a simplified version of this critique in the functionalist interpretation/rejection of Kant in *Dialektik der Aufklärung.* In *Negative Dialektik* he summarizes Kant's notion of freedom: "the experience of self in the moment of freedom is tied to consciousness; the subject knows him/herself to be free only insofar as his/her action appears to be identical with him/herself; and that is the case only when they are conscious" (*ND*, 226). The problem is that this leads to a "rationalistic narrowing" of the notion of freedom and free actions to pure reason ("But the insistence on this becomes rationalistically self-limiting" [*ND*, 226]), a move that links Kant to his precritical philosophical forebears. Indeed, it leads to a separation of rational from other motives and links Kant to Hamlet, in whom "the divergence of insight and action is paradigmatically inscribed" (*ND*, 227).[20] That is, the limitation of the free will to its rational side makes it impossible for this concept of freedom to include that other side which it requires to be free, namely its relation to nature, unconscious action, the real. This other side, which now becomes "irrational" according to the "rationalist rules of the game" (*ND*, 227), Adorno calls "the supplement, the something else" ("das Hinzutretende"): "*Das Hinzutretende* is the name for that which was expunged by that abstraction [of a will reduced to practical reason]; a will could never be real without it" (*ND*, 228).[21] Kant, and the other idealists, know that there is no (practical) consciousness without the will, but they reduce this necessary unity of opposites to "blank identity" (*ND*, 229), whereby the Other of Reason, which it needs to be free and is thus essentially also experienced in the will *together* with Reason, becomes reduced to (an appendage of) Reason:[22]

> But praxis needs an Other that is not covered fully by consciousness, that is corporeal, in mediation with reason and yet qualitatively different from it. Both moments are in no way experienced as separated; yet philosophical analysis has dealt with this phenomenon in such a way that the language of philosophy cannot express it otherwise than as if it were merely some Other added on to rationality. (*ND*, 228)

Kant's attempt to protect his practical philosophy (of free will) from the encroachments of the theoretical reveal his recognition of the need for a difference, even though he was unable to work out a dialectic of nonidentity in the concept of the will. As in the relationship between the will and representations, the denial of their mutual interdependence for the sake of separate spheres is an ultimately untenable position.

Adorno plays out this dialectic, which one could call "Kant's missed chance," in analyzing Kant's notion of "intelligibler Charkter" (*ND*, 283ff). I quote a passage at length since it not only indicates the limitations of the Kantian position but also states Adorno's own position and echoes the argument from *Dialektik der Aufklärung,* according to which Kant flips over into Sade. In this passage Adorno describes an inherent dialectic between nature and reason and the dangers of denying their mutual interpenetration:

> That reason is both nature's other and a moment of it, this belongs to its own prehistory and has become part of its immanent determination. Reason is natural since it is a mental force that splits off from others for self-preservation;

once split off from and contrasted to nature, however, reason becomes nature's Other. Rising above nature ephemerally, reason is simultaneously identical and not identical with it; the very concept of reason is dialectical. However, the more reason loses its inhibitions and makes itself in this dialectic the polar opposite of nature and leaves nature on its own, the more reason itself regresses to nature and self-preservation gone wild. Only as a reflection of nature can reason genuinely be more than nature (*Übernatur*). (*ND,* 284)

This movement could be mapped as follows: Beginning with a complete overlapping of nature and reason, which must undergo some separation for human agency to develop, one response to that separation might be the attempt to *impose* (or fold over) reason onto nature, which results in a (disastrous) reidentification.

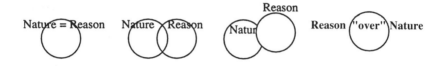

It is precisely the concept of the will that *could* occupy the unique position between the two spheres, which could, also according to Kant, be the scene of reason's "identical and nonidentical" reflection of/on nature. Without that space and the splitness in the subject it brings about, nature becomes eclipsed by reason in a brutal reduction to oneness.

In a section that will bring us back to Lacan and the "object," Adorno analyzes the contradiction between the two spheres that intersect in the concept of the will as *Ding an sich.* The binarisms he unfolds are familiar to us from the tradition of the will explored above. On the one hand, the will, defined parallel to reason, is a "thing in itself," a concept that unites the individual moments of actions and impulses. "In the face of individual impulses, the will is in fact independent, quasi thing-like, insofar as the unifying principle of the ego attains a modicum of independence by experiencing its phenomena as 'its own' " (*ND,* 236). Will, in this form, becomes the other of its "material," i.e., the sensations.[23] It is active, independent, determining, rational, unifying. And yet, this leads to a contradiction since, on the other hand, the will is that which goes beyond objectification, indeed is that movement out of which reason can develop and act in the first place (see the section on "The Pre-ego impulse" ["Der vor-ichliche Impuls"]; *ND,* 221–22).[24] It is prerational, arbitrary, transgressive, "groundless" (like Schelling's "Wille als Ursein").[25] This contradiction "may be inherent in the matter at hand (*in der Sache*)" (*ND,* 238) and has the following form as a true dialectic:

> Will without bodily impulses living on in weakened form in the imagination would not exist; at the same time, however, will sets itself up as the centralizing unity of impulses, as the instance that binds and potentially negates them. That necessitates its dialectical determination. Will is the force of consciousness by which it breaks out of its own circle (*Bannkreis*) and thereby changes what merely is; its activity (*Umschlag*) is resistance. Without question the transcendental rational doctrine of ethics never forgot this; hence we see Kant's admission of the way the moral law is independent of philosophical consciousness. (*ND*, 240)

Thus, Kant's positioning of the will as the place of nonidentical contact between reason and its other is a crucial "model" of freedom for Adorno, because precisely this "Umschlag" within the will of impulse to reason (developmentally) and from reason to "reality" not only makes up a prime example of negative dialectics but also shows the close connection between negative dialectics and freedom. Kant according to Adorno, however, like Sade according to Lacan, never analyzed this unique middle sphere, moving on a "sinuous curve" instead that reinstitutes the dangerous rationalist dualism and its potentially violent repressions and hierarchies as it gets forced into a unity.[26] At the core of Adorno's thought on freedom, then, is the attempt to make good on what the contradictions in Kant point to as a desperate need, a "dialektische Bestimmung des Willens" (*ND*, 238). To formulate this dialectic, Adorno calls for a different logic.

According to Adorno, what is needed is a logic of the nonidentical to appreciate the necessity of the contradiction inherent in the will. Confronted with the contradiction (antinomy) of Reason and the will (freedom)— namely, the subject is both free and unfree—Kant tried to solve the problem "with the means of undialectical logic, i.e., the distinction between the pure and empirical subject, without considering the mediation of these two concepts" (*ND*, 238f). Adorno draws the contradiction into reason itself, thereby revealing the necessity of a different logic: "The fact that reason cannot avoid contradiction indicates that contradiction eludes both reason and 'logic' " (*ND*, 238). This means that the contradiction of the will cannot be avoided by appealing to a constituting Reason, a pure guarantor of the Law and identity, because if such a "pure" noumenon were not in some essential way linked with its empirical, phenomenal self, it could not exist and be law giving.[27] Thus, identities granted to both the empirical and transcendental self by the Law (of Nature or Reason) are given their limits by some irreducible nonidentity: "[The] transcendental requires the irreducibly non-identical, which at the same time limits its autonomy (*Gesetzlichkeit*)" (*ND*, 239). What we see here is the will being used to resist rational determination. The will, as a "Ding an sich" that is nonetheless not "dingfest" (*ND*, 212), would be a place to begin analyzing this nonidentity. The problem lies not in the notion of will as "Ding an sich" but in *objectifying* this "thing" as a presence and identity when it must in fact be that which makes identity possible. Thus, Adorno writes in a footnote: "The construction of thing-in-itself and intelligible character makes a nonidentity the condition of possibility of identification even as it escapes identifying categories ("Die Konstruktion von Ding an sich und intelligiblem Charakter ist die eines Nichtidentischen als der Bedingung der Möglichkeit von Identifikation, aber auch die dessen, was der kategorialen Identifizierung entschlüpft"; *ND,* 286n). The (free) will is "Ding an sich," but only if it maintains its elusive character as "das Ding," or *objet petit a* in a Lacanian sense, a nonpresence that nonetheless acts as a condition of identity.

To see how it could be formulated, we need to consider the conclusion where Adorno states most explicitly how to read Kant as a "model" of negative dialectics. Here Adorno "dares" to provide the "true content" of Kant's "Ding." The key for Adorno is to see it neither as objectivized being nor as an abstract, empty form, but as a temporally intervening phenomenon:

> If one dared to grant the "X" of Kantian intelligible character its true content, which would assert itself against the total indeterminacy of its aporetic conceptualization, then it would have to be this: the historically most advanced consciousness that flares up and quickly dissipates, within which resides the impulse to do what is right ("das geschichtlich fortgeschrittenste, punktuell aufleuchtende, rasch verlöschende Bewußtsein, dem der Impuls innewohnt, das Richtige zu tun"). (*ND,* 292)

As long as the "intelligible character" or "pure will" is undialectically opposed to the "added on" empirical subject (or "das Hinzutretende") as two forms of being, human beings will feel themselves "mutilated . . . in their becoming, in their effective reality" ("verstümmelt . . . in dem, was sie wurden, in ihrer Wirklichkeit"; *ND,* 292).[28] In fact, the unique twist in the modern form of evil ("ein Scharnier im Mechanismus des Bösen"; [*ND,* 293]) has been to deform and weaken by splitting off precisely the forces in human beings that could overcome the deformation. Adorno's argument here echoes late-nineteenth-century discussions of psychopathology. The neuroses, for example,

> turn all instincts, which could press out beyond this false state of existence, back into narcissism, which finds satisfaction in the false state. . . . In the end, the intelligible character would be the paralyzed rational will. Whatever, on the contrary, had been considered its higher, more sublime and purer aspect becomes nothing but its own inadequacy and lack, the inability to change what demeans. Failure thus becomes stylized as purpose.

> Die Instinkte, die über den falschen Zustand hinausdrängen, stauen sie tendenziell auf den Narzißmus zurück, der im falschen Zustand sich befriedigt. . . .

Am Ende wäre der intelligble Charakter der gelähmte vernünftige Wille. Was dagegen an ihm für das Höhere, Sublimere, vom Niedrigen Unverschandelte gilt, ist wesentlich seine eigene Bedürftigkeit, die Unfähigkeit, das Erniedrigende zu verändern. Versagung, die sich zum Selbstzweck stilisiert. (ND, 293)

Thus, the truth of Kant shines through precisely there where there is "the shocking lack in his theory, the withdrawing, abstract form of the intelligible character" (ND, 293), namely the truth of the impossibility of giving fixed status to that which is "a becoming, not a being" ("ein Werdendes, kein Seiendes"; ND, 294). The contradictions in Kant come about because he moves the will back and forth from the spheres of desire and the law, rational and irrational, without examining its inherently paradoxical, absent-present position *in between,* a position that guarantees its movement and freedom. Thus, Adorno would still speak of the will (defined as "intelligible character"), but "only insofar as it doesn't float abstractly and powerlessly above what is; rather, it emerges time and again, indeed gains its temporality and reality, from the lacking relationality of what is" ("Trotzdem ist vom intelligiblen Charakter nur insofern zu reden, wie er nicht abstrakt und ohnmächtig über dem Seienden schwebt, sondern in dessen schuldhaftem Zusammenhang, und von ihm gezeitigt, stets wieder real aufgeht"; ND, 294). The will, therefore, needs to be understood in terms of the "way subjects experience themselves as now free, now unfree" (ND, 294). As Adorno says earlier in a footnote, the "good will" has "its medium in the continuity of life" (ND, 225), not in opposition to it. Its freedom means "critique and transformation of situations, not their confirmation by a decision in the midst of their imposing structure" (ND, 226).[29] The truth of human freedom is thus not grounded in an identity but in a movement mediating moments of identity (the self in its stasis under the Law) and nonidentity (the diffuse impulses of desire that break up the "compulsive character of identity"). This odd "grounding" is the process of willing that splits the self (alienates it) on its way to the only "free" subjecthood we know as beings thrust upon the Other. Lacan likewise uses Kant and Sade to take us to this limit where the will can be defined dialectically.

Lacan: The Will and the Dialectical Ethics of Desire

Lacan overlays onto Kant and Sade his own developmental model in order to work out the intersubjective relations that precipitate subjectivity. A key to his use of them beyond his apparent "rejection" comes at the conclusion of his essay when Lacan writes: "Sade thus stopped, at the point where desire is knotted together with the law" (KS, 74). Lacan uses Kant and Sade to reach this limit and to see how to move beyond it to a better understanding of how these contradictory elements are "knotted together." It should come as no surprise that this "knot" of the law and desire, reason and nature, is intimately connected to a conception of the will richer than its reductions to practical reason or the insistence on pleasure. The way to grasp this knot of desire and the law, in order to get to its "cause," is through a reading of "Kant with Sade" and the *Seminar VII, The Ethics of Psychoanalysis* (1959–60), out of which the essay grew, which emphasizes the unique status of the interpenetration of opposites as a kind of transcendental condition of subjectivity. My main goals in working through "Kant with Sade" are therefore the following: (1) to provide an interpretive gloss for some of the more difficult passages; (2) to show how Lacan uses Kant and Sade to work out a dynamic structural relationship between self and Other, desire and Law, Nature and Freedom, at the heart of which is a rich concept of the will (that takes into account the unconscious); (3) to isolate the structure of willing so that it can be used to understand Adorno's call for a "dialectical determination of the will"; and (4) to work out the significance of Kant's ethics today. The point of the present argument is to show how Lacan provides a "critique" of Kant that is not just the rejection of reason as a literal killjoy. Lacan maps out Kant's approach to its limit using Sade. He thereby reveals the (sadomasochist) dangers of an undialectical model so that we can reflect on the free "cause" of desire in the primal status of a will as interaction of self and Other. Such a will is not either active or passive, present or absent, law or nature, determined or indetermined; instead, such a will emerges as the very spacing that provides the condition for these either/or structures at the heart of the subject.

Lacan bridges the transition from Kant to Sade in his essay by referring to an "eroticism" in the *Kritik der praktischen Vernunft* that arises from the relationship to a special "object." To appreciate the "nature of the said object" he turns to Sade. He writes:

> One rediscovers what founds Kant's expression of the regret that, in the experience of the moral law, no intuition offers a phenomenal object.
> We would agree that, throughout the *Critique,* this object slips away. But it can be divined by the trace which is left by the implacable pursuit which Kant brings to demonstrating its elusiveness and out of which the work draws this eroticism, doubtless innocent, but perceptible, whose well-foundedness we will show in the nature of the said object. (*KS,* 57)

This is not the same dialectic that we saw in Adorno/Horkheimer (according to which expelling pleasure from science leads to the eroticization of science itself). Rather, Lacan is saying that Kant's eroticism (and Sade's and, indeed, all eroticism in general) is motivated by a peculiar object, whose significance is constituted precisely in its absence for the subject. Although it was Kant's transcendental Idealism that first posed the necessity and constitutive force of this object, as the *Ding an sich* that has the peculiar status of the "cause" of our freedom from causality, he did not show how it functions (erotically) as the *cause de désir.* To appreciate the force of this absent object and the position it has in a theory of the law and desire we turn to Lacan on Sade. Sade is the "truth" of Kant because he makes clearer, for Lacan, the position of this special *Ding* in the dialectical constitution of subjectivity. (Later we shall return to Kant to see how this "truth" is more fully present in his ethics than Lacan grants.)

In the seminar on ethics, Lacan establishes the connection between Kant and Sade by means of their common approach to the "Thing." He quotes Kant: "We can see a priori that the moral law as the determining principle of will, by reason of the fact that it sets itself against our inclinations, must produce a feeling that one could call pain" (*Seminar VII,* 80). And he then points out that this driving force of the will, this cause, is linked to Sade's own drive for the Thing: "In brief, Kant is of the same opinion as Sade. For in order to reach *das Ding* absolutely, to open the floodgates of desire, what does Sade show us on the horizon? In essence, pain" (*Seminar VII,* 80). The essay "Kant avec Sade" explores this horizon, this point of interaction between desire and the law, this Thing at the location of human willing.

Lacan begins by formulating the Sadian version of the categorical imperative. If Kant's version of the principle by which all actions and subjective maxims would by judged relies strictly on universalizability (act such that the maxims guiding your behavior could be generalized to everyone), Lacan's version of a Sadian imperative relates law and pleasure in a different way. Lacan derives this imperative mostly from Sade's argument in the section of *Philosophy in the Bedroom* entitled "Yet Another Effort, Frenchmen," in which lack of the right to *ownership* of another person grants each of us the right to *enjoyment.* It states to me, coming from the speaking position of some Other, that "I" (i.e., the Other) have the "right to possess/take pleasure in" ("droit de jouir de") "your" (i.e., my) body. Lacan initially makes use of this "imperative" in order to make three points that set up his general discussion of (Sadian) subjectivity. First, he takes the opportunity to point out that this maxim does not function on the basis of reciprocity. The very introduction of the law (the *right* to *jouissance*) shows that the relation between two subjects alone cannot account for the "logical time of any crossing-over of the subject in his relation to the signifier" (*KS,* 59). That is, psychic development and relations occur not merely between "subjects" but between a subject and the order of signifiers out of which the subject is constituted.[30] In the imperative, the two subjects relate to each other via the right that transcends them. Thus, although, as we shall see, fantasy plays a major role in the discussion of Kant and Sade, this fantasy is not merely in the reciprocal sphere of the Imaginary but brings something else, some other absent Thing and will, into play, because of the role of the Law.

Second, we have here at the beginning of Lacan's discussion a hint of his conclusion about the point where Sade "stopped," namely the intertwining of desire and Law. After all, what we can learn from both Kant and Sade is nothing about desire or pleasure but certainly a great deal about what lies behind desire, namely a confrontation between bodies and "rights," and the formation of the "free subject." In Lacanian terms, what we have in this formulation of a "Sadian principle" is the imperative placed upon the "brute subject" (abbreviated as "S") to pass through the effects of the order of law and the signifier (the Other). At issue is what arises out of this interaction and how the freedom of subjectivity can exist in neither the natural nor the legal subject but in the dialectic between the two spheres of nature and law. The subject develops freely only in a mutually violating interaction between the body and the signifying law. What our freedom is, then, depends on this dynamic middle ground that marks the overlapping of our purest self and the place of our alienation in the Other.

Third, the peculiar form of this Sadian principle introduces the fundamental split in the speaking subject. For Lacan, human beings are forced to develop a dialectical kind of freedom because as linguistic beings our wills share the spheres of the individual and universal.[31] Lacan presents the first part of the imperative in the first person ("I have the right of enjoyment over your body . . .") but then puts these words in another's mouth (". . . anyone can say to me . . ."). We are led to read the sentence dialectically,[32] reinterpreting the "I" of the first part not as "me" but as a voice beyond me, assigning me in fact to a subjected place. The Law addresses me as Other and the address comes from the Other. Usually, we forget the splitting of the subject that is inherent in any formulation of the "I" in language—a splitting into the subject of the enunciation and the subject of the statement, i.e., the enunciating I and the "I" named in the utterance. We assume that the speaking I and the "I" contained in the statement are the same. But they are not because the I has passed through language. (At the simplest level, consider how difficult it is for small children to make the leap from the "you" they hear in addresses to them to the "I" they must use when they speak.) The Sadian maxim "unmasks" this structure since it comes from an "I" that is not "me." Subjectivity, in terms of the speaking subject, what Lacan calls the "barred subject" (*sujet barré*), symbolized as $\$$, that can say "I," does not arise "out of itself" but only in response to a different voice of the Other that issues an imperative to it. To the extent that that Other is given the attribute of freedom (as we saw in the narrow reading of Kant), that imperative has a "murderous form," according to Lacan, because it issues a definition (or as Kant would say "gives a law") in the form of a "you are" (as in the Other's constant refrain: "You are John," "You are a good boy," "You are a hungry baby today"). This definition constitutes the subject within the field of meaning even as a part of that subject is always unnamed, killed off. (The pun here in French is between the "Tu es" that nominalistically constitutes the subject and the "Tuez!" that performatively murders.) Lacan writes: "It is thus indeed the Other as free, it is the freedom of the Other, which the discourse of the right to *jouissance* poses as the subject of its enunciation, and not in a manner which differs from the *You are* [*Tu es*] which is evoked in the murderous capital [*fonds tuant*] of any imperative" (*KS,* 60).[33] In a move paralleling that of Adorno, Lacan's point here is that the Sadian principle makes clearer than the Kantian imperative the violent intermixing of self and Other that guarantees freedom through the splitting of the subject.

Lacan has thus fused Kant and Sade not just to reject them but in order to present the dualistic structure out of which subjectivity and freedom are gained at the price some necessarily exacted losses. He has presented them in such a way that a dialectical mediation of opposites will be possible. The self arises neither out of the spontaneous act of its autonomous self-determination nor out of its complete definition by the Other but, rather, from the painful and alienating confrontation of the two.[34] He summarizes the relationship between the (free) discourse (of the Other) and the formation of the subject and its pleasure, in a dense formulation: "But this discourse is no less determining for the subject of the statement, in that each address suscitates him through its equivocal content: since *jouissance*, by shamelessly confessing itself even as it speaks, makes itself one pole of a couple of which the other is in the hollow which it is already drilling in the place of the Other in order to erect the cross of Sadian experience there" (*KS,* 60). How are we to understand these two "poles" and the process of "hollowing out" a space in the Other? To gloss this passage and to make Lacan's next pages clearer, I introduce here a variation of a diagram from Lacan's Seminar XI, *The Four Fundamental Concepts of Psycho-Analysis,* the Venn diagram we saw above in chapter 1. In the Sadian interaction between two individuals, fundamental structures of the psyche become clear. Not that the interaction is the norm; rather, the interaction is a reaction to normal processes of development and so Lacan uses Sade to work out general structures, as well as the structure of "perversions."[35]

In the chapter on "Alienation," a concept that will play a crucial role in Lacan's discussion of the Sadian/Kantian will, Lacan maps out two spheres (*FFC,* 211–12):

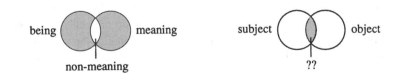

This model portrays graphically a number of Lacan's fundamental principles. First, at the most obvious level, we see the necessity of understanding the human psyche in terms of an interacting, indeed interlocking, of Self and Other. Lacan's vehement and sarcastic attacks against ego-psychology throughout his career are aimed against the view that the individual psyche can be understood and "cured" by examining and strengthening the independent ego. Here, on the contrary, one's individuality, freedom, and "health" depend not on one's independence but on the particular nature of the configuration formed between the Self and Other. In the Sadian interaction, which revolves around the importance of pain, Lacan sees a (per)version of this mutual dependency (a version also akin to Kant). The pain inflicted is not a reduction of *jouissance* to "contempt" or disgust or indifference vis-à-vis the Other (a reaction like the Stoic's " 'See you broke it,' he said, pointing to his leg" [*KS,* 60]). The sadist like any subject does not "get off" by effacing the other since the sadist is locked together with him/her. Rather, the interaction between sadist and victim relies on the *persistence* of the other/victim because the self/sadist identifies with him/her.[36] The self must experience itself somewhere, somehow "in the place" of the Other, whereby this means a partial effacement ("hollowing out") of the Other by the self and yet a maintenance of the Other where the self finds its place. Hence we shall see a persistent and contradictory set of behaviors that form (Sadian) subjectivity: on the one hand a "plugging up" of the apertures marking the body's opening toward the Other so that the self can emerge "whole" out of the Other; and on the other, an invasive, violent boring ("drilling") into the Other, as if the sadist could "get to the bottom" of the Other and locate himself there to take the place of that solid core. Such a dialectical relation between self and Other is like that between exhibitionism and modesty, in which the one's pleasure at being immodest depends precisely on the other's modesty. Lacan calls such a relation "amboceptive" and relates it to the fundamental interlocking of self and Other: "For modesty is amboceptive of the conjunctures of being: between the two, the immodesty of the one being by itself the rape of the modest of the other. A channel which would justify, were it necessary, what we first produced by the assertion, in the place of the Other, of the subject" (*KS,* 60). Modesty and immodesty, like the self and Other, are not mutually exclusive spheres, then, but depend upon each other in a crucial overlapping conjuncture. The overlapping section of the two circles conveys the duality of the crucial position of the subject "already drilling in the place of the Other" (*KS,* 60). The "assertion, in the place of the Other, of the subject" means that the subject is "inserted" (passively) into that place, but also "asserts itself" (actively); but, ironically, it can do so only with the Other's *words* (as an "assertion"). The sadist grapples with "undoing" this contradictory process that forms subjectivity.

A second fundamental feature of the psyche that Lacan can relate to Sadian experience follows from the first, namely the "conjuncture" formed between self and Other occurs inevitably by means of painful "cuts" into the spheres. "The assertion, in the place of the Other, of the subject," according to Lacan and Sade (or the formation and assertion of the free will, according to Kant), never takes place without pain, and the pain of castration, like the pain of duty in Kant, is constitutive of "free" subjectivity in the Symbolic. As "assertion" it involves the subject imposing and positing itself within the Other via language; and yet, because this language does not originate in the self, it is also that point where, precisely in asserting itself, the will of the individual subject depends on the universalizing law or structure of the Other.

We can view these cuts from two perspectives. On the one hand, from the perspective of the "brute subject," there is a cut into his/her sphere by the sphere of the Other (symbolized as "A" for *grand Autre*). If the Other is the battery of signifiers, the order of meaning, then that cut is necessary if the subject (S) is to become a signifying subject of language (Ꞩ). The cut is experienced as an impossible choice or double bind. Confronted with the necessary dependence on the Other, the brute subject could reject it for the sphere of pure "being" but then would have to give up that sliver of itself that is linked with A (which is itself not incomplete or split, symbolized by a slashed or barred A = Ꞛ). This peculiar middle space comes to be associated with the "objet petit a." Such a reaction would be experienced as psychosis or autism (but often it also exists as a fantasmatic hope to return to some brute state).

$$S \qquad A \qquad\qquad S \quad A$$

We shall see that the sadist strives for this kind of return to wholeness in a fantasmatic way, but longs for a unity by *being* the object (*objet petit a*) that would complete the Other and hence reinstate a totality.[37] Or the subject can opt for meaning, in which case it must tolerate the existence of part of A in itself (the discourse of the Other, the unconscious is the necessary result of adopting language). It also accepts that a part of itself is split off and forever a remnant of its tie to the Other:

In either case, the subject essentially loses its totality as it experiences "splitting," or "aphanasis." This impossible choice Lacan makes clear by the either/or of "Your money or your life": either way something is lost, namely the life/livelihood of the brute subject. It is significant that Lacan calls this choice the *vel,* the unique "or" of "alienation," whereby the "V" of *vel* will reappear both as the "V" of *volonté* and part of the movement of fantasy.

On the other hand, seen from the perspective of A, S is not merely absorbed into A. Rather, in order for a signifying subject, $, to develop, A must also be "decompleted," i.e., there must be some part of the battery of signifiers that the subject can "latch onto" and, in part, "make its own."

What saves any individual from the "totalitarianism" of the Other is the possibility of splitting off or cutting into it by the subject. In that process, which Lacan refers to as "separation" the counterpiece of alienation (and gives the movement ^ to oppose it to the v or alienation), the reverse "amboceptivity" becomes clear as a part ("partial object") of the Other is both part and not part of the Other and the Self. (Lacan always mentions four such objects: feces, phallus, gaze, and breast.)[38] This object, i.e., the zone between the spheres seen from the perspective of A, is called by Lacan the *objet petit a.* Having come from A at the very formation of the subject, it has a unique status for the subject, not being the object of desire but the *cause* of desire.[39] It is the "cause" because it arises at the moment of the subject's "assertion" and is the very condition of desire. As Lacan writes in the *Seminar VII: "das Ding* is at the center only in the sense that it is excluded. That is to say, in reality *das Ding* has to be posited as exterior, as the prehistoric Other that it is impossible to forget . . . something strange to me, although it is at the heart of me, something that on the level of the unconscious only a representation can represent" (71).

Third, by putting these two fundamental principles together, we see that the interaction between self and Other revolving around the cuts into their mutual spheres forms the basic structure of fantasy. Lacan gives fantasy the formula $ ◊ a. The operator connecting the two is multivalent, referring both to the twin countermovements of alienation (v) and separation (^) and to the general shape of the essential "losenge" formed between self and Other. In the Venn diagram it has the form:

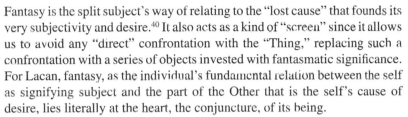

Fantasy is the split subject's way of relating to the "lost cause" that founds its very subjectivity and desire.[40] It also acts as a kind of "screen" since it allows us to avoid any "direct" confrontation with the "Thing," replacing such a confrontation with a series of objects invested with fantasmatic significance. For Lacan, fantasy, as the individual's fundamental relation between the self as signifying subject and the part of the Other that is the self's cause of desire, lies literally at the heart, the conjuncture, of its being.

Finally, there's the role of *jouissance*. In Kant and Sade it takes the form of a "will-to-*jouissance*," i.e., an attempt to make of this tripartite structure of interlocking spheres a forced, willed oneness. As an insistence on regaining for the self a sense of wholeness, it is related to what he calls "phallic *jouissance*." It is the guarantor of a "freedom," a "horrible freedom" because ultimately it is at the expense of the self ($) and Other. Lacan's goal is to "interrogate this *jouissance*, precarious in that it hangs in the Other, on an echo which it only suscitates as it abolishes it, by joining the intolerable to it. Doesn't it at also appear to us to exalt only in itself, in the manner of another, horrible freedom?" (*KS*, 60). We could gloss this by saying that the sadist self who would (violently) "hang in" the Other does so to restore its wholeness and thereby to "exalt" itself in an impossible way

To summarize the discussion thus far and to relate it to the dialectics of the will, we see that Lacan defines the formation of subjectivity out of a fundamental interaction of opposites. The space of that interaction is "transcendental" in the sense that it is the "condition of the possibility" of a subject. It is the space whose contours are given by a basic choice: to become a "subject" you must give up part of yourself to the Other in the place where the Other also loses part of itself. This is Lacan's variation, then, on the "free will": Our freedom and selfhood rest on a basic "choice," but it is not a choice made out of autonomous self-determination (*Willkür*) but within the interaction of self and Other. Indeed, as we shall see, the "horrible" freedom of Kant and Sade arises out of a *denial* of this dialectic of the impossible choice. That is, a dangerous subjectivity emerges where the dialectic of willing is not recognized.

Armed with these terms and this model, we must now consider the inherent *dynamism* of this interaction, since the self and Other are engaged in a constant movement. The notion of interlocking spheres must not be seen as merely static. The unique form of Sadian *jouissance* gives Lacan a particular way that these spheres interact: "it is *jouissance* by which Sadian experience is modified. For it forms the project of monopolizing a will only after having already traversed this will in order to install itself in the most intimate part of the subject which it provokes beyond, by touching its modesty" (*KS,* 60). We could thus say that the sadist subject is the exception that proves the rule, for in attempting to impose a unified will on another by splitting it and dominating that split other, it proves that its will is "horribly" trying to undo the very alienation that is at the root of its willing. The sadist subject's pleasure is derived from the impossible denial of the paradoxical nature of its own precondition.[41] The *jouissance* of the sadist, Lacan seems to be saying, gives us an informative variation of the constitution of subjectivity. It would control the other by traversing the *true* space of willing in order to so identify with it that its split, alienated constitution is denied.[42] The Sadian subject (split like the rest of us, $) strives to undo the effects of its splitting, i.e., reattain a position of Oneness, by passing through its own splitting, acting it out on another subjectivity that stands in as its Other. That Other can be split off and made a piece of brute (monstrous) being through torture, with which the subject then identifies. The subject ($) identifies with the "piece" (*objet petit a*) and thus would occupy that space and become the object of the Other's pleasure. All this occurs "in the aim that his subjective division be entirely sent back to him from the Other" (*KS,* 62). Here I read "sent back" in the sense also of "undone"; i.e., having reduced the Other to an apparently unsplit, brute subject (denying *its own* splitness and the space of *objet petit a*), the sadist subject identifies with it and "gets back" (falsely) its own brute subjectivity. Lacan puts this movement or modulation of the Sadian fantasy (or "a calculus of the subject" [*KS,* 63]) into the form of the "sinuous line," which I reproduce with the different glosses on the symbols:

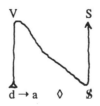

The starting point is *objet petit a,* which marks the splitting in the Other that decompletes it, giving the self a chance to develop by means of splitting itself ($).[43] This starting point is the domain of dialectical willing, the site of interpenetration of self and Other. Given the "cause" of its desire, the subject in this case (namely, of sadism) strives to work *back* through the *vel* and will (choice) that gave it its alienated freedom as a subject toward what would be a more absolute (and horrible) freedom (the "whole" self, S). Ironically, in moving toward a more radically independent subjectivity, it has turned itself even more into an object or instrument. Lacan summarizes this movement in a way that recalls Adorno's version of Sadian desire as "self-sacrifice to an Other" ("Selbstpreisgabe an ein Anderes"; *DA*, 112): "Sadism rejects the pain of existing into the Other, but without seeing that by this slant he himself changes into an 'eternal object' " (*KS*, 65).[44] The Sadian subject's desire for completeness leads him/her to deny the cut within the self. But, unlike the psychotic, the sadist does not merely withdraw back into the partial sphere without the Other. Rather, he/she strives to focus on the cut within the Other, impose that cut brutally and literally onto others, so that it can restore a kind of wholeness or oneness to itself. Hence, its desire is driven by a "*will*-to-*jouissance*" in the sense of a demand for unity. But in so doing, the split Other in fact, through a process of identification, flips back onto the self, making its subjectivity indistinguishable from its subjection, i.e., objectification, at the hands of the Other. It loses the possibility for genuine willing in striving for radical autonomy. This is why the "freedom" is both false and horrible: It occurs not through the dialectical mediation of self and Other but by a problematic denial of that relation that merely brings the Other back with even greater force as the motivation of the self. The movement of the sinuous line can thus be presented as a series of moves within the diagram of interlocking circles, with split subjectivity at the beginning and a fantasmatic wholeness at the end:

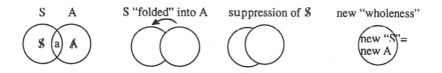

| S   A | S "folded" into A | suppression of $ | new "wholeness" |

In Kantian terms, as we shall explore below, this means that the greatest "freedom" to be achieved by a natural subject (who is caught in a chain of causality) is to take the Law (Reason) and to make it the real cause of the subject. The human, divided subject would become *heilig* by asserting full autonomy. It would gain a wholeness of sorts, but at the expense of the dialectic of alienation and separation that makes up the sphere of true human willing. An absolute and horrible freedom indeed.

The Sadian fantasy thus in a crucial sense reverses the normal relation. Fantasy is usually represented by Lacan as the split subject's ambivalent relation to the lost *objet petit a* ($ ◊ a). In the case of Sadism, however, we see a subject attempting to *undo,* as an act of freedom and "will," its own (split) subjectivity. It is dangerously paradoxical since its freedom and willing are in fact grounded in the very splitting and interlocking it would undo. The reversal appears in the transposed arrow in the "losenge" that is Lacan's formula for fantasy (i.e., in the model above we see a $\varnothing$ on the way back to S). If fantasy usually marks and masks the subject's primally split and dialectical origins (its will as *vel* and its relation *as* split subject to *objet petit a*), a splitness Lacan calls aphanisis,[45] in the case of the Sadian fantasy, the goal is to *undo* the split to end up via fantasy at an unsplit position, S. Lacan says: "One will see that there is a statics of the fantasy, by which the point of aphanisis, supposed in $\varnothing$, should be indefinitely recessed in the imagination" (*KS,* 63). Not unlike Kant's transcendental subject attempting to ground itself in a self-determining will, the Sadian subject attempts to pass through the will in order to take it, as the law, upon itself, making it the "cause" of its desire. In that way the subject could hope to constitute itself as absolute. But Lacan uses Sade to show the price paid by this movement: "It is thus indeed the will of Kant which is encountered in the place of this will which can be called-to-*jouissance* only to explain that it is the subject reconstituted from alienation at the price of being no more than the instrument of *jouissance*" (*KS,* 63). The fantasy of a subject that would (re)constitute itself as unalienated does so only at the price of losing its subjectivity and desire to the reign of the Other since they can only exist *dialectically* as a relation, even if alienated, between self and Other. A nondialectical, unsplit will loses its agency.[46]

Lacan argues that this disastrous movement is played out in Sade's own life in such a way that we see the actual loss of his subjectivity. This is why masochism represents the flip side or a variation of sadism. This is not to say that masochism is sadism turned against the self instead of the other; rather, masochism, the effacement of self, inheres within the very sadist fantasy for wholeness. Lacan depicts the masochist fantasy (although he does not use the term explicitly) in a second graph that modulates the first. The fantasy embedded in Sade's "imperative" to give up one's body to the *jouissance* of another is shown as only a quarter turn away from the sadist's. It seals like a crypt, in fact, the total disappearance of the subject. Lacan writes of Sade's literal disappearance behind the signifiers of his works: "For Sade, the $\varnothing$ (barred S), we see at last that, as subject, it is in his disappearance that he signs, things having reached their term. Unbelievably, Sade disappears without anything, even less than in the case of Shakespeare, remaining of his image, after in his will he had ordered that a thicket efface even the trace upon the stone of a name that would seal his destiny" (*KS,* 66). The "will" referred to here is, of course, a testament, Sade's "last will" that said he wanted all traces of his personhood effaced. If in the sadist we see the attempt willfully to undo the effects of the alienating will/*vel,* here we see the ironically tragic fate of that undoing: the will-as-law is imposed straight and simple as pure sign on the body of the subject (e.g., the incarceration of Sade). The effects of alienation, by means of a vain attempt to deny it, therefore become "administratively confirmed" (*KS,* 66).

Sade's problem, Lacan reiterates especially near the end of the essay, was that he did not work out the *relation* between desire and the Law (the two spheres). Thus, in "willing desire" (just as the revolution and Kant "willed freedom") he is both onto something (the "thing" beyond desire, its cause in a dialectical will) and yet off the mark (he exhausts himself in his imposition on objects, in a one-sided "willing," thereby not seeing its ambivalent structure). Indeed, this is the point of bringing together Kant and Sade, the Law and desire: What we must focus on, better than they did, is the way the site of interlocking, the point of intersection, the intermediate area, where self and Other join in a lost cause. Kant and Sade are close to this essential motivating force "beyond the pleasure principle" in so far as they define the will as the middle between law and desire, as the problematic *vel* that constitutes an alienated, phenomenal subjectivity. But they make the wrong use of this will and the "right-to-*jouissance*," turning away from the analysis of the fundamental fantasy and its cause in the (lost) object, focusing instead on an abstract and politically dangerous will that would impose an autonomy and wholeness. From that place of the Other, it imposes its Law on the self, annihilating the subjectivity Kant and Sade would have saved.

For Lacan, what is missing in both Sade and Kant is a dialectical determination of the *objet a,* the cause of the subject's desire. Instead, in their different ways, they both deny and reject the fundamentally mediating role of that sphere between and in the self and Other, in particular by projecting that primal (lost) object into a "transcendental" realm (Kant) or by masking that *objet a* by a (monotonous) series of instrumentalized and instrumentalizing objects of desire (Sade). We can now turn to what Kant does contribute to conceptualizing that sphere by means of his theory of the (good) will and the Good as the object/cause of the will.

Kant's Good/Dialectical Will

Since Adorno says that the contradictions in Kant also reveal the "truth content" (*ND,* 230, 238) of his thought, and since for Lacan the "truth" of Kant (enacted perversely and blindly by Sade) is the knotting of desire and the Law around an "object" that "is not one" (or also around a *jouissance* beyond the pleasure principle), let us now turn again to Kant to see how the dialectics are played out in his ethics. That is, we should not turn to the places where he either falls into dualisms or imposes a formal reason as a unifying force but to those where he *does* reveal the deeply rooted split nature of human subjectivity. We should look beyond his problematic "analysis" (his tendency to separate out what needs to be thought together) to his attempted synthesis. This occurs in the "dialectic" of practical reason, under the concept of the "Objekt" defined as "das Gute." What we find there, if we read it with Adorno and Lacan in mind, is a richer conception of the will than its dangerous identification with either practical reason or pathological inclinations.

The foundations for the ethical arguments that make up the *Kritik der praktischen Vernunft* are laid in the dialectical arguments near the end of the *Kritik der reinen Vernunft*. In particular, we need to consider the third antinomy between necessity and freedom. There Kant examines the contradiction that arises when one does not take into account the distinctions he calls for in his critical philosophy. It arises when one looks out into the world and sees all things connected inevitably by an unbroken chain of causality (this would be the basic premise of the argument). Either one assumes all objects are causally connected, in which case there is an infinite regress of causes, which is impossible, whereby one must posit a first cause (contradicting the basic premise, since such a cause breaks the chain); *or* one assumes that there is a concept of freedom, independent from the world of causally connected objects, in which case one is positing an empty concept by definition given the basic premise (since *all* things are presumed to be causally connected, what could this "freedom" be but a non-thing, by definition nothing?). Given these aporias (antinomies), something must be wrong in the basic premise, namely the world is a collection of causally connected things. Kant argues that we must instead distinguish between the world of objects (*Gegenstände*), i.e., the world of appearances (*Erscheinungen*) or nature, and the world of things in themselves. Then we could say that all "objects" (appearances) are related causally but not all "things" (in themselves).

What can we say about these *Dinge an sich?* Since they are not appearances, they are never objects of knowledge (hence they fall out of the realm of epistemology), they are the ground of things as they appear to us, and they are not determined in any way by the natural laws that govern appearances. Thus, the *Ding an sich* is the "freedom of reason" as the principle of self-determination. It is that which escapes the laws of causality.[47] The distinction between *Erscheinungen* and the *Ding(e) an sich,* the deduction and epistemological consequences of which are the focus of the *Kritik der reinen Vernunft,* leads Kant logically to the *Kritik der praktischen Vernunft* as the study of the limits and tasks of (human) freedom.[48] Ethics has a "transcendental" grounding in "something" within human beings that is nonetheless beyond the empirical subject. It can be a "something" (i.e., not nothing) because the realm of things is not limited to objects of knowledge (*Gegenstände*), but it is a unique nonreified "thing."

If freedom is defined as the self-determination of the transcendental subject, the agency guaranteeing its self-motivation is practical reason or the will as it provides its own ground.[49] What could this agency of willing look like? For Kant, the will, like the essence of human beings in general, is grounded in and bounded by the two spheres of nature and freedom. In the former, it belongs to the chain of causal connections and is "merely" the faculty that allows us to translate some external (or internal) compulsion or inclination into an action that we take in/upon the world. But in the sphere of freedom, the will takes the *form* of an "ought" (*Sollen*). The emphasis is on the word *form,* since a free will, or an action following a free will, could never arise from a specific command: "You ought to do x or y," since then the "x" or "y" would have a determining force. This would make the self-determining will dependent on its representations, a blatant contraction that Kant avoids by means of a strict formalism. That is, the justification of freedom, and the agency of the will, comes merely from the *form* of the ought, i.e., my freedom is grounded in the fact that I *can* say "I ought" regardless of the changeable character of what follows and regardless of whether I do or do not actually do what I ought. This constant law giving core of the self is thus called the "intelligible character" or "unity of personhood" (the "noumenal" as opposed to the "phenomenal" self). The individual actions that make up my behavior are grounded in subjectively formulated maxims, which in turn must be grounded in the most universal statement of a formalized law, the "categorical imperative" that prescribes no action but tells me what form my other maxims would have to take (namely, they would have, in principle, to be universalizable without contradiction, i.e., any of *my* maxims would have to be able to be accepted as the maxims of all rational beings). Like the transcendental precondition of knowledge in the "I think" that "must be able to accompany" my experiences, the "I ought" as the empty form of law giving becomes the transcendental precondition of freedom and ethical behavior (i.e., one could say it "must be able to accompany my actions" if there is to be any hope of morality).[50]

The best way to approach Kant with Lacan and Adorno in mind is to consider the way the dialectic of subjective and objective motivations unfolds around a fundamental gap in humankind, a gap that Kant sees as a priori and the condition of morality. If we keep this gap in mind we can avoid turning his transcendental argumentation into an *imposing* rational presence. According to Kant, the human will is moved or determined by two kinds of motivations or determinations (*Beweggründe* or *Bestimmungen*): subjective (especially the category of drives, needs, and inclinations) and objective (defined by the Law given by reason absolutely). In human beings, because the will in reality is motivated by the two sides, the objective law seems imposed on the subjective and is thus experienced as a "need" ("Nötigung," i.e., as an imposed necessity and as a lack).[51] Kant's goal is to find a way of formulating this gap between the objective law and our subjective being and a kind of bridge that would be "moral," i.e., which would be strictly according to the law. What he thinks of is the categorical imperative and a (problematic) way of making the objective motivations subjective.

In order to explore this gap more fully, let us look at Kant's discussion of different kinds of imperatives in the *Grundlegung zur Metaphysik der Sitten* (*Foundations of a Metaphysics of Morals*). We can say in general that imperatives can be defined as the formulas that map out gaps in human existence. "Thus, imperatives are only formulas that express the relationship between objective laws of willing generally to the subjective imperfection of the will of this or that particular rational being, e.g. of a human will" (*GzMdS*, 34). This means that the imperative in general has the function of Lacanian fantasy: a formula that expresses the relationship between the interlocking parts of a split human subjectivity. Given the diagrams we used above, we could make the following parallels:

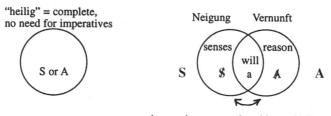

imperatives respond to this gap/difference

Similarly, we can say that Kant's formulations of the imperative are his attempts to come to grips with what Adorno called the fundamental *Nicht-identität* (albeit in his rationalist way).

Kant defines in particular three kinds of imperatives, i.e., three formulas that express, or respond to, the gaps in human existence: imperatives of "Geschicklichkeit" (or rules of action), imperatives of "Klugheit" or "Glückseligkeit" (or pieces of advice), and categorical imperatives of "Sittlichkeit" (or ethical laws). The first two grow out of concrete gaps in a person's psychical existence, namely the gap between a present state (desire) and an end state to be achieved, whereby the gap is bridged by some means (*Mittel*). The rules or advice give the best means of attaining a specific end, be it a state of affairs or something more general like "happiness." But the more difficult question arises for Kant when he asks how a *categorical imperative* is even possible, i.e., how he can find a nonempirical formula that bridges a gap in human existence.[52] This is the point where Kant can make his most important contribution to the dialectical model of will: He points to a gap in human existence that exists a priori, a gap in human subjectivity that is constitutive of that subjectivity. This gap is the "cause" of human willing. His goal is to map out formulations that express mediations or relationships across this gap.

By considering now why the categorical imperative takes the different forms it does (*GzMdS*, 42f), we understand how Kant is using the complex (self)determination of will to close the very gap it opens up.[53] Here we have arrived at the point where Kant offers both his most radical insight into the split origins of human agency and his retreat from that very openness into a rational determinism. Kant sets up the categorical imperative as that principle which would bridge the gap between subjective and objective determinations of the subject, the gap that makes up the essence of human (non-whole, non-holy) freedom, by making the former conform to the latter. That is, it gives the *form* of what it would look like to have my subjective motivation completely determined by objective determinations. If we define the expression of subjective motivations as "maxims" (they tell me what to do in a given case), and if we define the expression of objective determinations as universal laws (that exceed the individual subject, indeed which hold, as Kant repeats, for "all rational beings," not just humans), then to make objective determinations my subjective motivation means to consider my individual maxims as universal laws. Hence, the first form of the categorical imperative: "Act only according to those maxims that you could also will to become universal law" ("Handle nur nach derjenigen Maxime, durch die du zugleich wollen kannst, daß sie ein allgemeines Gesetz werde"; *GzMdS*, 42). Similarly, if I recognize that objective determinations must be universal and thus modeled on natural laws (which, by definition, do not just hold for isolated, arbitrary situations), then to make my subjective motivations conform to objective determinations means granting my maxims the status of natural law. Hence, the second form of the categorical imperative: "Act as if the maxims of your action could, through your will, become natural laws" ("Handle so, als ob die Maxime deiner Handlung durch deinen Willen zum allgemeinen Naturgesetze werden sollte"; *GzMdS*, 43).[54] Both these versions map a movement of and in the subject, a movement whose ambivalence we must now explore.

Kant's formulation of ethics in terms of a relation between subjective and objective determinations on the one hand positively opens up a space for a dialectical interpretation of the will, and, on the other, attempts to close up this space with a false sense of totality. The dialectical space that Kant illuminates is not so much a "beyond" (even though it is transcendentally defined and guaranteed) in the sense of a metaphysical or imagined place; rather it is a unique position "in between" the subjective and objective, between the empirical and "universal" self. It is a position that makes synthesis possible and is occupied by a dialectical version of the will and a special kind of "object" ("das Gute"). Kant's simultaneous efforts to close up this space can be considered his Idealist (and Sadian) turn that would deny or collapse a difference inhering in human beings for the sake of an absolute practical reason (often identified as a "good" will).

One way of seeing these different moves within Kant is to compare the "holy" with the "mere human" condition. In the former, what Kant calls "heilig" (*GzMdS,* 64), the subjective and objective determinations are united. We have in the "holy" being a fantasm of "wholeness"—to be "heilig" would mean to be "whole" in the sense that no gap is left between the law and the individual's behavior, between the "ought" (*Sollen*) and the "wanting" (*Wollen*) (see also *KpV,* 32). That is, such a "heiliges Wesen" could be said "not to be found wanting"; its (divine) will exists in a fullness of *jouissance.*[55] For the rest of us, however, this gap persists and can only be overcome by a sense of "commitment" (*Verbindlichkeit*) that we feel (e.g., according to Kant as "duty") to unite the two sides of the gap. The more driven we are by this sense of duty to fill the gap, the more Sadian becomes our "will-to-*jouissance.*" The very term *verbindlich* shows how the different strands are knotted together—neither absolute unity nor radical fragmentation. The human condition is thus at the same time marked by difference and committed to overcoming that difference. Humans, as willing or wanting beings, always run the risk of undialectically choosing either pure difference or pure unity.

This double movement in Kant creates two different conceptions of the will. On the one hand, the will in human beings overlaps in the two spheres that essentially split each subject into two subjects—empirical or phenomenal and transcendental or *Ding an sich* (see *GzMdS,* 86f). Kant writes:

> [A] rational being [must] view itself *as intelligence* (*als Intelligenz*), not from the perspective of its lower capacities, as belonging not to the sensual world but to the world of understanding. As a result, there are two ways (*Standpunkt*) that it can comprehend itself, the laws regulating the uses of its capacities, and thus all its actions: on the one hand, as belonging to the sensual world, under natural laws (heteronomy); on the other, as belonging to the intelligible world, under non-empirical laws that are grounded in reason alone, independent of nature. (*GzMdS,* 78)

It is precisely the will that occupies the place between these two spheres to the extent that the will acts based on the determinations that can come from either side. (Imagine, then, the center sliver between the two interlocking spheres being affected by both sides.) But on the other hand, Kant's other more problematic and ironically Sadian conception of the will places it completely on the side of the law. It is, in this conception, not essentially torn between autonomy and heteronomy (i.e., capable at times of being one or the other—its autonomy not being fully attainable) but, rather, radically autonomous. The will's existence in this form is called the "good will." It takes its violent turn or perversion, as both Adorno and Lacan show, when it imposes its will to unity.

There are, then, two "truths" of Kant. The first strives to maintain the status of the will in its dialectical position. This is the Kant who recognizes that the categorical imperative is essentially a "synthetic sentence" that must bridge two levels or spheres without collapsing them into sameness. The *principles* of a "good will," and the possibility that these principles have an effect on our will, are not contained within the concepts of the will or good will. These principles that connect the "pure" good will to its sensual existence are synthetic and need a connecting "third": "Such synthetic propositions are only possible by binding two recognitions through the mediation of a third that contains both" ("Solche synthetische Sätze sind aber nur dadurch möglich, daß beide Erkenntnisse durch die Verknüpfung mit einem Dritten, darin sie beiderseits anzutreffen sind, untereinander ver-bunden werden"; *GzMdS*, 72).[56] For Kant, this "third" is "the positive concept of freedom" ("der positive Begriff der *Freiheit*"). With this turn, Kant opens up the middle sphere in a crucial way. (Hence, Lacan was right to say that we need a "synthetic" approach to avoid the violent analytics of universalization, but he was mistaken to say there was not such a synthetic move already indicated in Kant.) This *Idea* of freedom is not something that can be grasped or imagined. Rather, it has the status of a "*Standpunkt*" (*GzMdS*, 85) that we must be able to take so that we can think of ourselves as rational, sensual, and ethical beings. This concept of freedom has the contradictory status of "causality" for us—Kant's famous notion of "Kausalität durch Freiheit." In fact, this "cause," he says, is not an "object" (otherwise it would be a part of nature's chain of cause and effect, and no freedom or ethics could be grounded in mere "objects of desire") nor strictly speaking a "thought" (which would likewise be under the conceptual chain of speculative reason), but, rather, is an "empty place" or gap in the self ("ein leerer Platz"; *KpV*, 49). I quote at length a passage from the *Kritik der praktischen Vernunft* in which we see how Kant envisions this hole (or wanting) at the core of human agency. Kant reiterates the third antinomy from the first *Kritik* that would demand a double perspective of humans (as phenomena and noumena). A site must therefore be held open and not become an "object" of knowledge. Unfortunately, Kant cannot maintain this openness:

> The determination of the causality of beings in the sensual world as such can never be unconditioned, and yet for every series of conditions there

must be something unconditioned, and consequently a causality which is entirely self-determining. Therefore, the idea of freedom as a faculty of absolute spontaneity was not just a desideratum but, as far as the possibility was concerned, an analytical principle of pure speculation. But because it is absolutely impossible to give an example of it from experience, since no absolutely unconditioned determination of causality can be found among the causes of things as appearances, we could defend the supposition of a freely acting cause when applied to a being in the sensual world only insofar as the being was regarded also as noumenon. This defense was made by showing that it was not self-contradictory to regard all its actions as physically conditioned so far as they are appearances, and yet at the same time to regard their causality as physically unconditioned so far as the acting being is regarded as a being of the understanding. Thus the concept of freedom is made the regulative principle of reason. *I thereby do not indeed learn what the object may be to which this kind of causality is attributed* [my emphasis]. I do, however, remove the difficulty, since, on the one hand, in the explanation of natural occurrences, including the actions of rational beings, I leave to the mechanism of natural necessity the right to ascend from conditioned to condition *ad infinitum,* while on the other hand, *I hold open for speculative reason the place which for it is vacant,* i.e., convert it into knowledge even of the possibility of a being acting in this way. Pure practical reason now *fills this vacant place with a definite law of causality in an intelligible world* (causality through freedom). *This is the moral law.* (my emphasis)

Die Bestimmung der Causalität der Wesen in der Sinnenwelt als einer solchen konnte niemals unbedingt sein, und dennoch muß es zu aller Reihe der Bedingungen nothwendig etwas Unbedingtes, mithin auch eine sich gänzlich von selbst bestimmende Causalität geben. Daher war die Idee der Freiheit als eines Vermögens absoluter Spontaneität nicht ein Bedürfniß, sondern, *was deren Möglichkeit betrifft,* ein analytischer Grundsatz der reinen speculativen Vernunft. Allein da es schlechterdings unmöglich ist, ihr gemäß ein Beispiel in irgend einer Erfahrung zu geben, weil unter den Ursachen der Dinge als Erscheinungen keine Bestimmung der Causalität, die schlechterdings unbedingt wäre, angetroffen werden kann, so konnten wir nur den *Gedanken* von einer freihandelnden Ursache, wenn wir diesen auf ein Wesen in der Sinnenwelt, so fern es andererseits auch als Noumenon betrachtet wird, anwenden, *verteidigen,* indem wir zeigten, daß es sich nicht widerspreche, alle seine Handlungen als physisch bedingt, so fern sie Erscheinungen sind, und doch zugleich die Causalität derselben, so fern das handelnde Wesen ein Verstandeswesen ist, als physisch unbedingt anzusehen und so den Begriff der Freiheit zum regulativen Princip der Vernunft zu machen, wodurch ich zwar den Gegenstand, dem dergleichen Causalität beigelegt wird, gar nicht erkenne, was er sei, aber doch das Hinderniß wegnehme, in dem ich einerseits in der Erklärung der Weltbegebenheiten, mithin auch der Handlungen vernünftiger Wesen, dem Mechanismus der Naturnothwendigkeit, vom Bedingten zur Bedingung ins Unendliche zurückzugehen, Gerechtigkeit widerfahren lasse, andererseits aber der speculativen Vernunft den für sie *leeren Platz offen erhalte,* nämlich das Intelligibele, *um das Unbedingte dahin zu versetzen* [here my emphasis]. Ich konnte aber diesen *Gedanken* nicht *realisieren,* d.i. ihn nicht in Erkenntniß eines so handelnden Wesens auch nur blos seiner

Möglichkeit nach verwandeln. *Diesen leeren Platz füllt nun reine praktische Vernunft durch ein bestimmtes Gesetz der Causalität in einer intelligibelen Welt (durch Freiheit), nämlich das moralische Gesetz, aus* [my emphasis]. (*KpV,* 48–49)

In other words, at the heart of human existence, that which makes freedom and action possible in the world, is a will defined not as a "wholeness" but as a "hole." This insight, not his "Sadian" call immediately to "fill it" with an abstract reason, needs to be maintained.

That this "hole" has an effect on us, indeed is the "cause" of our desire, means that it must also have *some* kind of status of an "object." Thus, Kant in the dialectic of practical reason works out some of the peculiar parameters of this "object," what he calls the "highest good" ("das höchste Gut"). This object is inextricably tied to the concept of the free will: "It is a priori (morally) necessary *to give rise to the highest good through freedom of the will*" (*KpV,* 113). Its dual status is already clear (*KpV,* 109–10) from the way Kant on the one hand emphasizes that *as object* it could never be the determining ground (*Bestimmungsgrund*) of the pure will (since only the moral law could be such a ground), and yet on the other stresses that it is "not merely an object" ("nicht blos Object"), since it contains the moral law within itself. Thus, it is a kind of thing that, unlike the other objects of our desire, can also function with the moral law as a determination of the will. It belongs to both spheres—that of objects and that of the law.

Moreover, Kant argues, the highest good unites contradictory elements in a way that demands a unique synthesis. In particular, he says that the highest good contains both *Glückseligkeit* and *Sittlichkeit* (the two features of *wohl* and *gut* that we saw initially—"well being" and "doing good"): "namely that happiness and morality are two specific and completely different elements of the highest good; their union therefore cannot be grasped analytically . . . but must be a synthesis of the concepts"[57] (*KpV,* 112–13) If we recall that Lacan had himself rejected the strictly "analytic" deduction of morality (the dangerous tautology and nominalism of the categorical imperative), we see here that Kant already turns to a needed synthesis. Contradictory determinations are entailed in the concept of the highest good, such that pursuing it leads to both happiness and virtue, but these opposites cannot be reduced to an identity. Rather, they can only be "synthesized" as opposites within the concept of the highest good.

Kant conceptualizes this synthesis, what he calls the dialectical or critical "solution" to the antinomy of practical reason, through an analysis of desire. Desires and inclinations are by definition unfulfillable: "For inclinations change and grow with the favor one shows them, and they always leave behind a greater sense of emptiness (*ein noch größeres Leeres*)" (*KpV,*

118). In Lacan's terms, desire is driven by a metonymic chain of endlessly substitutable objects.[58] But this "Leeres," which is the positive remainder of desire, recalls the "leeren Platz" (*KpV,* 49) that is the site of the causality of the intelligible subject. That is, desire circulates around an emptiness that is its "cause" and the place of that emptiness is the point of "freedom" and the source of a different kind of feeling, the "self-contentment" ("Selbstfrieden-heit") of "independence" ("Unabhängigkeit") from inclinations (*KpV,* 117). In this way the dialectic of practical reason is "solved" in the object of the highest good: In pursuing it we experience our freedom of will and desire, so to speak, arches around that empty space.[59] The dangerous and violent "dialectic of Enlightenment" arises, on this reading, not actually from Kant's own dialectic but from the Enlightenment denial of this void, its "filling" it with some "object" (a reified Kantian *Ding* or the Sadian body).

We can now see that Kant *avec* Lacan and Adorno allows for a formulation of the "dialectical determination of the will" in terms of the splitting of the subject and the alienation that makes a certain "thing" the cause of our desire—even as Kant then attempts to determine that peculiarly indeterminate cause. He characterizes the will as an interstice, for example: "the will is at the midpoint between it's a priori, formal principle, and it's a posteriori material motivations, as if it were located at the crossroads (*gleichsam auf einem Scheidewege*)" (*GzMdS,* 18). But then he follows this immediately with a determination by the rational: "and yet since it must be determined by something, it must be determined by the formal principle of willing itself, whenever an action occurs out of duty, since there all material principle is absent" (*GzMdS,* 18). The dialectical opening of this uniquely causal will at this "crossroads" or intersection becomes closed or "sutured" by the imposition of a partial determination, namely reason as a metaphysical cause.[60]

In Sade, we encounter such a forced closure in a graphic form infused with perverse pleasure. Lacan concludes his essay with a reference to the final scene of *Philosophy in the Bedroom* in which Eugenie's mother's vagina (and other orifices) is sewed up during a truly sadistic orgy. It represents according to Lacan's implications the crowning domination of the Oedipal law in Sade, who seems to argue for desire *against* the law. It is Dolmancé, Eugenie's sodomistic instructor, "who—did Sade see it?—closes the affair with a *Noli tangere matrem*" (*KS,* 75). The act is an ambiguous one that Lacan captures with an ambivalent elision: "V . . . ed and sewn up, the mother remains forbidden. Our verdict upon the submission of Sade to the Law is confirmed" (*KS,* 75). The act is one of violation ("V . . . ée" can thus stand for *violée*). But the forceful act that would open up a space at the heart of the formation of the (Oedipal) law is a willful one that in fact covers up (*voilée*) the possibility of such an opening.[61] That is, the object/absence that is marked by the mother and that is the cause of desire is denied and refused in a process that inflicts pain on her so that the subject, in pursuing desire, does not have to confront the *cause* of its desire. Lacan playfully hints at Eugenie's *penisneid* and Dolmancé's explicit fear of the vagina, not in order to fix these in a literal sense but rather because were it not for the absence in/of the (M)Other, i.e., were it not for the hollowing out in the Other (by means, e.g., of the mother's absence, the incompleteness of the battery of signifiers) the subject would not be constituted. This constituted subject, however, is not a whole subject but is split and alienated. The problem is that both Kant and Sade would deny this painful process of the constitution of a split self in relation to an Other marked by absence (the "leerer Platz" of the *objet petit a*) by imposing a dangerous fantasy of totality, i.e., would deny the alienated, dialectical will constituted out of the *vel* for the sake of a violent "will-to-*jouissance*" that is not an ambivalent "cause" but a totalizing identity.[62]

Kant discovered the basic void in the subject, indeed the subject as void, and yet covers it over and plugs it up in different ways—epistemological, metaphysical, and ethical: He discovered that the pure "I think" of apperception is "outside" the purview of its own perception and is thus a radical lack that grounds the very possibility of the subject. Hence he says it is "–X." This destroys all metaphysics. But then he also identifies this with the "Thing-in-itself," turning it into an *objet petit a* that fills in the void and relates to the world of phenomena. Also, he plugs the void up with my freedom as a noumenal entity, or more precisely, the law, whereby he loses the point that my freedom is grounded in the void that makes me inaccessible to myself.[63]

Sade, then, can indeed be seen as the "truth" of Kant in a double sense. Both show that behind the identity of the subject there is a split will, a nonidentity, a gap, a peculiarly absent or empty (transcendental) "thing," which makes up the *cause* of the subject's desire. But both also show the dangers that come from denying that split, striving to fuse the "brute subject" with the dictates of the Other, since what seems like a fantasy of recapturing a totalized subjectivity in fact instrumentalizes the self. Only a will that is defined as an ambivalent "cause of desire," that is itself not "conceptual/comprehensible" (*begreiflich*) but whose "Unbegreiflichkeit"[64] is, i.e., a will whose central dialectical space is circumscribed by a dialectical determination, can guarantee freedom and the "truth" of the subject.

Will, Power, Will to Power: Nietzsche, Foucault, Habermas

> Characteristically, Foucault dislocates a conventional understanding of the individual will in political action.
>
> EVE KOSOFSKY SEDGWICK, in *Redrawing the Boundaries,* 1992

> The question arises concerning the democratization of the very processes that form a common opinion and will (Meinungs- und Willens-bildungsprozesse).
>
> JÜRGEN HABERMAS, in *Die Moderne,* 1992

It is almost impossible for us to think of the will without adding the epithet "to power." Nietzsche's influence on us has become so strong that the concept of the will is inseparable from that of power. And yet, this conceptual fusion harbors confusion in the form of a problematic and even dangerous reduction of the will to a manifestation of power, or, in philosophical discussions, the reduction of conceptualizations of the will to theories of power. This chapter reexamines the relationships between Habermas and Foucault via Nietzsche by analyzing their responses to the collapsing of will and power. What we encounter here is a series of aporias that arise when the will is interpreted undialectically as power, because such a limited definition of will as power cannot account for the contradictory determinations of willing. The three authors dealt with in this chapter all recognize the problem of a nondialectical conception of will, each in his own way pointing to the resulting aporias and taking different approaches to evading them. I shall play off Habermas and Foucault against each other and use Nietzsche to lead to a broader, dialectical interpretation of will to power.

To summarize the positions of these three thinkers: Habermas, although arguing persuasively in principle against the reduction of philosophy to theories of power, provides in fact a one-sided reading of Nietzsche that attributes to him such a reduction; on the basis of that reading he then dismisses

Foucault. This still leaves the will undertheorized within Habermas's own political theory. Foucault, undoubtedly thanks to his antimetaphysical stance, indeed does tend in numerous formulations to reductive analyses based on a positivistic concept of power, but his thought, I shall argue, is most fruitful in those places where he strives to resist such a reduction. That nonreductionist side is the strong sense in which Foucault could be said to be Nietzschean, for Nietzsche's understanding of the will is not only nonreductionist but in fact resists and gives us a response to the very reductions Habermas finds so dangerous. My reading of the *will* back into the will to power therefore uses Nietzsche to bring the fundamental motives of Habermas and Foucault conceptually closer.

These three thinkers share a common enterprise that can be defined in terms of an attempt to avoid four problematic philosophical positions: (1) the aestheticization of life (at the expense of ethics, ontology, and epistemology), (2) the instrumentalization of thought (as positivism or structuralism), (3) a hidden metaphysics (i.e., a reification of a substance "behind" the existing world), and (4) nihilism (with its protofascistic political consequences). My point is that a broad conceptualization of the will avoids these pitfalls because willing, as we have seen, is most fruitfully understood as a dialectical activity that is both empirical and transcendental, individual and supraindividual, determined and innovative, rational and irrational. Since Nietzsche strove to map out these dialectical possibilities in his conception of "will to power" he can serve as a bridge between the otherwise antagonistic positions of Habermas and Foucault once we can show that their thought, too, relies on an often submerged theory of will. To do this, however, I shall first have to "undo" the reductive readings of Nietzsche, i.e., the reduction of "will to power" to mere "power" found in Habermas and Foucault. What I can develop through the interaction of these thinkers is a richer formulation of agency that accounts for both determinacy and change, structural forces and individual activity, embeddedness in the empirical and transgression of its limits. Had Habermas and Foucault focused more on the dialectical possibilities of their own implicit, in part Nietzschean conceptions of the will, they would have recognized their mutual proximity to such a form of agency.

One clarification needs to be made in advance of this argument. All three of these thinkers have rejected any expectation or injunction to provide a "theory" of the will, especially in some foundationalist sense (as if the theory would illuminate some prelinguistic or preaction concept that would then be put into language or action). Hence, my aim here should not be interpreted as providing the theoretical foundation they thought (and often demonstrated to be) impossible. But all three do offer accounts of individual and collective human agency, the ability of human beings to exercise power while being in its grips. And despite their different, even polemical approaches to this issue, they share an understanding of the complex, contradictory, dialectical nature of human agency. This commonality can be both illuminated and strengthened by recognizing its relation to conceptions of willing.[1] Moreover, our general understanding of agency will be enriched by the models of willing that emerge from the interaction of these three thinkers.

Habermas's Reduction of Nietzsche

In *Erkenntnis und Interesse* (*Knowledge and Human Interest*) Habermas gives Nietzsche a unique status at the close of the book. Indeed, because of his position as telos of a development that Habermas sees in intellectual history, Nietzsche is already present implicitly from the beginning. Habermas's goal in the book is to reveal the historical origins of positivism. He defines positivism in terms that reveal the target of his criticism to be a particular form of reductionism, namely the abandonment of (self-)reflection. He says: "That we deny reflection, *that* is positivism" (*EI,* 9). He traces how from Kant onward epistemology became reduced to nothing but a concern for method, a concern or process of reflection that cancels itself since scientific method rejects self-reflection for the sake of grasping the "object." Nietzsche, Habermas claims at the end of the book, completes the work begun by Hegel and continued by Marx. Nietzsche does not just continue the process that unfolded the self-contradictions of nonreflexive epistemology; his philosophy, according to Habermas, takes the additional step of "self-rejection of reflection" ("Selbstverleugnung der Reflexion") itself (*EI,* 353). That is, Nietzsche, confronted with the nineteenth-century turn toward scientificism and its fixation on objectivizing methods, rejects not this self-effacing mode of thought but rational thinking in and of itself. Nietzsche appears, in this reading, as the ultimate positivist and reductionist.

To argue this, Habermas must show that Nietzsche shares "a view of scientific knowledge with positivism" (*EI,* 354). Habermas must make this point indirectly, however, since Nietzsche's early writing, especially his essay *Vom Nutzen und Nachteil der Historie für das Leben,* in fact contains a *rejection* of a positivistic mode of history-writing (*EI,* 357–58). Thus, Habermas cannot simply show that Nietzsche embraces the positivism and science of his day. Rather, Habermas attempts to demonstrate that Nietzsche makes a series of associations that lead to a radical separation of philosophical reflection and science. Specifically, Habermas claims, Nietzsche links the search for knowledge in general to the narrower field of positivistic science, so that by then rejecting the latter he simultaneously abandons the enterprise of epistemology in general. In this way science is disconnected from philosophy (defined as self-reflexive thought) and vice versa. Science then becomes "liberated" from the need to legitimate itself in a process of self-reflection and is allowed to pursue its most radically positivistic tendencies. Philosophy, on the other hand, must give up its claims to knowledge (*Wissenschaft*) and values and becomes linked to myth or art. That is, positivistic science is seen in Habermas's Nietzsche as the sole mode of knowing. In casting the former out of philosophy, Nietzsche would be accomplishing a double reduction: Science becomes the domain of efficiency alone, since it is no longer beholden to something like philosophical arguments justifying its methods; and philosophy, unable to contribute to knowledge, loses its status as the site of reasoned legitimation of other disciplines.[2] The results of such a reduction that isolates science (as the only kind of knowledge) from philosophical activity are ethically, politically, and conceptually disastrous.

Not only does Habermas's argument have an elegant logic, but he is also motivated by a fully legitimate concern to avoid the effects of the reductive tears that rip through the modern and postmodern intellectual fabric. And were Nietzsche the one who argued for and accomplished such a split between knowledge and life, science and morality, epistemology and values, reflective reason and our "pre-scientific ties to the unhistorical and suprahistorical" ("vorwissenschaftliche Bindungen an das Unhistorische und Überhistorische"; *EI*, 358), then Habermas's conclusions would be justified. And yet, even while maintaining the same antipositivistic concerns, we could approach Nietzsche otherwise. Namely, where Habermas sees an "ambivalence" issuing out of Nietzsche, pulling both Nietzsche and postmodern thought in contradictory ways, he could see a genuine dialectical alternative, a *response* by Nietzsche to the debilitating ambivalence he called "nihilism." That response motivates (and is motivated by) his interest in a complex and dialectical model of willing.

Let us first pursue Habermas's argument. He characterizes the ambivalence as follows:

> With Nietzsche, the positivistic concept of science becomes ambivalent in a unique way. On the one hand, modern science is granted a monopoly on knowledge, which is confirmed by the devaluation of metaphysical knowledge. On the other, the monopolized knowledge in turn becomes devalued by forcefully dispensing with the connection to praxis that was peculiar to metaphysics and thus losing our interest. (*EI*, 356)

One can certainly find passages in Nietzsche that link science, and knowledge in general, to objectivizing instrumentality. And one can find numerous passages in which Nietzsche argues how literally deadening such developments could be. But rather than accepting this divide between a dead letter of science and a living spirit of aestheticized myth, Nietzsche, contrary to Habermas's interpretation, sought to synthesize the possibility of knowing and unknowability, activity and passivity, unity and fragmentation, facticity and transcendence ("overcoming"). Given the way those very oppositions have been played out in the history of thinking about the will, it is not surprising that willing occupies such a central place in Nietzsche's thought. In Nietzsche's version of the will, as I will unfold later in this chapter, we find a resistance to positivistic reduction to instrumental power and to nihilistic senselessness, a resistance that strives to provide a complex account of agency, values, knowledge, and "being" (actually, "becoming"). For now, however, it is important to note that the concept of the will is totally absent from Habermas's early discussion of Nietzsche, even though it would be central to Nietzsche's understanding of *Erkenntnistheorie,* the powers and limits of reflection, the position of instrumental science, and the interrelation of thought, "life," and morality. That is, *Erkenntnis und Interesse* builds up a powerful argument against Nietzsche as a radically undialectical, positivist thinker; but this argument rests on the exclusion of Nietzsche's central dialectical concept, the will, which could come to grips with the dangerous contradictions of positivism. By taking this concept into account, we save Nietzsche from the devastating argument Habermas makes against his supposed positivism of power.

In Habermas's later treatment of Nietzsche, the will does appear, but it is not treated as a synthetic category. Instead it is split into the two poles of aesthetic mythologizing and technical or instrumental power.[3] (This way of isolating moments as merely opposed, which are actually dialectically joined within the will, recalls the reception of Kant we saw in the last chapter. There, the will was split into its components of autonomous self-determination, or law, and natural inclination, or desire.)[4] In *Der philosophische Diskurs der Moderne* (*The Philosophical Discourse of Modernity*) Habermas locates Nietzsche in a developmental history that ends up abandoning the positive and fruitful (not Adorno's and Horkheimer's) "dialectic of the Enlightenment." The project of the Enlightenment, according to Habermas, unfolded on many levels. But fundamental to them all was the concept of Reason which, though often implicated in the problems of the Enlightenment, was the only valid means of their solution (hence, "dialectic"). Reason was defined as absolute by Hegel, as materialist and instrumental (*Zweckrationalität*) by the Young (Left) Hegelians, and as compensatory historical memory by the neoconservative Right Hegelians. Through these redefinitions Reason progressively lost its ability to respond to its own contradictions. Nietzsche, according to Habermas, abandons the dialectic entirely by rejecting the unique dialectical force of Reason.

Although this argument also has an entirely persuasive logic, it does not do justice to the will and its reconceptualization as the will to power, which become for Nietzsche the alternative to a "dialectic of the

Enlightenment" based on Reason. After all, the will, as we have seen, has had from the beginning of the Western tradition a uniquely dialectical relationship to Reason since it both grounds and disrupts rational knowledge. But rather than pursue this dialectic of the will in Nietzsche, Habermas focuses on Nietzsche's so-called aesthetic solution, according to which Nietzsche rejects reason (and all dialectic) for a cult of irrational creativity. This approach to Nietzsche leads Habermas to see in the will to power a kind of unsynthesized "ambivalence" between art and power—in the way we saw thought split between science and myth in *Erkenntnis und Interesse*—but not a complex dialectic at work on a different level. Let us look at how Habermas reduces Nietzsche to a set of contradictory positions, isolating elements that are in fact knotted together in his understanding of the will.

Habermas, following the lead of Manfred Frank,[5] interprets Nietzsche in terms of the cult around the god Dionysos that developed during and after Romanticism. Nietzsche, according to Habermas, picks up this cult of ecstatic experience and purges it of all but its *aesthetic* content: "Nietzsche continues the Romantic purification of the aesthetic phenomenon from all theoretical and moral contamination" (*PDM*, 116). The new world that art opens up would therefore offer an escape "from nihilistically devoided modernity" but only "at the price of a painful loss of differentiation, an abandonment of the ego's borders, an internal and external fusing with some amorphous Nature" (*PDM*, 117). Dionysos, in Habermas's reading of Nietzsche, offers not salvation but a combination of Schopenhauerian will as disindividuating force and modern art as a sphere independent of cognitive and ethical claims.

This interpretation of Nietzsche through Dionysos leads Habermas to a twofold reduction of the will to power. On the one hand, he sees in the will to power an "aesthetic kernel" ("ästhetischen Kern"; *PDM*, 118). Nietzsche's metaphysics become reduced to a "metaphysics of the artist" ("Artistenmetaphysik"; *PDM*, 118) and the will to power is reduced to the "metaphysical version of the dionysian principle" (*PDM*, 119). On the other hand, Habermas also sees behind Nietzsche's aestheticism a hidden "metaphysics" of power, a will beyond all individual subjects that exists merely as a field of objectified power forces: "The suprasubjective will to power manifests itself in the ebbing and waning of processes that overwhelm the individual" ("Überwältigungsprozesse"; *PDM*, 118). Nietzsche thereby becomes at one and the same time a pure aestheticist, a pure positivist of instrumental power "processes," and a hidden metaphysicist as the will to power becomes godlike (Dionysian) power. What is lost in this interpretation, however, is the prominent place of the *will* in Nietzsche's thought, for the will fuses these positions at the same time it dialectically modifies them.

Thus, the will is totally eclipsed by other features in Habermas's summary of Nietzsche's position and the will to power becomes "power":

Nietzsche owes his concept of modernity, which unfolds out of a theory of pure power, to an unmasking version of rational critique that places itself beyond the horizon of reason. This mode of critique does suggest a certain plausibility, since it at least implicitly appeals to criteria borrowed from the fundamental experiences of modernity. Nietzsche enthrones, for example, taste, "the yes and no of the tongue," as the organ of knowledge, beyond true and false, beyond good and evil. (*PDM*, 119)

Habermas can then go on to show that this position is incapable of accomplishing its intention, namely criticizing its other (Reason), since its reductive status has given up all claims to critique. And Habermas is right: If Nietzsche abandoned all self-reflection for either aesthetizing or instrumentalizing processes, he would abandon the ground of critique. But the question remains: Is this untenable position really to be attributed to Nietzsche, or is it in fact *Habermas* who reduces the will to power in Nietzsche to unsynthesized and hence self-cancelling opposites?

Of course, Habermas's goal in setting up Nietzsche in this way is to prepare for a broader critique of postmodern thought. From the "ambivalence" between "Artistenmetaphysik" and "Machttheorie," Habermas sees two ungrounded and inherently contradictory strands emerge in the twentieth century: an aestheticized ontology (Heidegger through Derrida) and a genealogy based on instrumentalizing concepts of power (Bataille and Foucault). And yet, Habermas has waged a brilliant and fully appropriate attack against a *straw man*, a Nietzsche (and followers) devoid of the central idea that was intended to be the conceptual counterforce to Reason and aestheticism and mere power, namely the will to power. Habermas's elision of the will in the *will* to power in Nietzsche is thus central to his critique of Foucault.

Habermas's Reduction of Foucault

Habermas's extensive critique of Foucault in *Der philosophische Diskurs der Moderne* opens with parallels to the approach to Nietzsche. As he had done with Nietzsche, Habermas locates Foucault's intellectual roots close to Romanticism. For example, he connects *Madness and Civilization* via Hölderlin to motifs in Schelling. In the case of Foucault, as opposed to Nietzsche, however, Habermas claims that he is not limited by his Romantic origins. This means that with the exception of particular thematic continuities between Foucault's early and later work (Habermas indicates four; *PDM*, 284–90), a methodological and conceptual break occurs between Foucault and Romanticism. That is, Habermas does not look for mythic and aestheticized moments in Foucault (he saves those for Heidegger and Adorno) but, rather, asks whether Foucault's radically antihermeneutic critique of reason can be carried out without becoming caught in aporias. The direction of

Habermas's argument is thus clear from his reading of Nietzsche: Nietzsche was, for Habermas, at least "ambivalent" (caught between the poles of aestheticism and power, myth and positivism); Foucault is not even ambivalent any more but reduced to merely *one* side, namely a concept of modernity that is identified with theory of pure power (*PDM*, 298–301). If this positioning of Foucault is correct, and if the theories of power could be shown to contain fundamental aporias, then Foucault would be trapped by them. Here, too, Habermas's argument has a powerful logic, although its conclusions rest on a reading that overlooks the dialectical possibilities contained in Foucault's (implicit) conceptualization of the will to power.

Habermas is explicit about his reduction of Foucault to a theory of power. He writes: "In the same way that 'Life' was raised by Bergson, Dilthey, and Simmel to the fundamental transcendental concept of their philosophies, and indeed still formed the background of Heidegger's existential analysis of *Dasein,* so Foucault raises 'Power' to the fundamental transcendental-historical concept of his critical writing of history" (*PDM*, 298). Likewise he claims later that the original subtitle of the first volume of the *History of Sexuality*—"La Volonté de savoir"—has lost all "transcendental meaning contained in the notion of a structurally produced will to self-empowerment" and becomes merely "the empirical form of a specific technology of power" (*PDM*, 321). Here we see the first hint of the positive role a richer notion of will has for Habermas and the place it could have in Foucault as borrowed from Nietzsche ("la *volonté* de savoir"). Yet Habermas suppresses this line of inquiry. Instead, the implication here is that Foucault has abandoned the oppositions and dualities that make up the very activity of willing. Thus, Habermas litotically evaluates the position of this concept as "in no way trivial" and correctly calls it an "irritating fundamental concept" ("irritierende[r] Grundbegriff"; *PDM*, 298), for it would unsettle a reductive theory of power. But what is in fact irritating is that in the pages following this fundamental assertion about the bedrock of Foucault's thought, Habermas does not give a single reference from Foucault himself. Instead, he argues by implication and parallelism that Foucault's so-postulated *Grundbegriff* can be linked to Heidegger's "pseudo-religiously . . . contaminated" concept of Being (*PDM*, 299–301).[6] Habermas thereby fails to explore the full role of the concept of the will in Foucault, linking it instead to a problematic and inadequate notion of power.

Habermas's initial charge against the concept of power in Foucault underlies the rest of the critical argument against him. He claims that it is on the one hand "non-dialectical" (*PDM*, 299) and on the other formulated of "paradoxically" (*PDM*, 301). The paradoxes in the concept of power—and one might wonder why Foucault is not given the benefit of the doubt so that they might be called dialectical turns—all revolve around a basic conjunction of its "transcendental" status with the historical, particular, bodily, and contingent nature of power structures. That is, according to Habermas, Foucault wants to see power as both transcendental—a structural horizon escaping the grasp of the world it defines—and concretely analyzable with scientific methods. Habermas thus strives after all to impose onto Foucault the same "ambivalence" he read in Nietzsche between a quasi-mythic hidden metaphysics and a strictly instrumentalizing positivism. Unfortunately, Habermas never pursues the argument that could strengthen Foucault's philosophy and bring the two thinkers closer, namely that the tension between these positions belongs to the historical dialectics of the will and that Foucault could be inserted into this history as a thinker who attempted a synthesis (even if a necessarily "paradoxical" one).[7]

Habermas sees the untenable ambivalence in Foucault arising out of the *origin* of the theory of power in a *Willensbegriff*, but, rather than trace Foucault's *Machttheorie* back to the richer understanding of will, he focuses on reducing the richness of the will to a limited concept of power. In this he is undoubtedly encouraged by some of Foucault's own formulations, and yet he systematically misreads Foucault as well. He argues that Foucault transforms the concept of the will into the category of power by means of two operations.[8] Habermas's argument in fact has major flaws but is crucial for his approach to Foucault. He claims first that Foucault reduces will to mere power by proposing *one* will for all times, "one truth-constituting will for *all* times and *all* societies" (*PDM*, 317). And yet, the passage cited from Foucault as evidence states just the opposite, namely the unique formation of a will to truth in every individual society: "*Each* society has its *own order* of truth, its general politics of truth: that is, it accepts certain discourses that it allows to function as true ones" (*PDM*, 317; cited from *Discipline and Punish; my emphasis*). Habermas clearly sees "order of truth" ("Ordnung der Wahrheit") and "politics of truth" ("Politik der Wahrheit") as substitutes for "will to truth" ("Willen zur Wahrheit")— a move Foucault also might make—and yet he overlooks the historical specificity that Foucault would attach to this "will" which is both changing and constant.

Second, Habermas claims that in making the move from a "will to truth" governing scientific knowledge to a more general "will to power" governing discourse-formation in general, Foucault completes the transformation of will into a single concept of instrumental power. Habermas calls this a "neutralization of the issue" ("sachliche Neutralisierung"), whereby Foucault "makes the will to truth undistinguishable from a general will to power which supposedly inhabits *all* discourses, not just those specializing in truth" (*PDM*, 317). Having claimed that Foucault offers nothing but a theory of power, Habermas feels he can criticize him solely on the basis of his concept of power. And yet here too the conclusion is ungrounded, for the generalization from "will to truth" to "will to power" does not entail the reduction of "will" to nothing but "power." That is, although Foucault may very well see the "will to truth" as a special case of the "will to power," this does not make the "will" a mere by-product of power. Given Habermas's more rhetorical than logical arguments, we can presume that there is clearly something at stake for Habermas that he should so deliberately underestimate the role of the will in Foucault.

Throughout the lectures Habermas plays a kind of argumentative cat and mouse with Foucault's theories of power and of the will (to power, knowledge, and truth), both recognizing the significance that these theories could have and then undermining them. For example, he wonders rhetorically why Foucault would have chosen theories of power as the foundation of his critical thought: "It . . . demands an explanation why Foucault decided to point his theory of science, which is based on a critique of reason, in the direction of a theory of power" (*PDM,* 301). He gives a biographical explanation based on the reactions to the student uprisings of May 1968, namely Foucault's disappointment with (certain kinds of) political action.[9] But then, he also gives Foucault credit for attempting to avoid three crucial conceptual problems: (1) Heidegger's history of knowledge as a history of metaphysics, (2) a dependence on structuralism's hidden anthrocentric metaphysics (structures as "metasubjects"), and (3) the untenable assumption of self-regulating discourses that subordinate practice. Habermas agrees with the need to avoid these philosophical traps, and I think he is correct in seeing their avoidance as the framework within which to understand Foucault's thought; and yet whereas Foucault addresses these problems through the working of a complex will (to truth, knowledge, power), Habermas undermines Foucault by claiming that he would try to take care of these problems with the single stroke of the concept of power. That—Habermas is right—cannot be done. The question is, then, why Habermas limits Foucault's conceptual apparatus completely to the inadequate term of *power?* The answer is so that he can implicate him in the "aporias of a theory of power" ("Aporien einer Machttheorie"; lecture 10 of *PDM*).

Through his reductive readings, Habermas has Foucault where he wants him because any thinker so reduced to a one-sided concept of power can only get caught up in aporias. (Adorno, we recall, does the same through his functionalized reduction of Kant, who then falls prey to a disastrous "dialectic" under such a reading.) If Foucault's critical enterprise is to avoid the basic problems that Habermas has identified, he must develop an approach that is both empirical and "transcendental" (i.e., constitutive of experience, knowledge). And the fact is, as Habermas persuasively argues, the concept of *power* alone is not up to fulfilling this double function. Because it is not inherently dialectical (in the way willing is), it collapses under the weight of fundamental aporias. In Hegelian terms, because power is only a partial determination (empirical, instrumental, caught in the determinacy of cause and effect, rationally purposive), it cannot assume broader scope and opposite determinations (transcendental, self-reflexive, innovative, irrational) without conceptual confusion. Habermas brilliantly presents the origin of these aporias. The Western philosophy of subjectivity, he argues, conceives of two relationships between "subjects" and "objects": truth and success (power), whereby the latter depends on the former since one needs to "accurately" measure successful actions. A theory of power, Habermas continues, would remain bound to the constraints of philosophies of the subject because such a theory keeps the basic operators, merely reversing their dependencies. Any objectivizing, i.e., positivistic, empirical, and instrumental analysis of "technologies" of power results, accordingly, in its opposite: "incurable subjectivism" (*PDM*, 324).

Specifically, Habermas's tenth lecture on the philosophical discourse of modernity works out three aporias that Foucault, reduced to a theory of power, could not escape (*PDM*, 325–36). The first he calls "presentism," i.e., the situation in which Foucault's critique of the past presumes his own position in the present without a hermeneutic or evaluative reflection on the *grounds* of his present position. The second is relativism, which would compromise Foucault to the extent that all forms of knowledge, including Foucault's own, would be relativized vis-à-vis "power." And the third involves the implicit normative claims for a politics of liberation Foucault raises without grounds for their validation, again since the only ground appears to be power, which legitimates everything. Habermas points to those places in Foucault's work—especially his interviews—where he either avoided the questions raised by these aporias or has indeed been intellectually embarrassed by these impasses (*PDM*, 333f).[10] Foucault, I would say in partial agreement with Habermas, often did not see the answer he had to offer in terms of the will which accounts for its knowability and unknowability, for its unique presence-absence as "groundless ground" (Schelling's *Ursein*), for its individual and supraindividual status, and for its simultaneous determinacy and emancipatory resistance to determination. Unfortunately, in other words, he also often did reduce his own thought to an untenable position as a theory of power, a position that excludes "all traces of communicative actions embedded in life-world contexts" (*PDM*, 336). Thus, Habermas's claim that Foucault, or at least the Foucault who does suppress will for the sake of power, cannot address such fundamental issues as how the individual and groups act innovatively within a social order that crystallizes and defines relationships between them, does partially apply.

And yet, we can still ask: If power cannot avoid these aporias, what about the "will to power"? What I shall show is that Foucault, despite himself at times, cannot be limited to theories of power since the will (to truth, knowledge, power) remains a force in his thought. And then I shall show that the will to power can avoid the aporias in which Habermas would ensnare Foucault; indeed, via a discussion of Nietzsche, I shall show that the will to power works through those very aporias in ways that are similar to Habermas's solutions. That nonreductive interpretation of willing gives us a more adequate account of human agency.

Foucault's "Morphology of the Will"

Interpreters have tended to divide Foucault's work into two or three stages. The first two have received the most attention and they are formulated in terms of supposed oppositions between early and late, or structuralist and anti/poststructuralist, or pre- and post-Nietzsche, or pre- and post-theory of power, or archeology and genealogy.[11] The third stage involves a supposed turn to the heretofore excluded subject and issues of selfhood.[12] In the following discussion, I shall be exploring a different kind of conceptual gap that runs through Foucault's work, that between "power" and "will to power," where by power I understand his positivistic and strictly structuralist-relational approach to either society or science, and under "will" I include concerns with intentionality and directed agency.[13] That is, by keeping a focus on the "will" in Foucault's work, rather than reducing him to a theorist of mere power, I can bring into play the richness of dialectical determinations we saw in chapter 1. These two concepts, power and will, are, of course, less strict oppositions than the difference between a partial and fuller determination (since, as we know from the historical dialectics, the will has often been reduced to a merely empirical interaction of other forces). Foucault's strength, which Habermas refused to allow in its totality, lies in those places throughout his work where he maintained this difference, although he certainly does not always formulate the conceptual determinations of the will adequately. It is only this gap that saves him from charges of mere instrumentality, nihilistic or cynical "presentism" (which could not deal with change) and a hidden metaphysics of "suprasubjectivity."

In 1970–71, his first year of teaching at the College de France, Foucault offered a course that was "to initiate a series of individual analyses that will gradually form a 'morphology of the will to knowledge' " (*LCMP,* 199), thereby offering a conceptual frame for his future work. But this frame is less a break from than a conceptualization of something already underlying his past work. He writes in the summary to the seminar about his "earlier studies" that isolated discursive practices and regularities (*LCMP,* 199–200). He puts them "under the heading of archeology" and characterizes his present turn as follows: "Studies conducted in relation to the will to knowledge should now be able to supply the theoretical justification for these earlier investigations" (*LCMP*, 201). What does Foucault hope to gain theoretically from the reformulation of his project in terms of this central category, the "will to knowledge"?

Foucault summarizes the "general direction" of his work in terms that show the advantages of foregrounding this concept: It allows for "establishing a distinction between knowledge and the rules necessary to its acquisition; the difference between the will to knowledge and the will to truth; the position of the subject and subjects in relation to this will" (*LCMP*, 201). All of these elements will have to be analyzed as we proceed through Foucault's work from the 1970s and 1980s. A "morphology of the will," which he also comes to call genealogy, as opposed to an archeology, makes it possible for Foucault to legitimate his own enterprise through the distinction between the will to knowledge and the will to truth, since the regime of the latter is contained within that of the former. Indeed, as he says in the essay, "Nietzsche, History, Genealogy," the will to truth may have to be "sacrificed" for the "endless deployment of the will to knowledge" (*LCMP*, 164).[14] Moreover, the introduction of the will allows for, indeed demands, the theoretization of both the position of the subject and a nonreduction of knowledge to the subjective "agent" since the will is *both* "anonymous, polymorphous, susceptible to regular transformations, and determined by the play of identifiable dependencies" (*LCMP*, 200–201) *and* acts through an individual (as he says in the essay on genealogy, rejecting with Nietzsche the way objective history denies the individual will; *LCMP*, 158–59)

Foucault's reformulation of his project in 1970–71 in terms of the Nietzschean concepts surrounding the will thus points him in the direction of working through the aporias in which a pure archeology would entrap him. We see him use the will as a means of escaping a self-contradiction in the inaugural lecture, "Discourse on Language," where he discusses three different systems of exclusion. The first two—organized prohibition and institutionalization —are limited in scope. But the third is broader, operating around the division between truth and falsehood. He immediately recognizes the clear danger of an error in propositional logic that would result from an attempt to critique such a division (since the proposition of a critique, as a proposition, falls under the sway of the system—truth/falsehood—it is critiquing). Thus, he realizes the necessity of "putting the question in different terms . . . asking what has been, what still is, throughout our discourse, this *will* to truth which has survived throughout so many centuries of our history; or if we ask what is, in its very general form, the kind of division governing our will to knowledge" (*AK*, 218; my emphasis). The "will" (to truth or knowledge) is thus introduced to shift levels, or types, and thus to avoid a performative contradiction. That is, the statement: "Truth versus falsehood is a division of exclusion" is self-canceling; but not the statement: "There are many forms of will (to power), among them forms of the will to knowledge and, as a subset, the will to truth, all of which are historically modifiable and exercise constraint (power) on discourse—whereby the will to truth dominates today with its specific formulation of the division between truth and falsehood."

By definition, archeology and its fundamentally structural framework, is not the tool to deal with the *will* to knowledge, because the former would disregard at least half of the determinations (individuality, innovation, intention, etc.) that make up the will. He writes: "We are faced with the unavoidable fact that the tools that permit the analysis of the will to knowledge must be constructed and defined as we proceed, according to the needs and possibilities that arise from a series of concrete studies" (*LCMP*, 201). His work from 1970 onward then has to be seen under the heading of "morphology of the will" and not, strictly speaking in terms of either "archeology" or "theories of power." Therefore, when he says in a lecture from 1976 that "the course of study that I have been following until now—roughly since 1970/71—has been concerned with the *how* of power" (*PK*, 92), the "how" points not just to instrumental and positivistic technologies but also, more important, to what we can call a "will to power" (even if Foucault does not, unfortunately, always refer to it as such).

In many of his pronouncements throughout the 1970s, Foucault was at pains to introduce terms that circumscribe the will inhering in, motivating, and organizing power relations. Without using the word "will," Foucault in an interview from 1977 says that even from the beginning he was interested in the *force* organizing scientific statements. This is not an "external power imposed on science" but rather "their internal regime of power" (*PK*, 112). When he says that this interest leads him to reject analyses that remain on the level of structure for the sake of "analyses in terms of the *genealogy* of relations of force, *strategic* developments, and *tactics*" (*PK*, 114; my emphasis), he is conceiving of a nonstructural, nonpositivisitic motivation inhering in power relations. As he says in the afterword to Dreyfus and Rabinow's monograph, he needed a *broader* conception of power than the merely legal or institutional (or economic) to deal with the creation of subjects. My point is that this richer conception is linked with the will and its dialectical determinations.

In response to a question in 1977, Foucault narrates his "transition" from "The Order of Discourse" to the *History of Sexuality* in terms of a shift in the concept of power that likewise implies the introduction of the will, especially its dialectical relation to the Law. The earlier studies employed an essentially "juridical" model of power. For Foucault, this meant that discourse functioned as a coherent structure that excluded statements for strictly structural reasons; i.e., the "law" dominated by a nonindividualized prohibition. But in his post-1970 work he came to view power in terms of "technology, of tactics and strategy" (*PK*, 184). Precisely the strategic "intentionality" inhering in power became his focus, not just the "structural" feature of exclusion. When he tries to characterize this in a discussion he uses the term "rationality" (*PK*, 197), admittedly, as Jacques-Alain Miller, one of the participants in the discussion, points out, not the best term.[15] Rather, it is like a "strategy without a subject" (*PK*, 202). In terms that we will see echo Nietzsche's, Foucault rejects the Darwinistic reading of organizing force, since "the problem isn't one of self-preservation. When I speak of strategy, I am taking the term seriously: in order for a certain relation of forces not only to maintain itself, but to accentuate, stabilize and broaden itself, a certain kind of manoeuvre is necessary" (*PK*, 206).[16] This "strategy" or "manoeuvre" occupies for Foucault the same position as the "will to power" in Nietzsche, namely an active force that makes possible a paradoxical agency in human beings. Human willing, after all, must work with the forces (desires, drives, impulses) of the body, such that we cannot will without them even as our willing, strategies, tactics are not determined by them.

We encounter here a problem that demands a certain kind of reading. Although I see Foucault providing his own version of agency with the full historical and conceptual complexity associated with willing, he typically describes his enterprise with other terms. We therefore need to draw out of his writings the conceptualization of willing that lies behind his discussions of power. In this way we save him from his own reductions (and from Habermas's critique), since the analysis of power can make most sense if it is seen in the light of a newly illuminated "will to power." We will also then be able to bring Nietzsche's analysis of the will to bear on Foucault and thereby bring him closer to Habermas.

How can *Discipline and Punish*, which is alluded to in its earliest stages in 1970 as "the seminar during this past year (with) its general framework the study of the penal system in France during the nineteenth century" (*LCMP*, 204), be understood as a contribution to the study of the "morphology of the will to knowledge" when "will" never plays an explicit role? The answer is to be found in the way Foucault formulates the process "at the heart of all mechanisms of punishment" (*DP*, 55), and by implication behind power itself. The process is called the "truth-power relation" (*DP*, 55), or "power-knowledge" (*DP*, 27–28). It involves a special "mapping of the social body" (*DP*, 79, 82). What is important here is that for all the tendency to put the technologies of power into strictly structural and functional terms—or to make them, as Habermas called them, "success-oriented"— Foucault's argument resists such a reduction thanks to the maintenance of a dynamic force that plays itself out on and through individuals (though it is not subjective in origin) and that affects the physical/social body even as it involves nonempirical *conditions* of truth/power. The "truth-power relation" (or "power-knowledge") is, then, the *will* to truth/power motivating particular formations through tensions and intentions among individuals.[17] It is *both* individual *and* supraindividual. To ask whether it originates in the individuals or in the structure in which they are embedded mistakenly isolates the elements that are co-original (*gleichursprünglich*) in the will.

In the *History of Sexuality* and his later essays, Foucault, despite the weight he places on the concept of *pouvoir*, is more explicit about avoiding the reduction of his thought to a theory of power. The French subtitle of the *History of Sexuality*—"La Volonté de savoir"—Habermas's denial notwithstanding (see above), is thus a clue to his conceptualization. When Foucault says that "the object . . . is to define the regime of power-knowledge-pleasure that sustains the discourse on human sexuality in our part of the world" (*HS*, 11), he is defining the will, which operates on all three levels and whose conceptualization has traditionally related them in dialectical ways. The will functions precisely at the intersection of power, knowledge, and pleasure (in Kantian terms, "at the crossroads"), involving each yet resisting reduction to any one. Thus, Foucault implicitly picks up on the tradition of interpretations of the will when, echoing the formulation we saw in the summary of his 1970–71 seminar on "morphology of the will," he writes that he is not concerned with the truth or falsehood of statements about sex but, rather, "the essential aim is . . . to bring out the 'will to knowledge' that serves as both their support and their instrument" (*HS*, 12–13). The broader "regime" is therefore a formation of will that is neither an abstract metaphysical nor a reductively empirical entity but the very conditions of the dynamic interaction of elements involved in human agency.

To appreciate the significance of this reading for Foucault's theory of power let us look at a detail with implications for translation and Foucault's reception. Near the end of the *History of Sexuality* Foucault refers to the "great technologies of power in the nineteenth century," the deployment of sexuality being one of the most important. These formations are not, he insists, speculative discourses but "concrete arrangements" (*HS*, 140). The excellent translation by Robert Hurley includes the original French for this phrase: "agencements concrets." Not only is this term a neologism that escapes direct translation into English but, more important, the French reminds us of a feature of "power relations" too easily missed in the notion of positivistic "arrangements," namely the connotation of agency. This richer conception of *agencements* allows Foucault to distance himself from the limitations of a structuralist theory of power.[18]

Foucault addresses the unique nature of this "agency" inhering in power in the fourth of his five propositions on his method. It reads: "Power relations are both intentional and nonsubjective" (*HS,* 94). His gloss on this proposition shows how he navigates a passage between metaphysics, structuralism, and subjectivism. He rules out some other "instance" that " 'explains' " power relations, i.e., some quasi-metaphysical force *behind* power relations as a cause producing them as effects; he likewise rules out the possibility that power "results from the choice or decision of an individual subject" (*HS,* 95); and he rules out a collective subjectivity—class, caste, or state apparatus. Instead of these possibilities he proposes the inseparability of the structural network making up relations from the "aims and objectives" or "tactics" of "calculation" imbuing the network. As John Rajchman states:

> For Foucault, the "will" in the "will-to-knowledge" is therefore not constitutive agency. It is not the will of a people, a nation, or a race. It is many people acting and struggling with each other at once, some dominating others, within a tacit system of action. There are many different such wills; to analyze the "will-to-knowledge" is to analyze how they emerge and are transformed. Freedom is thus not the agency of Reason in History; it is a struggle within the "politics of truth" of the knowledge about us.[19]

And in the same vein, Foucault states as a "methodological precaution" in a lecture from January 14, 1976, that the "will to power" is neither located in a special place in or outside the social body, nor is it the preformed and independent wills of the individuals. Rather it is that which allows power to "circulate" such that individuals "are always in the position of simultaneously undergoing and exercising this power" (*PK,* 98) All these formulations play out variations of the dialectical determinations of willing: activity and passivity, determinism and freedom, subjective and supraindividual, empirical and transcendental. The will, for Foucault, seems to be an "in-between" or "non-place" that allows for the circulation of power and the exercise of individual practices.

If we retain the inherence of will in power, we can better understand the nature of the "third shift" (*UP,* 6) that Foucault seems to have made as he continued working on the history of sexuality. He summarizes his thought in three stages: (1) focus on discursive practices of the human sciences, (2) "manifestations of power," (3) an analysis of "what is termed 'the subject.' " His turn to the "practices of the self," "the forms and modalities of the relation to self by which the individual constitutes and recognizes himself *qua* subject" do seem to take him "far from (his) original project" (*UP,* 6).[20] And yet, in fact it is most appropriate to see this "shift" as a continuation of the investigation of the "morpholology of the will (to knowledge)" that he had embarked upon in 1970. Since the will is the *conjuncture* of power-knowledge-pleasure, it was in fact the occasional collapsing of categories into monolithic power during the 1970s that represented the departure from the original project. That is, as opposed to Habermas's reductive reading, we can see the emphasis on mere power as but a limited phase of Foucault's overall "morphology of the will."[21]

Foucault's essay on Cassian offers the most extensive conceptual deployment of the concept of the will as the fusion of power-knowledge-pleasure. Foucault argues that Cassian's monastic institutions define the regime of a new will to truth/knowledge in terms of sexuality and the body. Much has been made for centuries of the difference between Greek and Christian attitudes toward the body and sex (*UP,* 36). But Foucault maps this divide in terms of regimes (formations, morphologies) of the will. For the Greeks, as he argues in *The Use of Pleasure,* the will, or the way in which pleasure became an "ethical problem," took the form of a control and regulation of sexual acts in order to promote mastery, balance, and greater enjoyment. For Christianity, however, the focus is on something quite different: "The whole essence of the fight for chastity is that it aims at a target which has nothing to do with actions or relationships; it concerns a different reality to that of a sexual connection between two individuals" (*PPC,* 233). This other reality is the will, dialectically defined precisely by its presence-absence and activity-passivity, since it exists thanks to the fact that its nonexistence calls it into existence (see also *PPC,* 261). At its root we find an ambiguous "wanting" (as we did in Lacan's *manque-à-être*). That is, the very impossibility of a will that can control desire engenders the will that strives to control itself. The very impossibility of self-mastery creates the drive toward autonomous self-determination. Like the knotting of law and desire in Kant, Lacan, and Adorno, the Christian will according to Foucault exemplifies the unique structure of willing in general.[22]

With Christianity, the will to knowledge attains a level of self-reflexivity as it internalizes an essential contradiction. Where in Greco-Roman practices and philosophy dichotomies (like mind-body) reigned and had to be related via complex codifications, for Cassian the battle became that of the will against itself. In this regard, Foucault's reading conforms with other interpretations of how the conception of man as a "willing being" emerges with such Christian thinkers as Augustine and Duns Scotus.[23] Foucault argues: "Now two opposing poles appear, not, one has to realize, those of mind versus body. They are, firstly, the involuntary pole, which consists either of physical movements or of feelings evoked by memories and images that survive from the past and ferment in the mind, besieging and enticing the will, and secondly the pole of the will itself, which accepts or repels, averts its eyes or allows itself to be ensnared, holds back or consents" (*PPC,* 234–35). These two are locked together in a dialectical battle such that "the aim is that the subject should never be affected in his effort by the obscurest or the most seemingly 'unwilled' presence of will" (*PPC,* 235). The self-involvement of the will with itself is precisely what creates the "different reality" by removing the practices of the self out of the realm of actions and relationships and into the realm of the "subject" and its "libido (and later sex) itself" (*PPC,* 235). The dangers and nihilism of this position can only be countered by alternative conceptualizations of the will.[24]

I have focused on this one essay because I find it exemplary of Foucault's work in his final years and, more broadly, because it makes explicit fundamental moments of his thought.[25] The different regimes are not reducible to "arrangements" or positivistic networks of power since what is at stake in each is a formation of will (*agencement,* or as we will see in Habermas, "Willensbildung")—the point of intersection of drive, body, ethical control, self, intersubjective relations, and the social strategies of a historical moment. With the creation of modern social norms in the West out of Christian belief, this will turns in on itself, becoming not only the forming "agency" but also the object of its own self control. The will to knowledge, in becoming the will to the truth (of sex), hypostatizes and renders itself abstract, disassociates itself from its own individual and social agency (see *PPC,* 235). And because this development can be recognized as *one* formation, there is potential for change; bodies, selves, wills are not just caught up in a regime of "power" but participate in forming its nonsubjective intentionality.

We have thus in Foucault's theoretical and historical elaboration of the formations and morphology of the will details of a model I outlined in the introduction during the discussion of Butler. Beginning as a kind of non-place or in-between, it opens up at the interstices of empirical forces a kind of retrograde arc that *creates* a subject and makes possible actions on objects in the world. I had diagrammed this process earlier[26] as follows:

$$s \longleftarrow \quad w \longrightarrow o$$
$$\text{subject} \quad \text{willing} \quad \text{objects}$$

Its nonempirical and nonmetaphysical status, in the sense that it is not a thing in the world or a substance underlying the self (a "mini-agent" within the self), guarantees that "it" cannot be reduced to a play of power or to the subject that emerges out of it. It makes possible "tactics" and "strategies" that allow for action in the context of power, pleasures in the context of the law, and knowledge in the context of a priori structures.

Nietzsche's Theory of Will to Power

Foucault, in one of those places where he was his own worst conceptual enemy, claims that he is a Nietzschean in an essential sense (e.g., *PPC,* 32, 250) and that Nietzsche is a "philosopher of power" (*PK,* 53). But if this were the case, they would both fall prey to the aporias Habermas outlined. As we have seen, however, Foucault, despite such pronouncements, cannot be reduced to a theory of power. Now we must examine Nietzsche's conception of the will to show that Nietzsche is not best understood as a "philosopher of power" and that Foucault is Nietzschean not in the way Foucault thought but according to this richer interpretation of Nietzsche's will.[27] The issues we must address concerning Nietzsche's "will to power" are the same as those that Habermas raised in his criticisms of both Nietzsche and Foucault: (1) To what extent is Nietzsche's understanding of the will to power reducible to a theory of power? (2) To the extent that Nietzsche offers a "materialist" account of will and power, does he become, paralleling Foucault's (perhaps) ironic self-description, a "gay positivist" (*positiviste heureux*)? (3) To the extent that Nietzsche resists positivism, does he succumb to "bad metaphysics" of the kind he rejects in Western culture in general and in (Schopenhauerian) Idealism in particular, i.e., a hypersubjectivism? That is, does the "will" become in Nietzsche a special kind of substance or entity? (4) Does Nietzsche's position result in nihilism, a dangerous senseless and relativistic protofascism, even if everything can be explained only in terms of the will to power? And finally, (5) should the will to power, as Heidegger says in his first lectures devoted to Nietzsche, be equated with art, in which case Nietzsche's theory becomes "mere" aestheticism (as Habermas charges)?[28] My argument will be that Nietzsche uses the *will* to power as his way to walk the dialectical tightrope that spans these conflicting positions, i.e., to avoid each position, even though each one makes up an extreme conclusion of certain lines of his thought.

To see the necessary disjunction in Nietzsche's thought between power and will to power, we can look at two passages from Nietzsche's *Nachlaß* in which he distinguishes himself from Darwin.[29] Nietzsche opposes Darwinism as a reductive theory of self-preserving forces. In the first passage (*Nachlaß, Werke* III, 748–51), Nietzsche rejects Darwin because the "undesirable drama" ("unerwünschte Schauspiel") of the day shows how the strongest are being overwhelmed by the "Typen der *décadence*," a fact that could not be explained in terms of mere materialist force.[30] He says that only his concept of will to power, which he calls the "last ground and character of all change" ("letzten Grund und Charakter aller Veränderung"), explains why natural selection does not work. This formulation captures ironically the duality of fixation and innovation, stability and change, that we saw in chapter 1, for the will has traditionally been defined as both human "character" and the potential for spontaneity. His implication is that although the strong have the power, the weak exercise the stronger *will* to power since willing does not only preserve but can also destabilize relations (of power). That is, according to Darwin (in Nietzsche's reading), the strongest win the struggle to preserve their position—that is why they are strongest. But for Nietzsche, the mediocre or weak can win if they have the stronger or more directed *will* to power. In fact, Nietzsche rejects the notion of self-preservation since, he says, the goal of life (will to power) is not the achievement or maintenance of power relations but an increase or change, even at the expense of particular forms of successful power.[31]

In the second passage, Nietzsche rejects Darwin for setting "usefulness" ("Nützlichkeit") as his highest goal (*Nachlaß, Werke* III, 894–95; comp. also *Genealogie der Moral, Werke* II, 817–20). "Progress" and struggle occur, for Nietzsche, not in order to create that which will last but for the sake of that which encourages change. Here we can recall the terms in which Habermas cast the fundamental aporia of Western subject-object philosophy, namely truth versus success (power). Nietzsche is *not* siding with the latter. Instead, he skirts the contradiction that emerges when an objectivizing category (success, efficiency) becomes dependent on a subjective one (truth) since he turns to the will, which, as we shall see, implicates subject and object in a different process. The process is both self-directed and directional—the will wills, it wants more and therefore is constantly changing, turning, and "growing." It is not merely a structural relation of forces. Thus, he writes in *Jenseits von Gut und Böse*: "The physiologists should think twice before positing self-preservation as the cardinal drive of an organic being. Above all something living wants to *release* its force—life itself is will to power—; self-preservation is only one of the indirect and most common effects of it" (*Werke* II, 578).

The association of will with *Leben* is crucial for Nietzsche. It runs throughout his thought and Habermas, we saw, used it to establish a connection between Nietzsche's master concept and that of Dilthey and Simmel. But if we look at the arguments, we see that Nietzsche is pursuing the Habermasian goal of critiquing mechanistic science by attacking its reduction of will to the notion of cause and effect. The will is therefore central to any attempt to distinguish Nietzschean thought from positivism. "Life" fulfills a dual function associated with the will, since it is both antimetaphysical and antiempirical (since clearly life is "of this world," although what *makes* something *alive* as opposed to a collection of interacting atoms is more than the sum of its parts), systematic and innovative, active and passive, self-contained and self-transcending, unified and fragmenting.

One of the most confusing features of Nietzsche's discussions of the will is the fact that he is using a concept that has been taken over and reinterpreted by mechanistic sciences even as he strives to distance himself fundamentally from them. (He is also rejecting the concept as it has been taken over by the metaphysical morality or moralizing metaphysics of Christianity; see below.) Thus, in this philosopher of the will (to power) we find constant pronouncements *against* the existence of the will. And yet, these rejections of the will are generally rejections of the will as cast in terms of *cause and effect.* That is, Nietzsche rejects the nondialectical, reductionist formulations that are ultimately associated with a form of determinism. Zarathustra, for example, attacks the "spirit of gravity" ("Geist der Schwere," whereby in the term "Schwere" we hear the echoes of the origins of modern mechanics in Newton's analysis of gravitational laws) with its basic concepts "compulsion, statutes, necessity and consequence and purpose and will and good and evil" ("Zwang, Satzung, Not und Folge und Zweck und Wille und Gut und Böse"; *Also Sprach Zarathustra, Werke* II, 444). Likewise, in an aphorism from the *Gay Science* that contains some ideas he will later revise, Nietzsche stresses an association that he opposes throughout his life, namely the quasi-religious belief in the will as "effective force" ("wirkende Kraft") or "cause" ("Ursache," *Werke* II, 128). In the *Nachlaß* he attempts to formulate a theory of the "organic functions" in terms of a "fundamental will, the will to power" (*Werke* III, 449). The important thing is that he casts it in self-reflexive terms that would not be reduced to mechanistic explanation: "There is no other causality [although even this word is problematic here] besides that working from will to will. Not explicable mechanistically." Ironically, this formulation links Nietzsche to Kant, who also defined the will in terms of a peculiar "cause of freedom," although, as we shall see, Nietzsche does not identify this "causality" with Kant's. And in two often-quoted aphorisms from the *Nachlaß,* Nietzsche addresses directly the relationship between " 'will to power' and causalism" and formulates a "critique of mechanism." He argues that cause and effect are secondary concepts, psychological projections back into phenomena. Mechanistic explanations are an "imagistic speech" ("Bilderrede," *Werke* III, 775) or "Semiotik" ("sign language," *Werke* III, 776) or a "translation into the human language of the senses" (*Werke* III, 777). The predictability of cause and effect does not prove that there "are" causes and then there "are" effects. Rather, he postulates a continuous process of "striving," which he again opposes to the Darwinistic and mechanistic notions of self-preservation: "not self-preservation (*Selbstbewahrung*), but wanting to appropriate, dominate, become more, become stronger" (*Werke* III, 367–68). He rejects the opposition of things and forces, arguing instead for a unified and directed order of "Willens-Quanta" (*Werke* III, 776) or "ein Quantum 'Willen zur Macht' " (*Werke* III, 777). The will is neither some *thing* "in addition" to the mere "things," nor is it reduced to them. As he says in the late work, *Der Antichrist:* "The old word, 'will,' serves only to indicate a resulting action, a kind of individual reaction that necessarily follows upon a series of partially contradictory, partially harmonizing partial stimuli— the will no longer 'effects' or 'moves' " (*Werke* II, 1174). This follows an avowed approval of Descartes's view of *homme machine,* yet demonstrates that Nietzsche's version of the will cannot be accommodated fully by a mechanistic account. The supposed basis of mechanistic explanations are instead interpretations of the process of the will to power (whereby "interpretation" is a mode of willing and "interpretations of" has both us and the will itself as subject; see *Nachlaß, Werke* III, 489: "Der Wille zur Macht *interpretiert* . . .").[32] Thus, far from being a positivist in the sense of striving to offer a non-self-reflexive mechanical explanation, Nietzsche would rather strive for a paradoxical theory of the will. Such contradictory formulations locate Nietzsche's formulations squarely in the midst of the dialectical tensions that make up the history of conceptualizations of willing.[33]

Nietzsche not only avoids the aporias of positivism, he sees through them and offers the "will to power" as a necessary alternative. The problem with mechanistic positivism, he argues, is that it is implicitly dualist, leading to a self-contradictory metaphysics. That is, the reduction of man or world to machine leads to a postulation (often implicit) of something else (spirit). And eventually, once that contradiction is revealed, one is left with the nihilism of senselessness.

Nietzsche plays this process out on the "bad" or "old" concept of will that has dominated Western culture so that he can salvage a new one as the basis of his overall philosophy. He points to the way the tradition of thinking on the will has tended to shift back and forth between partial determinations. Namely, the reduction of will to cause and effect leads to its opposite, the postulation of a "free will," which, if it is ultimately rejected, leaves us with the nihilistic "Geist der Schwere." Instead, Nietzsche develops a "third" position. Let us pursue this in greater detail.

Nietzsche never tires of reformulating the dialectically structured argument that mechanistic science contains an implicit dualism that leads it to flip into its opposite. The first section of *Jenseits von Gut und Böse,* "On the Prejudices of the Philosophers," revolves around this self-contradictory structure inherent in Western thought. He places the theory of "materialistische Atomistik" among "the best-refuted things that exists" (*Werke* II, 576) and yet still declares war on the "need for (or lack in) atomism" ("atomistisches Bedürfnis"; *Werke* II, 577). The reason is that he finds the belief in "mere things out there" always associated with a belief in something like the soul—and vice versa. The latter he calls "soul-atomism" ("Seelen-Atomistik"), the belief "that takes the soul as something indestructible, eternal, indivisible, as a monad, as an *atomon*" (*Werke* II, 577). In the twenty-first aphorism, Nietzsche brings these two beliefs together in one of his sharpest dialectical arguments.

The target of the aphorism is the concept of a "cause in and of itself": "The *causa sui* is the best self-contradiction that has thus far been thought up" (*Werke* II, 584). It is linked with the concept of "free will": "The longing for 'freedom of the will' . . . the longing to carry the entire and final responsibility for one's actions . . . is nothing less than the desire to be that *causa sui.*" And to attack *this* notion, he looks at its opposite, "den 'unfreien Willen,'" which, he says, can be traced back to inappropriate mechanistic thinking, i.e., thought "which leads to the misuse of the notions of cause and effect" (*Werke* II, 585). Once one abandons the belief in a world of "laws" in which the will would be unfree, one no longer feels the longing for a will that escapes these laws and is a cause unto itself. (See also *Nachlaß, Werke* III, 774–77, where he points out that the belief in "laws" connecting "things" creates the need to postulate a "doer" making the connection. This parallels the discussion in the thirteenth aphorism of section 1 of the *Genealogy of Morals.*) Nietzsche would thus drop the opposing yet inextricably linked concepts of free and unfree will—subjectivism and mechanism—for a different order: "The 'unfree will' (like the 'free' one) is mythology—in real life it's only a question of *strong* and *weak* wills" (*Werke* II, 585). The key here is that he does not drop the will altogether.

This fundamental argument underlies many of Nietzsche's positions. He rejects Kant, for example, for proposing two forms of causality, "causality of the will" and "causality of nature" (*Jenseits von Gut und Böse, Werke* II, 600–601). And in the later work, *Götzendämmerung,* Nietzsche attacks "The Four Great Errors": (1) "Error of confusing cause and effect," (2) "the error of false causality," (3) "the error of imaginary causes," and (4) "the error of free will." Nietzsche pursues the irony that emerges when one believes in the mechanistic account of the world in terms only of cause and effect and one is then forced to invert and extend the concept of cause. This means that one is first forced to invent causes in the "soul" and then to exempt them from the very order of cause and effect by positing some as "free." This is the argument we saw recurring within the Western tradition for some concept of *Willkür* or *arbitrium librerum.* The reason *why* one is forced to invent an untenable notion of "free will" is to avoid the nihilism of the opposing position.

Nihilism, according to Nietzsche, is associated with two conditions that result from two forms or experiences of meaninglessness (which he often calls "psychological" conditions, but I agree with Heidegger who says that if Nietzsche sees the world as will, then "psychological condition" is both individual and ontological).[34] In the first, meaninglessness arises from the disappointment one would experience when one's implicit dualism is reduced to one position. It would be something like: "You mean the world is really *nothing but* cause and effect?" The "nothing but" implies that one had wanted more, namely the opposite of cause and effect, "freedom." In the second, meaninglessness arises when one's dualism is experienced as a false choice with no other option available. One might imagine this to be the result of Reason's facing Kant's antinomies (especially the third on causality and freedom). This is, in fact, the state in which Nietzsche finds the majority of "advanced" Western minds. (He formulates the relation between these two positions clearly in his notes: "futility of mechanistic theory—it gives the impression of meaninglessness. The entire history of human *Idealism* is in the process of flipping over into Nihilism—that is, into the belief in absolute *worth*lessness and *meaning*lessness"; *Nachlaß, Werke* III, 896.)

The worst form nihilism takes is the self-reflexive one that arises around the very aporias of the will we have been analyzing, specifically when the dialectics are not embraced as such. With the untenability of the opposition between free and unfree will, or between *causa sui* and laws of cause and effect, the entire concept and life-giving activity of the will is placed into question. This is the self-annihilating state described at the end of the *Genealogie der Moral* as a result of the development and collapse of "ascetic ideals," whereby human beings would rather will nihilism than lose all ability to will ("Lieber will der Mensch *das Nichts* wollen als *nicht* wollen"; *Werke* II, 839, 900). Nihilism, then, has its roots for Nietzsche—and here he is fully in agreement with Habermas—in a dangerous reductionism. It is linked to mechanistic theories of cause and effect and power that have no place for the "driving force" ("treibende Kraft") that necessarily inheres in structures and relations (see *Nachlaß, Werke* III, 750). We must now see whether Nietzsche's theory of the will to power can avoid precisely this charge of reductionism, since that "Kraft" (will) must not itself be reducible to a quasi-substance.

Confronted with what seems like an impossible choice among a mechanistic metaphysics of things, or a subjectivist metaphysics of "freedom" (Kant's *Ding an sich*, Schopenhauer's *Wille*), or a nihilistic metaphysics of nothing, Nietzsche neither chooses any of these nor gives up the will to choose (a response he often calls "European Buddhism"). Instead, he formulates a comprehensive, literally all-embracing (hence active, choosing, willing) conception of the will as becoming, change, totality.[35] Nietzsche's "solution" is neither positivistic, metaphysical, nor aestheticist, since the will as becoming (*Werden*) forms a paradoxical ontology that undermines all fixations on substances and also contains the ordering and normative principles for an epistemology and ethics. Faced with nihilism, Nietzsche cuts through its binarisms to a more inclusive perspective. This operation is important since Foucault, in Habermas's reading, was torn between a "historical-pragmatic" and "transcendental" conception of power. Habermas did not allow Foucault the Nietzschean option of a rich understanding of the will that works through the aporias of power.

First, we should examine how Nietzsche generalizes the strategy of working through the binarisms. (I would call this argumentation "dialectical," although not in the sense of Kaufmann, since the two poles are more left behind than *aufgehoben*.)[36] In *Götzendämmerung* (*Werke* II, 693) Nietzsche plays out the "history of an error" in terms of a "fable" about the "true world." It is modelled on his analysis of the development of the concept of the will. There are six stages: (1) the "true world" as an ideal sphere attainable for the wise (Platonic Idealism); (2) the "true world" as attainable only for the virtuous after death (Christianity); (3) the "true world" as unattainable yet as imperative (Kant); (4) the "true world" as unattained and unknown, and therefore not a source of consolation or ethical prescriptions ("Hahnenschrei des Positivismus"); (5) the rejection of the concept, "true world," as useless; (6) and finally, with the rejection of the "true world," the realization that the belief in this world as illusion has also been destroyed (*"mit der wahren Welt haben wir auch die scheinbare abgeschafft"*). This endpoint is, for Nietzsche, the "midday; moment of the shortest shadow; end of the longest error; highpoint of humankind" ("Mittag; Augenblick des kürzesten Schattens; Ende des längsten Irrtums; Höhepunkt der Menschheit") and the birth of Zarathstra. If we replace "true world" with "free will" and "illusory world" (or positivistic, unconsoling world) with "unfree will," then we see that we have worked through the binarism that has formed the long history of Western thought on willing, and its nihilistic flip-flopping, for the sake of a new dialectical conceptualization.

What does Nietzsche oppose to the pair "free" or "unfree" will? Throughout his entire philosophy the same series of words appears in different constellations to characterize the will to power. The most "philosophical" of these terms is "Werden" (becoming); and the general "metaphorical" imagery surrounding it involves either water ("Strom" or "Fluß") or "Leben." Already in *Menschliches, Allzumenschliches* (1879) we have the foundation of his argument:

> *The Freedom of the Will and the Isolation of Facts.*— Our usual, imprecise way of looking at things takes a group of phenomena as one entity and calls them a fact: between it and another fact we imagine an empty space, whereby we *isolate* each fact. In truth, however, all our action and knowledge is not the effect of facts and empty intermediary space, but a continual flux. Now, the belief in freedom of the will is precisely incompatible with the idea of a continual, uniform, undivided, indivisible flow. . . . [free will] is itself a form of atomism in the sphere of willing and knowing.

> *Die Freiheit des Willens und die Isolation der Fakta.*— Unsere gewohnte ungenaue Beobachtung nimmt eine Gruppe von Erscheinungen als eins und nennt sie ein Faktum: zwischen ihm und einem andern Faktum denkt sie sich einen leeren Raum hinzu, sie *isoliert* jedes Faktum. In Wahrheit aber

ist all unser Handeln und Erkennen keine Folge von Fakten und leeren Zwischenräumen, sondern ein beständiger Fluß. Nun ist der Glaube an die Freiheit des Willens gerade mit der Vorstellung eines beständigen, einartigen, ungeteilten, unteilbaren Fließens unverträglich . . . er ist eine *Atomistik* im Bereiche des Wollens und Erkennens. (*Werke* I, 878)

Here we see the intimate connection between positivism and a belief in the free will. Nietzsche is opposed *not* to willing (or knowing), but only to a reification of that dialectical activity into an opposition between an atomistic will and an atomistic world of facts.

Nietzsche develops these ideas and images elsewhere. In the central section of *Also sprach Zarathustra*, "On Self-Overcoming" ("Von der Selbst-Überwindung"), Nietzsche links the "flow of becoming" ("Fluß des Werdens") with "life" (*Leben*) (*Werke* II, 369–72). And in *Götzendämmerung* he clearly opposes the "error of free will" to the "innocence of becoming" ("Unschuld des Werdens," *Werke* II, 977). The philosophy of the will to power, therefore, is unfolded in terms of a dialectical philosophy of *Werden*.

The vitalistic response to mechanism and subjectivism needs to be understood, then, not in terms of biologism but as a special and paradoxical ontological position that places *Werden* above *Sein* (see the semi-ironic passage from the *Die fröhliche Wissenschaft* where he says: "We Germans are Hegelians, even if there had never been a Hegel, insofar as we instinctively attribute to becoming, to development, a deeper significance and higher value than that which 'is'—we hardly believe in the legitimacy of the concept of 'being' "; *Werke* II, 226–27). One of the many formulations of this position occurs in the *Nachlaß*, an aphorism entitled with a pun lost in English: "Vom Wert des 'Werdens' " ("On the Value of 'Becoming' "). It begins by showing how a rejection of mechanism has motivated his own thought:

> If the movement of the world had a final state, it would have been arrived at already. The only fundamental fact is, however, that there is *no* final state; and any philosophy or scientific hypothesis (e.g., mechanism) that posits such a state as a necessity is *refuted* by that very fact.
>
> I seek a conception of the world that does justice to *this* fundamental fact. Becoming must be explained *without* taking refuge in such notions as final ends or purposes. (*Werke* III, 684)

And he goes on to reject all notions of being ("das Seiende") as the foundation of the world: *"one ought not accept anything as being at all"* (*"man darf nichts Seiendes überhaupt zulassen"*).

There are a number of consequences that follow from this identification of will to power as his fundamental concept and *Werdensphilosophie*. The first is the necessary linguistic paradox that arises when the copula is used with either *Werden* or will to power because "linguistic means of expression are useless in talking about becoming" (*Nachlaß, Werke* III, 685). In fact, the will to power also cannot be expressed adequately with the concept of becoming: "one shouldn't want to understand it as 'becoming,' and even less as having become. . . . The 'will to power' cannot 'have become' " ("man soll es nicht as 'werdend' verstehn wollen, noch weniger als geworden. . . . Der 'Wille zur Macht' kann nicht geworden sein"; *Nachlaß, Werke* III, 690). That is, the very phrases "The will to power *is Werden*" or "*Werden is* so-and-so" are contradictory and reductive. This position connects back to the rejection of subjectivism as the flip side of metaphysics, since as we saw the postulation of "being" sown together by laws of causality forces one to postulate also a doer beyond the activity. As he formulates it in one note from the *Nachlaß:* "My demand is that one reintroduce the *doer* into the doing, now that he has been understandably abstracted out of it, thereby emptying out doing. . . . All 'ends,' 'goals,' 'senses' are but ways of expressing, and variations of, the *one* will inherent in all occurrences: the will to power" (*Werke* III, 679). That is, the statement: "The will is" leads to the statement: "The will does," turning it into the kind of mega-subject, as cause outside of its effect, that Nietzsche wants to avoid.

Second, following directly from the first point, Nietzsche must continually try to reformulate his conception of the will to power so that it does not become a unitary substance. We therefore find statements, like the one just quoted, claiming that he wants to see the world only in terms of the will to power *and* that he does not see the will to power as an *Einheit*. In *Jenseits von Gut und Böse,* he writes: "Willing seems to me above all as something *complicated,* something that is a unity only insofar as there is one word for it" ("Wollen scheint mir vor allem etwas *Kompliziertes,* etwas, das nur als Wort eine Einheit ist"; *Werke* II, 581). He is constantly opposing the reduction of will to *one* thing because as *Werden* it can only be an aggregation and disgregation of forces, impulses. Thus, as we saw, he needs to distinguish his use of "will to power" from "the old word, 'will' " since he is referring to "a group of partially self-contradicting, partially harmonizing stimuli" (*Der Anti-Christ, Werke* II, 1174). He even goes so far as to say at times there *is no* will so that his "will to power" as complex phenomena not be mistakenly reduced to the "old will." Thus, in the *Nachlaß* we read: "There is not will: there are only will-punctuations" ("Es gibt keinen Willen: es gibt Willens-Punktationen"; *Werke* III, 685) and "there is no will, and therefore neither a strong or a weak will. The plurality and disgregation of impulses, the lack of system among them, results in a 'weak will'; the coordination of forces under the domination of a single one results in a 'strong will' " (*Werke* III, 696). But we should not be distracted by his pronouncements against the "old will" since in fact we hear in these passages the echoes of the age-old dialectic of the will as a unifying and fragmented force of selfhood. What

Nietzsche rejects as "old" are the partial determinations of that tradition. He can affirm the past only in its contradictory totality.

In this context we can also appreciate his metaphor of the "dance" for the activity of willing and becoming, since the dance captures for Nietzsche the movement and complexity whose status as "being" is constantly being undermined. In *Zarathustra*, for example, he writes of his visions of the future beyond the "Geist der Schwere" (with its older philosophical concepts, like "the will")

> where all becoming seems to me to be divine dance and divine willfulness, and the world loses itself, gives itself out, only to flee back to itself:— as an eternal flight from self and self-discovery of many gods, as a blissful self-contradicting, self-dialoguing, self-belonging of many gods.

> wo alles Werden mich Götter-Tanz und Götter-Mutwillen dünkte, und die Welt los- und ausgelassen und zu sich selber zurückfliehend:— als ein ewiges Sich-Fliehn und -Wiedersuchen vieler Götter, als das selige Sich-Widersprechen, Sich-Wiederhören, Sich-Wieder-Zugehören vieler Götter. (*Werke* II, 460)

These passages challenge the language and conceptualization of the will as an "entity," as a "partial determination," for the sake of a richer, dialectical understanding. The will to power as *Werden* is thus not the same "thing" as the (supposed) "metaphysical" substance/subject, "will"; and it is certainly not reducible to empirical or mechanistic "power." Thus, by linking the will to power to the concept of *Werden* and its peculiar status, we can understand the more profound philosophical reason why the will to power cannot be reduced to a theory of power (as entity or force, i.e., a kind of being).[37]

Third, Nietzsche attempts to explain how the insistence on "reducing" the will to power to one thing, to a form of being, comes about as the result of a psychological and moral disposition. We saw how metaphysics, in its reductive approach, undermines itself by falling into binarisms and aporias. But Nietzsche also argues that this position is a fusion of morality and epistemology. In particular, he sees the acceptance of the metaphysical binarisms of being (substance/subject) as motivated by a fear and inability to deal with change. He unites these responses under the term "will to truth": "Contempt and hate against anything that passes, changes, transforms:— where does the positive evaluation of stability come from? Evidently the will to truth is merely the longing for a world of *stability*" (*Nachlaß*, *Werke* III, 548; also 541). It is not so much that this position is "wrong" as that it gives its necessary projections a status as being and involves itself in aporias that it cannot accept on its own terms. It is connected with the need to believe in something firm—a need that itself arises from the will to power (*Die fröhliche Wissenschaft*, *Werke* II, 213; and *Nachlaß*, *Werke* III, 896). It is the need that motivates Christianity, Idealism, and positivism. What is lost in this "will to truth" is the "innocence of becoming," a certain *ethical* position that Nietzsche wants to regain.

Fourth, then, the ethics that Nietzsche sees linked to his philosophy of *Werden* or will to power must be based on the acceptance of the inevitability of change (whereby both the inevitability and the change receive the same emphasis). Thus, in the passage from *Zarathustra* on dance quoted above, Nietzsche also speaks of the point "where necessity and freedom are one" ("wo die Notwendigkeit die Freiheit selber war"; *Werke* II, 444). Or, as Zarathustra and Nietzsche say time and again, using an untranslatable word-play based on the literal meaning of necessity: the will is the "turning of my need—my necessity" ("Wende meiner Not—meine Notwendigkeit"; *Also sprach Zarathustra, Werke* II, 460; also earlier formulations in *Menschliches, Allzumenschliches, Werke* I, 509, 587, 877). He says in *Götzendämmerung* that it was from the ancients that he learned this "eternal pleasure of becoming *what one is*" ("ewige Lust des Werdens *selbst zu sein*"; *Werke* II, 1030–32). It is a position that is possible only if one accepts the totality of *Werden:* "There is nothing outside the whole" ("Es gibt nichts außer dem Ganzen"; *Götzendämmerung, Werke* II, 978). Moreover, as we saw in the passage from *Zarathustra* on the dance, given this totality, there follows an acceptance of the present as the necessity of *Werden* at that moment. "Becoming is equally valuable . . ." ("Das Werden ist wertgleich . . ."; *Nachlaß, Werke* III, 685) in the sense that it is always present.[38]

But if we recall that *Werden* is identified with will to power, and will to power is not a thing but "will-punctuations that constantly increase or decrease their power" (*Nachlaß, Werke* III, 685), then there is a new way of evaluating the movement according to the process of *Streben* or development without appealing to an outside measure. In this sense Nietzsche could be said to have a kind of aesthetic solution, not in terms of an abandonment of ethics and epistemology and ontology for the sake of aesthetization but a conception of value, truth, and "world" in terms of locally measured increases or decreases of will (i.e., amounts of and toleration for change and differentiation). The slogan, "The will is creative" ("Der Wille ist ein Schaffender"; *Zarathustra, Werke* II, 394) is not reductive once we link it to his philosophy of *Werden.* The "will to power," with its innovative potential, thus offers a rich response to the reductivist theories of Western thought even as it grows out of them.

Foucault, Habermas, and a Nonreductive Will

Because the "will" is not a concept that enjoys great popularity in the late twentieth century, the terms of Nietzsche's philosophy are in good measure foreign to both Habermas and Foucault. As we saw, even the Nietzschean

Foucault often replaces the "will to power" with mere "power." But Habermas is correct in arguing that that substitution is disastrous for Foucault's own position. What Habermas does not do, however, is explicitly *re*introduce the will to help "save" Foucault's position and relate it to his own. My point is that some one hundred years before Habermas, Nietzsche used the concept of the will to power to work through (and beyond) the aporias of mechanism, subjectivism, "metaphysics," nihilism, and aestheticism, and that Foucault, precisely to the extent that he is Nietzschean in the sense of further conceptualizing the *will* to power, approaches Habermas's call for antireductivism. At least I hope to have shown that the master concepts in Nietzsche and Foucault do fulfill the antipositivist function that Habermas finds crucial for any tenable (and fundamentally "anti-nihilist/fascist") philosophical position. But just showing that Nietzsche's and Foucault's concepts of the will to power do the same work that Habermas calls for is not yet enough; I must now briefly consider the relationship between the will to power and the concept that Habermas uses to escape the aporias of traditional Western philosophy, communicative reason/action.

First, we need to consider how the call for a nonreductive understanding of reason in *Knowledge and Human Interest* could be identified with will to power in its broader, nonreduced sense. What I propose is a *rapprochement* between Habermas on the one hand and Nietzsche/Foucault on the other by linking Habermas's crucial discussion of the "interests of reason" (*Vernunftinteresse*) to implicit or explicit concepts of the will in the other two thinkers. Indeed, one might wonder whether Habermas was perhaps not offering a reductive reading of Nietzsche precisely in order to differentiate his *Vernunftinteresse* from the will to power or *Wille zur Erkenntnis* (as opposed to the "will to truth" and its inevitable collapse into positivism)? How can we reestablish the connections broken by the polemics?

At the center of *Erkenntnis und Interesse,* Habermas turns to the concept of *Vernunftinteresse* in Kant and Fichte to recover the tool he needs to fight against the twin dangers of positivism (namely a reason emptied of its connection to life because of its reduction to methodology and irrational vitalism). Habermas analyzes the central passages in Kant's *Grundlegung zur Metaphysik der Sitten* that have the task of explaining the freedom of the will. Kant's problem is "paradoxical" (*EI,* 246), as we have seen at greater length in the last chapter, because the will is located between the spheres of the pure law (the "ought" of the formalized imperative) and empirical motivations (desires, needs, inclinations). To be strictly moral, the will must be motivated solely by the dictates of the law, but the will must also have an effect on the real world and the side of the will that is tied to nature must also experience some kind of pleasure (*Wohlgefallen*). Kant bridges this unique status of the will with a "limit-concept" ("Grenzbegriff"; *EI,* 249) at the margins of his own practical philosophy, namely the concept of the "interest of reason." In Habermas's terms, "inhabiting reason is a drive toward the realization of reason" ("der Vernunft wohnt ein Trieb zur Realisierung der Vernunft inne"; *EI*, 248). This interest has the same status according to Habermas that we attributed to the will as cause of desire in Lacan because it cannot be a mere "object" (or goal) of desire. In Habermas's terms: "The (pathological) interest of the senses in what is pleasurable or useful *originates* in need; the (practical, ethical) interest of reason in what is good *awakens* a need" ("Das [pathologische] Interesse der Sinne am Angenehmen oder Nützlichen *entspringt* dem Bedürfnis; das [praktische] Interesse der Vernunft am Guten *weckt* ein Bedürfnis"; *EI*, 245). In other words, we see Habermas here taking recourse to a concept that is closely identified with the will as a kind of motivating "wanting" and that fulfills the same function of synthesizing opposites dialectically. For example, Habermas writes:

> The cause of freedom is not empirical, but it is also not purely intelligible; we can characterize it as a fact, but not comprehend it. The term "pure" interest alludes to a basis of reason which simply guarantees the conditions of the realization of reason. That basis cannot be traced back to principles of reason since they, as facts of a higher order, have it as their ground.

> Die Ursache der Freiheit ist nicht empirisch, aber sie ist auch nicht nur intelligibel; wir können sie als ein Faktum bezeichnen, aber nicht begreifen. Der Titel des reinen Interesses verweist uns auf eine Basis der Vernunft, welche allein die Bedingungen der Realisierung von Vernunft garantiert, aber nicht ihrerseits auf Prinzipien der Vernunft zurückgeführt werden kann, vielmehr diesen, als ein Faktum höherer Ordnung, zum Grunde liegt. (*EI*, 249)

In the concept of (*Vernunft*) *Interesse* Habermas has a tool to do the work that the will was able to accomplish for Nietzsche. Neither the will to power nor the notion of an *Interesse* inhering in *Erkenntnis* does away with the significance of reason, or of knowledge for "life." Nietzsche is *not* against "knowledge," just against any conception of knowledge that denies the "will's pleasure in creating and becoming" ("Willens Zeuge- und Werde-Lust"; *Zarathustra, Werke* II, 345) that motivates it—in the way that Habermas struggles against any form of *Erkenntnis* that would deny its own inhering will as *Interesse*. It is true that a mechanistic reduction of knowledge and interest to the "technologies of power" would undermine Habermas's intention. But precisely the will to power avoids this move by finding a place for both reason and the interest in reason.[39]

Conversely, just as a nonreductive reading brings Nietzsche closer to Habermas, a nonreductive Habermas comes closer to Nietzsche. In the lectures on the philosophical discourse of modernity, Habermas refers to a choice that he wishes Hegel and Marx could have made, namely to explicate "ethical totality" ("sittliche Totalität") in terms of communicative reason, i.e., "according to the model of un-compelled *formation of a common will* by a communicative community under conditions of cooperation" ("nach dem Modell der ungezwungenen *Willensbildung* in einer under Kooperationszwängen stehenden Kommunikationsgemeinschaft"; *PDM*, 345; my emphasis). By placing "Willensbildung"—rather than reason—at the core of the "Kommunikationsgemeinschaft" Habermas opens the door to a broader conception of the will in his thought.[40] That is, either a broad theory of the will is necessary to supplement his concept of communicative reason or a theory of communication that takes the vicissitudes of the will's formation into account. In this way we see that although "power" in some sense is "the Other of reason" ("das Andere der Vernunft"; e.g., *PDM*, 358), the formation of will and the formative power of will, at the subjective and intersubjective levels (recall Foucault's concept of *agencement!*), are central to the project of communicative reason (and vice versa).[41] Unfortunately, Habermas does not develop either fully because he chooses *argumentation* as the powerful, yet limited, model of communication (with the famous "zwangloser Zwang des besseren Arguments," i.e., argumentative consensus, as the model for *Willensbildung*).

Because Habermas himself engages in a reduction of central concepts, the concept of communicative action in particular must and can be saved from *its* reduction to mere argumentative reason by associating it with will to power. What joins the two is the conception of language as including functions beyond the constative and of human action as including aspects beyond the rational. Habermas's appeal to language was, of course, motivated by the traditional reduction of the notion of knowledge to a reflexive model (both "pure self reflexion" and the belief in "true" language as "reflecting" reality). Thus he does recognize the need to introduce the pragmatic functions of language into the very heart of reason. But the will to power includes, as Habermas does not, the expressive as well as the performative—and the performative as creative (for a summary, see *PDM*, 360–79). (Recall Nietzsche's formulations: "der Wille ist ein Schaffender" and "der Wille zur Macht *interpretiert*"). In attempting to *reduce* Nietzsche to aestheticism, Habermas in fact blinds himself to the exclusion of the expressive/creative from his theory. As Nietzsche shows, *Willensbildung,* as opposed perhaps to traditional notions of truth, does not result exclusively from communicative reason. Therefore, communicative reason as argument (the will to truth) is, and can be, only *one* of the grounds for any ontology, ethics, or epistemology.

Given my "generous" readings of Nietzsche and Foucault, we can close the circle by returning to the debate or split in contemporary theory. Certainly Foucault and Habermas yield different research strategies—the critical focus of discourse analysis versus the pragmatics of communicative consensus. But my point is that there is a more fundamental connection between the two theories. Where Habermas and Foucault do overlap, then, is in their mutual concern with "un-compelled *formation of a common will by* a communicative community under restrictive conditions of cooperation" ("ungezwungenge Willensbildung in einer unter Kooperationszwängen stehenden Kommunikationsgemeinschaft"; *PDM,* 345) and what they both need, and to varying degrees get from Nietzsche, is a nonreductive theory of the will (to power) that accounts for the tensions between force and freedom, coercion and cooperation, power and reason.

4

The Will to Interpretation: Gadamer, Derrida, Heidegger's Nietzsche

Der Wille zur Macht *interpretiert.*

NIETZSCHE, *Nachlaß, Werke* III, 489.

In April 1981, Hans-Georg Gadamer and Jacques Derrida met at the Goethe Institute in Paris for what was intended to be the first serious, explicit, and extended encounter between representatives of the modes of thought associated with the two sides of the Rhine. The exchange has been documented over the past fifteen years and, given the apparent collapse of the actual dialogue between the two men, the responses have often been more fruitful than the encounter itself.[1] The goal of this chapter is neither to review the "improbable debate" (Derrida; *DD*, 52) for its own sake nor to play out the positions of hermeneutics and deconstruction with or against each other in the abstract. Rather, I shall use the way the exchange both explicitly and, even more so, implicitly, revolves around conflicting views of the will to argue for the significance (usefulness) of that concept in the theory and practice of interpretation. By using this encounter to develop a dialectical conception of the will of interpretation—in the double sense of the will *to* interpret and the will as the *object of interpretation*—we shall better understand the stakes and difficulty of the debate between hermeneutics and deconstruction. We shall see that the human agency involved in interpretation unfolds in a process of unification and fragmentation, individuality and structure, activity and passivity, repetition and innovation. Hence, the "debate" between deconstruction and hermeneutics over the status of human understanding becomes comprehensible and fruitful when seen as itself playing out the dialectics of willing.

At the core of the exchange in and after Paris are opposing approaches to the will to interpret. Gadamer, in his lecture, summarized some of the basic principles of hermeneutics as he developed it after Heidegger. Derrida, in the most "notorious" part of his three-question response, picked up on a comment that Gadamer made almost in passing: the idea that for understanding in a conversation to take place there must be "good will" on the part of the speakers. Derrida associated this concept of "good will" with Kant's definition in the *Grundlegung zu einer Metaphysik der Moral (Foundation of a Metaphysics of Morals)* and implied that such categorical "good will" contains, as Nietzsche has shown, an element of "will to power."[2] Gadamer rejected this association with Nietzsche for the sake of a different one, namely Plato's concept of "eumeneis elenxoi," the maieutic "good will" to make the other's argument as strong as possible. In his written response, Derrida then avoided this line of questioning completely, subjecting instead Heidegger's interpretation of Nietzsche to a deconstructive reading.[3] The thrust of Derrida's reading is that Heidegger's insistence on the "unity" of Nietzsche's thought may, in some sense, have been motivated by the "good will" to save Nietzsche from problematically ambiguous interpretations, but in so doing Heidegger also reduces Nietzsche's profoundly antimetaphysical, disseminating thought and style—his fragmenting and fragmented will—to a uniform metaphysics of subjectivity. That Heidegger charges Nietzsche with being the "last metaphysical thinker" becomes, for Derrida, in fact a displacement of Heidegger's own unifying will to "logocentrism." The connection to Gadamer is implicit but clear, since Derrida likewise would play Nietzsche's antimetaphysical willfulness against Gadamer's embeddedness in "a particular epoch, namely, that of a metaphysics of the will" (*DD,* 53).

Although all these positions will have to be unfolded in greater detail below, it is important to see that the issues at the center of this discussion can be framed in terms of conflicting conceptions of the will that have become an integral part of that concept's historical effects (its *Wirkungsgeschichte*). The improbability, or in speech-act terminology, the "infelicity," of the debate, arises from the way contradictory definitions, which are knotted together dialectically in the will of interpretation, were never explicitly connected in the dialogue; therefore, partners could only contradict each other instead of engaging in a dialectical exchange. The particular contradictions that are subsumed under the concept of the will—in its role in interpretation—are: (1) the will as an individual vs. the will as a supraindividual (transcendental and intersubjective) agency; (2) the will as a unifying force vs. the will as that which always supersedes itself and is thus internally split; (3) the will as that which thrusts the self onto the world of objects vs. the will as that which, in an act of unique self-reflexivity, can "cancel itself" (*sich selbst aufheben*) in order to "let things be"; and finally, (4) the will as the object of our interpretation (in the sense of the *vouloir dire* of an utterance or speaker to be understood) vs. the will as that which makes fixed meaning impossible (in the sense that the "want" of "wanting to say" implies as well a primordial *lack* of meaning at the "origin" of an utterance). One can recognize in these historically embedded, conflicting features of the will other layers of conflict played out in theory: the conflicting positions embraced under the terms hermeneutics and deconstruction and the conflicting possibilities of any reading of Heidegger reading Nietzsche. By working through these specific philosophical and theoretical positions in terms of the more general way the central concept of the will is inherently (historically) defined as a dialectic of contradictions, we can establish, I think, a new, dialectical relationship between the positions that circumscribe the art of interpretation.

A useful way to get to this dialectical relationship would be to consider the tensions between the concepts of the spirit and the letter. This opposition runs through the history of hermeneutics and its deconstruction and can, I believe, be fruitfully mediated by the concept of the will. Culminating in the late eighteenth century, arguments against the centuries-old methods of rhetorical and philological interpretation, pedagogy, and production rejected the traditional emphasis on *verba* (letter), turning instead to the illumination of the *res* (spirit) "behind" and informing texts. Gadamer, for all his attention to the medium of language, fully pursues this form of hermeneutics.[4] But against this association of hermeneutics with the "spirit" of a text, recent developments have allowed a renewed attention to the "letter."[5] My point in this chapter is that the will could function as a hermeneutic category that mediates between the positions of this "debate" since the contradictory determinations of the will account for those of both the unifying spirit and the disseminating letter in interpretation.

Gadamer's Good Will

It seems both odd and obvious that the touchstone of the interaction between Gadamer and Derrida should have been the mention of the (good) will. It is odd because Gadamer does not stress this concept in general in his writings. Yet it is obvious because, knowing Derrida, one would expect him to select an odd reference to use as the opening in another's argument into which he can insert his deconstructive machinery. Let us then turn to the exchange briefly in order to see where the question of the will leads us first in Gadamer's hermeneutics and second in the matter of understanding generally. The goal is not to argue whether Derrida was justified or not in seizing upon the will in Gadamer's talk, i.e., whether he understood or intentionally misunderstood

Gadamer's message.[6] Rather, having pointed out the place of the (good) will in Gadamer, Derrida enables us to initiate a line of questioning that will reflect back on the twin projects of hermeneutics and deconstruction. In a way that perhaps neither Gadamer nor Derrida have thought through, a connection has been established between their projects and the tradition that plays out a dialectic of the will. We shall work through the place of the will in their projects in order to rethink them in light of the dialectic residing there.

Working outward in concentric circles of context, I begin with the passage in the Paris lecture, "Text and Interpretation," where Gadamer raises the issue of the "good will." Referring to the "basic condition" ("Grundbedingung") that holds for both written and oral conversations Gadamer says: "Both have the good will to understand each other. Thus, wherever understanding is sought, there exists good will" ("Beide[7] haben den guten Willen, einander zu verstehen. So liegt überall, wo Verständigung gesucht wird, guter Wille vor"; *TI,* 38; see *DD,* 33f). The formulation, as Derrida correctly points out, treats the good will as an axiom or transcendental condition (in the Kantian sense, he implies, of a "condition of the possibility" of understanding). It is powerful in its counterfactual status: Where it does not exist, there can be no understanding, therefore it is a necessary precondition.

The immediate context of Gadamer's statement, which is clearly made in passing despite its fundamental character, deals with the issue that would separate hermeneutics from deconstruction, namely the differences involved in oral and written communication. Gadamer's basic assumption is that all understanding is modeled on the situation of the oral conversation. In this case, understanding happens or unfolds ("geschieht" or "sich ereignet") through an ongoing process in which each partner is thrust both upon the other and into the intersubjective medium of the common language in order to express him- or herself. In contrast, the concept of the "text," according to Gadamer in these passages, results in an interesting way from a *breakdown* of understanding. It is that which is appealed to in order to secure a common basis for understanding, or an identity of meaning, when some kind of doubt or confusion arises. As opposed to a purely oral conversation, there is something like an appeal to the "text" whenever we have to go back and repeat/reformulate what we have said because the other did not comprehend our meaning. The more serious the breakdown in understanding, the more we must (or wish to) turn to some "transcript" of the problematic statements. Similarly, one could say that philology and the art of textual interpretation arise when we can no longer "forget" the medium (as, he says, we do when we simulate an oral exchange in reading a letter). Thus Gadamer says

> Only when it [i.e., the forgetting of the linguistic medium] is disturbed, i.e. where understanding fails, do we inquire into the verbatim formulation of

the text, and only then can the reconstruction of the text become a task in its own right.

> Nur wenn dieselbe [i.e., Sprachvergessenheit] gestört ist, d.h. wo das Verständnis nicht gelingen will, wird nach dem Wortlaut des Textes gefragt und kann die Erstellung des Textes zu einer eigenen Aufgabe werden. (*TI*, 37; modified from *DD*, 32)

His argument culminates in the extraordinary formulation of a thesis: "They [texts] are actually only there when there is re-course to them" ("Sie [Texte] sind immer erst im Zurückkommen auf sie eigentlich da"; *TI*, 46; my translation; see *DD*, 41f).[8]

One of the immediate implications of this argument, which Gadamer addresses only partially, arises when one asks the question of what it would mean to "appeal" to the (understanding of a) text in order to guarantee the continuity of (oral) understanding that was broken. That is, if misunderstanding occurs or if there is a dispute over understandings, then the partners appeal to some text as a "message" (*Kunde*) whose "original authenticity" ("ursprüngliche Authentizität") they attempt to recover (*DD*, 35; *TI*, 39). But the problem arises when the appeal to the "text" opens up not only a potential ground of common understanding but also a potential object for further misunderstanding. The regression to the "original authenticity" or "identity of meaning" ("sinnhaft Identisches") of the original message (*Urkunde*) is as potentially infinite as it is necessary. It is certainly true that two partners could, after a point of disagreement, look to the "text" and find in their common search a point of agreement (which may not be the same as either starting position). In that way they would be led back through the text (a highlighting of the medium) to a renewed "forgetfulness" of the medium so that they could "so to speak return without a break into the conversation" ("sozusagen bruchlos in die . . . Gesprächssituation ein[gehen]"; *TI*, 38; *DD*, 33). But it might not function so smoothly, the appeal to a common text might itself yield two conflicting interpretations that would force the partners back again to a now different common text, and so on. This continued source of disagreement is, after all, what keeps philologists and many others in business. Given this problem, Gadamer clearly needs something outside of the process of understanding that functions in principle to prevent this infinite regress.

That which accompanies all understanding and guarantees the possibility of returning from textuality to the *Sprachvergessenheit* of oral dialogue is the "good will." The *fact* that understanding occurs, that is, that some basis for the identity of meaning is found (through or despite misunderstandings) means that the partners must be willing to agree, i.e., to "reach an understanding," on that basis. (See below on the double meaning of *Verständigung* that Gadamer emphasizes in *Wahrheit und Methode.*) Since Gadamer does not want to hypostatize such an identity "in" the text, it must reside rather in the will of the partners to come together "over" the text.

Given this crucial position occupied by the "good will," at least the first part of Derrida's responding question is very much to the point. He asks, for example, albeit in the form of a peculiar (rhetorical? ironic?) question, about the counterfactual nature of the precondition of the good will: "How could one avoid the temptation of underwriting the powerful self-evidence of this axiom?" (*TI,* 56; *DD,* 52).[9] Derrida clearly recognizes the strength of the hermeneutic position. And although his move to connect Gadamer's "good will" to Kant's from the *Grundlegung zur Metaphysik der Sitten* certainly twists the superficial role of the concept in Gadamer's argument,[10] Derrida does thereby get at the heart of its deeper function, since in both Gadamer and Kant the good will has a transcendental status. The four questions that he subsumes under his "first" question go in a number of different directions:

> Doesn't this unconditional axiom nevertheless presuppose that the *will* is the form of that unconditionality, its last resort, its ultimate determination? What is the will if, as Kant says, nothing is absolutely good except the good will? Would not this determination belong to what Heidegger has rightly called "the determination of the being of beings as will, or willing subjectivity?" Does not this way of speaking, in its very necessity, belong to a particular epoch, namely that of a metaphysics of the will? (*DD,* 52f)[11]

Since Gadamer felt that these questions indicated how deeply he was being misunderstood—evidenced by the way he essentially deflects from them[12]—let me reformulate them such that it becomes essential (and I hope fruitful) for hermeneutics to respond: What form would this "will" have to have in order to fulfill the criteria of a transcendental condition for intersubjective understanding *without* falling back into the epoch of "willing subjectivity" long since deconstructed (or "destroyed" by Heideggerian *Destruktion*)? Let us look at some of the answers that Gadamer could have provided, and perhaps indirectly did provide, in various works, predominantly in his Paris talk and in a series of essays he wrote throughout the 1970s and 1980s (after *Wahrheit und Methode*). In this way we can try to bring out a nonsubjectivist, nonmetaphysical, dialecticized will for hermeneutics.

First, let us consider what might initially come to mind when thinking of "good will," namely an "attitude" that the partners take up as they engage in a conversation. Gadamer describes this, without using the term will, in a brief essay called "The Inability to Carry on a Conversation" ("Die Unfähigkeit zum Gespräch"; 1972). He describes the conditions for a successful conversation and the reasons for its failure. A conversation succeeds thanks to:

patience, sensitivity, sympathy, tolerance, and absolute confidence in reason, which is part of us all. "The inability to carry on a conversation" appears to me to be a criticism that one raises against someone who does not *want* to follow one's thought, rather than a lack that the other really has. (my emphasis)

durch Geduld, durch Feinfühligkeit, durch Sympathie und Toleranz und durch das unbedingte Vertrauen auf die Vernunft, die uns aller Teil ist. "Unfähigkeit zum Gespräch" scheint mir mehr der Vorwurf, den einer gegen den erhebt, der seinen Gedanken nicht folgen *will,* als der Mangel, den der andere wirklich besitzt.[13]

The success of understanding rests then on the willingness (not so much the ability) of the partner, which expresses itself in the qualities that begin this citation. What is important for me here is neither the deeply moving and genuine *Humanität* that Gadamer wishes to express (and which may or may not be debunked by a Derridean/Nietzschean critique of the will to power) nor the appeal to a common "reason" (which could, à la Rorty, be given a pragmatic, nonlogocentric interpretation), but, rather, the double valence of such an attitude as both subjective and nonsubjective. As an attitude, or *Einstellung,* it is something beyond the individual, a position that is open before the subject places him- or herself into it. It is a subject position that defines the subject who occupies it. But on the other hand, it is also a position that does not fully mark the subject. There is the option for the subject to "take up" this position or not.[14] The subject must "want" to. The "inability" therefore is related to the "wanting" of the subject in the sense of the lack of a decision to enter the conversation with an attitude of "good will"; it is a subjective lack of will, not an objective inadequacy. In Kantian terms, the good will is a transcendental condition of (ethical) subjectivity and for this reason is accessible to all who want it (or, who are wanting).

Second, if we consider the "identity" of the text to which partners appeal to overcome misunderstanding, we see that Gadamer does have to address the notion of the subjective origin of meaning since his hermeneutic principles are based on the concept of the good will. In particular, the meaning of a partner's speech (or text), if expressed with good will, would be located in the partner's *vouloir dire.* Gadamer summarizes what he means by the "task" of interpretation to understand the Kunde of the other:

The task of interpretation always poses itself when the meaning content of the printed word is disputable and it is a matter of attaining the correct understanding of what is being announced. However, this "thing that is being conveyed" is not what the speaker or writer originally said, but rather what he *would have wanted to say* to me if I had been his original interlocutor. (*DD,* 35)

Die Aufgabe der Interpretation stellt sich immer dann, wenn der Sinngehalt des Fixierten strittig ist und es gilt, das richtige Verständnis der 'Kunde' zu gewinnen. 'Kunde' aber ist nicht, was der Sprechende bzw. der Schreibende ursprünglich gesagt hat, sondern *was er hat sagen wollen,* wenn ich sein ursprünglicher Gesprächspartner gewesen wäre. (*TI,* 39; my emphasis)

To understand any speech act (he gives the example of the command) is to grasp it "according to its meaning/intention" (*sinngemäß; TI,* 39; or "according to its general sense"; *DD,* 35), and that is to get to the originary (good) will-to-meaning placed into the act. The identity of meaning is thus guaranteed, or at least assumed, on the basis of the (presumed) will of the speaker/writer. Indeed, this will forms the very ethos of hermeneutics. As Gadamer wrote in the short essay, "Early Romanticism, Hermeneutics, Deconstruction" (1987):[15] "The art of hermeneutics is not to nail someone down to what he or she actually said. Rather, it is the art of perceiving [taking up] what he or she actually *wanted to say*" ("Das ist nicht die Kunst der Hermeneutik, jemanden auf etwas festzunageln, was er gesagt hat. Sie ist die Kunst, das, was er hat eigentlich *sagen wollen,* aufzunehmen"; *AF,* 254; my emphasis). Here we see how we can begin to connect an interpretation by the spirit (*sinngemäß*) with a sense of will (*sagen wollen*). The latter needs to be investigated, i.e., it has to be determined what is involved in any (*Sagen*)*Wollen.*

Third, just as directly as Gadamer would locate the task of under-standing in the uncovering of a subjective will-to-meaning, he also rejects the reduction of meaning to individual *vouloir dire,* i.e., he rejects the one-to-one identification of words with their abstract or subjectively fixed meanings. In two paragraphs preceding the passage just cited on "the art of hermeneutics," Gadamer states:

> A conversation is defined precisely by the fact that the essence of understand-ing and agreeing consists not in some "vouloir dire," which the words are supposed to represent, but in what "is wanting to be said" beyond all the found and sought words.

> Gespräch definiert sich gerade dadurch, daß nicht im "vouloir dire," das das Wort sein soll, sondern in dem, was über alle gefundenen oder gesuchten Worte hinaus *gesagt sein will,* das Wesen des Verstehens und der Verständigung besteht. (*AF,* 254; my emphasis)

Since meaning is located only in the context of conversation (hence his rejection of semiotics as a starting point, since the theory of the sign would isolate the functioning of language from the context of speaking), it can never be reduced to either a nonsubjective (structural) meaning or the strictly subjective will of one of the partners.[16] What is important here is that Gadamer, since he is working with the "axiom" of good will as the ground of understanding, cannot *dislodge* meaning from a willing (as structuralists would in seeing the origin of meaning in a supersubjective *langue*) even as he does not want to *reduce* meaning to subjective intention. Thus he must formulate this "good will" as a paradoxically "wanting" nonsubject (grammatically passive: "was gesagt sein will"). Meaning arises from a wanting-to-mean that is beyond the immediate grasp of an individual speaker.

Finally, the very notion of a "good will" that provides the transcendental condition of dialogue and understanding has the peculiar quality of cancelling itself in the very exercise of itself—and vice versa, of exercising itself there where it cancels itself. We saw that Gadamer would associate the concept of the good will to interpretation with the movement of understanding in a Platonic dialogue. This will, he says, is neither individual nor a "metasubject" (as Manfred Frank would have it in his criticism of Gadamer);[17] rather, it is a simultaneity of willing and nonwilling, leading and being led. Gadamer writes in the essay, "Destruction and Deconstruction" (1985):[18]

> The Socratic dialogue in its Platonic form is certainly a very peculiar kind of conversation which is led by the one partner and which the other willingly or unwillingly [willy-nilly, *nolens-volens*] has to follow. But in this way it remains the model of all dialogical unfolding insofar as it is not the words but the spirit of the other that is refuted. (*DD*, 111)

> Der sokratische Dialog platonischer Gestaltung ist gewiß eine sehr besondere Art von Gespräch, das von dem einen geführt wird und dem der andere willig-unwillig zu folgen hat, aber insofern bleibt es doch das Vorbild allen Gesprächsvollzugs, daß in ihm nicht die Worte, sondern die Seele des anderen widerlegt wird. (*Hermeneutik II*, 370)

This statement, in echoing one of the most famous lines from *Wahrheit und Methode*—"To lead [carry on] a conversation means to follow the lead of the matter at hand" ("Ein Gespräch führen heißt, sich unter die Führung der Sache stellen, auf die die Gesprächs partner gerichtet sind"; *WM*, 373)— reveals that at the heart of Gadamer's main text on hermeneutics is an (implicit) conception of the will that is both individual and intersubjectively transcendental, both self-affirming and self-cancelling, active and passive, indeed willing and unwilling. We shall see below how this contradictory will is to be found in Heidegger, who, rather than exploiting its dialectical possibilities problematically turns instead to a nonwilling form of *Denken* and *Sein*.[19]

Although this dialectical and internally contradictory concept of the (good) will does not appear in *Wahrheit und Methode,* we now know what to look for there in terms of its traces. I refer to two key argumentative turns. We saw earlier, for example, that understanding occurs on the basis of a willingness of the partners in an interpretive context (conversation or reading a text) to agree on a common basis of their hermeneutic effort. In *Wahrheit und Methode* Gadamer emphasizes this early on (albeit without explicit reference to the will) in his analysis of the ambiguities in the German word *Verständigung* and related cognates.[20] In English as well, the phrase "to reach an understanding" contains the double sense of comprehension and agreement, whereby the latter aspect clearly implies a willingness on the part of the partners. That is, since no agreement can occur by definition without the willingness of the parties, and since Gadamer (via linguistic usage) connects agreement with understanding in general, all understanding presumes noncompulsive willingness ("good will").

The duality and ambivalence of this will becomes clear in Gadamer's discussion of the "prestructure" of understanding. Never using the noun, "will" (*Wille*), Gadamer nonetheless writes about the status or position that one must occupy if one *wants* to understand (a text).

> Whoever wants to understand (*Wer verstehen will*) ought not give oneself over in advance to the arbitrariness of one's own pre-conceptions, consistently and stubbornly paying no heed (*vorbeihören*) to the conception of the text—until it makes itself heard and refutes the presumed understanding. Whoever wants to understand a text is, rather, prepared to be told something by it. Therefore, a hermeneutically schooled consciousness must be receptive to the otherness of the text. Such receptivity presumes neither a "neutrality" on the issues nor a self-annihilation, but instead includes the differentiating appropriation of ones own preconceptions and prejudices. (*WM*, 253)

Such a hermeneutic will, or more precisely, such a state or attitude of "being willing" to understand, is by no means a vestige of a "metaphysics of subjectivity," if by that we mean an insistence on autonomy of the self.[21] On the contrary, the will here is necessarily marked by its "openness" (*Offenheit, WM*, 253) to the other person or text even as the givenness of the opening position of the interpreter enters actively into the process of understanding. Gadamer insists, therefore, that this process relies on both turning to larger forces that subsume the acts of human will *and* the inability to do without the will of the self and other, I and thou.[22]

To summarize Gadamer's position, then, we see that he postulates the (good) will as a transcendental precondition of understanding in order to guarantee the unity and identity, indeed the very possibility, of meaning. This will, however, despite its centrality for the project of a "universal" hermeneutics, remains largely implicit and only sketchily drawn. What begins to emerge as we expose its contours is the way it is involved in an complex dialectic—subjective and nonindividual, powerfully imposing and self-effacing, unifying and differentiating, empirical and transcendental. And yet, since Gadamer did not work out the dialectical ground of the will that understanding is based on (because of his dependence on Heidegger, who turned away from the dialectics of willing), one is left with what looks like an emphasis on one side of the process.[23] Gadamer makes a strong case for the appeal to the will as the necessary, i.e., counterfactually unavoidable, guarantor of communication and interpretation. Without it there is no identity, and the fact is we use this unifying will—whether good or not, as we shall see—in any exchange. And yet, Derrida's intervention, his highlighting of a submerged conception of the will, reveals the one-sidedness of Gadamer's grounding. I would thus agree with the charge that Gadamer falls into a "Metaphysik des Willens" if by "metaphysics" one means a model whose dialectic has not been worked out. Of course, on these terms, as I hope now to show, Derrida falls prey to the same charge since he, coming from the opposite direction, also fails to work out a dialectical model of the will to interpretation. Let us see how Derrida can catch Gadamer, with his overemphasis of unity (*sinngemäße Identität*) in an aporia, but because he, too, has an unreflected and too limited understanding of the will, Derrida gets caught in aporetic positions as well. Not by chance Derrida's critique is played out in terms of Nietzsche and Heidegger's *Nietzsche,* since what is at stake for Derrida is the will of interpretation in its two forms: the process (which he sees Heidegger playing out) and Nietzsche's conception of it (which was the object of Heidegger's interpretation). That is, we shall have to pursue how the will plays a role both as a submerged concept in Derrida's (critique of the) practice of interpretation and as a more explicit object of his reading of Heidegger and Nietzsche.

Interpreting Derrida's Split Will

Derrida's position in the "improbable debate" with Gadamer is, as many critics have pointed out, an "impossible" one. The assumptions of hermeneutics concerning the universality of understanding force him into either understanding Gadamer (in which case Gadamer has him where he wants him) or misunderstanding Gadamer (in which case Derrida seems to make a point against hermeneutics but at the cost of all good faith—also Gadamer's point). That is, in entering into a genuine dialogue, Derrida submits to the "axioms" of conversational behavior proposed by Gadamer; and in refusing to enter, he employs the strategy of Hegel's figure of "unhappy consciousness," who in order to contradict the other contradicts himself.[24] Derrida has been generally criticized or credited with taking the second option. Both the comment about the Kantian good will and the written response on Heidegger and naming can certainly be considered so askew to the debate that he must have been making a point out of his act of misunderstanding.[25] How does his position look in terms of the concept of the will?

Let us see how both Derrida and Gadamer are trapped in the dialectic between "subjective" and "objective" versions of the will. Assume the worst case: Derrida did not understand Gadamer. One possibility is that he did this "unwillingly," or "against his will," that is he *wanted* to understand Gadamer but could not for linguistic, philosophical, educational, or ideological reasons. Clearly in this case Gadamer's position is unaffected, since the principle of the good will to understanding still holds, even under conditions where good will "is not enough" to actually understand the other.[26] Misunderstanding would then be explained as something like a gap between an individual's will and its execution. (A similar argument appears in Kant, where one's inability to be good in actuality does not affect the moral principle or duty to be good. Good will in its pure determination is unaffected by its empirical limitations.) But the other possibility is that Derrida showed "ill will," i.e., he did *not want* to understand Gadamer. And yet, in this case Derrida would be caught in an awkward position of having already understood Gadamer as saying x so that he can be sure to willingly misunderstand him in claiming that he said y. Moreover, he must assume his audience understood Gadamer as saying x so that they would appreciate the import of his willful misunderstanding when he claims that Gadamer said y. Such an approach by Derrida would assume that Gadamer's actual words support both readings, x and y, and the question how *they* want to be understood is open.[27] It would fail to dislodge Gadamer's fundamental assumption, however, since it reveals that beneath Derrida's willful misunderstanding is both his and his audience's understanding (even if that understanding differs from Gadamer's intention and occurs, ironically, "unwillingly").

The point here is not to "catch" Derrida in a contradiction but to reveal a dynamic inherent in the way we use the will in matters of understanding. Derrida's position demonstrates, I would say, a "universality" of the will to understand, but one that does not cover either Derrida's or Gadamer's concept of interpretation (or more precisely, it reflects aspects of both). We see that Gadamer's notion of "good will" may indeed be too subjectivist, since it always holds when the partner adopts that attitude, even if the actual communication fails for other reasons (as in the first scenario sketched above). But what Derrida nonetheless shows, even in the case of responding with "bad will," is that a nonsubjective positionality of the will to understand is in fact unavoidable, since the subjective intention to misunderstand always already presumes a condition of understanding. (I must have understood you, unwillingly perhaps, if I am then to willfully misunderstand you.) Moreover, Derrida can unmask the subjectivist implications lurking in Gadamer's notion of "good will" only by himself *willfully* separating out what he thinks Gadamer *wants to say* from his polyvalent text in order to show that *it* can (want to) say something else.[28] We see, in other words, a dialectic unfolding in their exchange that follows the same logic as those we saw in chapter 1, only here played out around the specific "will to understand." What I now want to show is how these competing and contradictory strategies of interpretation, strategies that at different times presume and reject the subjectivist and transcendental status of the will to understand, traverse a number of Derrida's essays on the will and understanding.

The three texts by Derrida that I shall focus on are *Of Spirit: Heidegger and the Question,* "Interpreting Signatures," and "Otobiographies."[29] The connections between these texts, on the one hand, and the issues raised by Gadamer, on the other, arise via the concept of the will in four ways: (1) "Interpreting Signatures," often considered a nonresponse to Gadamer's Paris talk, in fact addresses the central issue. Since Gadamer proposes the (good) will as a unifying force of interpretation, Derrida takes an example of one such unifying interpretation (providing the "identity of meaning" necessary for understanding), Heidegger's *Nietzsche,* in order to question the effect and effectiveness of a totalizing will to understand. Derrida strives to show how the unifying will to interpretation represses (always unsuccessfully) a textual force of splitting. Unfortunately, since in this essay Derrida does not explore the will at all, he has missed an opportunity to account for the simultaneity of unity and splitting in an adequate way. (2) As we saw in the peculiar formulation (in German) of Derrida's rhetorical question to Gadamer, it is apparently impossible *not* to "underwrite" (*unterschreiben*) the transcendental axiom of hermeneutics, the good will. The formulation points out, however, that the transcendentality of the axiom guarantees the autonomy of the interpreting subject (the way Kant's good will or law guarantees the autonomy of the ethical subject), but *only* if that autonomy is interrupted (and in some ways *undermined*) by the subject's "underwriting," i.e., its naming signature. "Otobiographies" deals precisely with the introduction of the heteronomous "name"/sign into the very act of establishing autonomous unity. The will to understand, in other words, is dependent on representations that are needed to "underwrite" or "sign" it. (3) In all these essays, Nietzsche, directly or indirectly, is the object—and not by chance because precisely his multivalent concept of the will (as unifying and splitting, as subjective and suprasubjective) is being refracted through Heidegger to incomplete and competing conceptualizations in Gadamer and Derrida. (4) And finally, the tensions these essays raise play out a confrontation between the spirit and the letter (whereby hermeneutics is identified with the former, and deconstruction with the latter), a confrontation that Derrida brings to bear on Heidegger. Thus, Derrida seems to be summing up his reflections on Heidegger, and making them explicit, when he deals with the power, danger, and limitation of the unifying *Geist* vis-à-vis the ghost of writing. And yet, my point is that this confrontational approach, as appropriate as it may be, remains ultimately unsatisfactory since the deconstruction of spirit by the material body of the letter leaves the dialectic of the will unaddressed; indeed, that deconstruction points to the even more powerful position of the dialectic of the will to the extent that it addresses many of the problems raised by the deconstruction (namely the will occupies precisely the dual position of fragmenting and unifying force, self-contained yet self-overcoming, which neither the spirit nor letter can account for).

Derrida's written response, or contribution, to the encounter with Gadamer seems at first to be even more beside the point than were his oral questions. Rather than address directly any of the points in Gadamer's lecture, Derrida published a reading of Heidegger's interpretation of Nietzsche, "Interpreting Signatures." Although we may never know whether this was intended as a cynical avoidance of debate or as a clever conceptual turn, my hermeneutic principle will be to pursue the latter possibility since it allows us to raise fundamental issues. Indeed, Derrida's essay can be read as a response, even if an indirect one, to a central argument of hermeneutics. Gadamer proposes, namely, the interpretive conversation as the model of the interaction between interpreter and text. Such a conversation, in presuming "good will," presumes as well a *Sinneseinheit,* an identity/unity of meaning, constituting the text and forming the goal of the interpretive effort. In his reading of Heidegger, Derrida addresses first and foremost this assumption of unity.[30] In so doing he is addressing one of the fundamental features ascribed to the (good) will: its unifying force.

Heidegger's argument, as Derrida highlights it, focuses precisely on the issue of the unity of Nietzsche's thought, a unity that is the same as the history of metaphysics (or *Seinsgeschichte*) in the West. Thus there is a further unity implied between the individual's and the *seinsgeschichtliche* unfolding of thought. If this unity can be shown to be split, or based on the repression of a more primary split, then Derrida will have at least placed one (if not *the*) basic hermeneutic assumption into doubt. My point will be that Derrida does succeed in radically challenging this supposed unity, but that both Derrida and Heidegger misconceive the nature of that unity/split, thereby missing an opportunity to define the inherent interrelatedness of unity and disunity in the movement of the will. That is, at least one strand of Heidegger's philosophy (as we shall see in greater detail below) sees the unity constituted in thought and Being, while Derrida sees the seeds of disunity in the disseminating power of the "name" (sign). And yet the relation that obtains between Spirit and Letter is much less one of unity (Heidegger, hermeneutics) versus deconstruction (Derrida) than the necessity of the interpreting will *both* to project unity *and* to split itself. By pointing out the kinds of aporias Heidegger and Derrida get involved in, we can see that the dialectical point has been missed.

Derrida opens up a dualistic reading from the beginning. He summarizes Heidegger's position and the point of his own critique early on (I quote at length since it gives away his strategy):

> [According to Heidegger] . . . there is a unity in Nietzschean thought even if it is not that of a system in the classical sense. This unity is also its uniqueness, its singularity. A thesis explicitly advanced by Heidegger is that every great thinker has only one thought. This uniqueness was neither constituted nor threatened, neither gathered together or brought about, through a name or proper name—nor by the life of Nietzsche, either normal or insane. This unique unity is something it draws from the unity of Western metaphysics which is gathered together there at its crest, which one could also compare to the simple unity of a line created by a fold. The result of all this is that biography, autobiography, the scene or the powers of the proper name, of proper names of signatures, and so on, are again accorded minority status, are again given the inessential place they have always occupied in the history of metaphysics. This points to the necessity and place of a questioning which I can only sketch here. (*DD*, 59)

The oppositions are clear: thought vs. life, idea vs. sign(nature), history of metaphysics vs. forces of the (proper)name, essence vs. the unessential, etc. Derrida's strategy is well-known enough. If he can show any of the secondary features to be involved in the constitution of the former, even as they are repressed, then he will have "deconstructed" the primacy of unity.

And indeed he can easily show how Heidegger falls into an aporia in trying to insist on unity. Heidegger assigns to Nietzsche the status of the "last thinker of metaphysics." This status first of all grants unity to all of Nietzsche's thought, according to Heidegger. It also enables Heidegger to position himself as the (first) one to go beyond Nietzsche by overcoming metaphysics. And yet Heidegger can position Nietzsche in this way only by himself making a "classical gesture" of metaphysics, namely the separation of the oppositions listed above: "This classical gesture also reappears in his dissociating the matter of life or of proper name from the matter of thought" (*DD*, 62). The *name* "Nietzsche" is clearly important for Heidegger, but only as a marker after the fact of a more basic and self-defining unity of thought. Heidegger's unity is thus metaphysical since it is based on an *exclusion* of that which would disrupt it; i.e., it is a unity only in a realm beyond the sphere where unity is disrupted. As Derrida puts it, Heidegger's unity is based on the united forces of repression: "Now what happens when a proper name is put between quotation marks? Heidegger never asks himself. Still, his whole undertaking, although entitled 'Nietzsche,' has perhaps put all its powers together in such a way as to nullify the urgency and necessity of this question" (*DD*, 60). A unity based on the repression of the active force of difference self-deconstructs; but further (as I shall show) we can also move beyond this aporetic impasse by means of a higher level of dialectical conceptualization in the will.

Derrida can be likewise shown to fall into aporias on the flip side of this argument. Does not Derrida have to presume the unity of Heidegger's thought in order to deconstruct it? Consider the opening justification of his focus on a couple of passages from Heidegger's massive study. This risky choice is legitimate, Derrida says, "[i]n view of the fact that the same interpretation is regularly at work throughout. . . . In each instance, a single system of reading is powerfully concentrated and gathered together" (*DD*, 58). Despite the attempt to replace organistic metaphors with mechanistic ones, Derrida must still argue for a unity in Heidegger's reading. He must presume to know the desire (and this will be important) for a unity in Heidegger's text. Derrida time and again sets up Heidegger's will to interpret Nietzsche, even if he then demonstrates that the object of that unified reading (Nietzsche) escapes the unifying force imposed on it. Derrida, in other words, himself presumes that there is a uniform *vouloir dire* in Heidegger's *Nietzsche* to which he must have access en route to his deconstruction.

We get closer to the core of the issue if we consider that for Derrida (and Heidegger, and indeed any reader) any interpretation addresses the question: "Who or what is some person, P?" For Heidegger, this question, asked of a thinker, involves a search not for an empirical person but for the "one thought" ("*einen* Gedanken") that unifies his (not her)[31] writing, a thought that has one particular location in the history of metaphysics. In so doing, Heidegger must exclude all that is nonunifying—the life, the signs, the particularities of the individual. The unifying Thought (or spirit) locates the thinker for Heidegger unequivocally in the history of Being, so the interpreter's (Heidegger's) goal is to disregard any aspect (the letter) that would distract him from getting at the core thought. Appropriate for a study of Nietzsche, Heidegger calls this focus of his interpretation getting to the "innermost will" ("innersten Willen"; *DD*, 65) of the thinker (since, after all, the "one thought" in Nietzsche seems to be the will to power). But we see how problematic this approach is by looking at how Derrida gets Heidegger and himself caught in aporias. Derrida rightly shows that the "thought" that makes up an oeuvre is not unified. But in turning to the "name" as the primary force, the peculiar "origin" of difference, and thereby rejecting the "will" completely, he is also himself blind to the unifying force of the will that *is also* at work. That is, Derrida seems to be setting up a false dichotomy between a unifying spirit and a fragmenting name/sign, prioritizing the latter, and thereby not accounting for the complex unifying *and* fragmenting will to interpret that is (always already) at work. We saw it at work not only in the way Derrida presumes unity in Heidegger (his will), but it is also at work in Derrida's phrases that can only attach attributes of the will to nonwilling entities, e.g., "One can also ask what *interest* is served by this Heideggerian discourse being carried out along these lines" (*DD*, 65; my emphasis),[32] or the reference to the "axiomatic structure of metaphysics, inasmuch as *metaphysics itself* desires . . . its own unity" (*DD*,

67). These formulations imply the insistence of an agency and *vouloir dire* that Derrida himself cannot escape. He merely makes it awkward by not having a developed exploration of the will that can explain the source and force of these phrases.[33] Thus, although Derrida can legitimately reject a *merely* unifying will in Heidegger's interpretation, he cannot avoid bringing in some kind of willing into his own.

There is more at stake here than an apparent blindness or lack of self-reflexivity in Derrida's approach. The aporias appear as such in Derrida (and Heidegger, as we shall see in greater detail below) because they are addressing a fundamentally contradictory phenomenon with nondialectical tools. The will to interpret contains within itself, we have seen, twin movements: one toward unity and one toward self-overcoming (self-splitting). To will to interpret or understand is thus to engage in these two movements. Derrida, unfortunately, seems to take Heidegger too much at his word that true thought and interpretation involve absolute unity; he therefore assumes that to discover moments of disunity in Heidegger's interpretation somehow undermines the hermeneutic effort. But that is no more the case than it would be to undermine Derrida's effort whenever we point to places where he must presume unity. Derrida's dualism, as we saw, opposes the "matter of thought" to the "matter of life or the proper name" (*DD*, 62); but he thereby must put all that opposes the unity of thought onto the same (other) side of the equation. The linking of "life" (*Leben*) and "proper name," is, however, problematic. Since *Leben* is associated with will, perhaps it would be better to see the activity of life in terms of the will to interpret, which involves moving back and forth between the unity of thought and the disunity of the individual(izing) name. In proposing his dualism (thought vs. life/name), Derrida is led to make critical pronouncements, for example, against a general hermeneutic, where he is in fact merely pointing out what we all do when performing the dialectical will of hermeneutics, namely dance around and within a contradiction (between thought and name).[34] That is, Heidegger insists on the unity of thought and Derrida points out the disunity of the name; but in doing so, Derrida also engages in acts of unifying understanding. The more productive way to look at this process would be to say that Derrida does point to the places where the will to interpret reveals itself as a disseminating "will to power," but that he also reveals how the will to interpret continues at the same time to exert its unifying force (also on him). It is thus less a matter of deconstructing hermeneutics, of deconstruction vs. hermeneutics, or of hermeneutics despite deconstruction than a working out of the will to interpret that engages always in both activities.[35]

Derrida's essay on Nietzsche, "Otobiographies," more than the "response" to Gadamer, highlights in many ways the contradictions inherent in the will to interpret, and so we can use it to work out the productive structure of these contradictions. A direct way to work out the bundle of issues that connect the apparently arbitrary or at least loose arrangement of arguments in Derrida's essay—which includes a reading of Nietzsche's autobiographical *Ecce Homo,* a discussion of the relation between the state and educational institutions by means of Nietzsche's *On the Future of our Institutes of Education,* a seminar held in Paris on life and death, and the later debate with Gadamer on the will of hermeneutics—is to look at a series of questions Derrida poses at the end of an introduction he wrote for a different presentation of this lecture. That is, when asked to hold a lecture in Virginia on the bicentennial of the Declaration of Independence, Derrida held the Nietzsche lecture (*OTO*) but with a short preamble.[36] In it he asks:

> How does something like a state come about? On what is it based or founded? How does it make itself "independent"? Or more important, how does independence declare itself and the auto-nomy of that which underwrites (signs, *unterzeichnen*) its own law? Who underwrites (*unterzeichnet*) these authorizations to sign (*unterzeichnen*), these representatives, procurations, delegations? Despite my promise, I will not continue down this path today. (*OTO,* 69)

Although it is true that the openly "political" questions are not pursued in this or the later essay, the issues they raise remain central since they in fact connect with discussions of the will from Kant to Nietzsche.[37]

It was Kant, as we saw, who defined the will, at least in its rationally determined form, as that which gives itself its own law. It does so in the form of a prescription (*Vorschrift*) that the subject gives to him- or herself. Derrida is asking here who is doing the writing of this inscription of the law into the self and who "underwrites" it, i.e., how the subject guarantees that the *Vorschrift* of the self-given law receives its authority. The law is not merely present in us but is re-presented to us in a certain form, and precisely this form, as a form of *écriture,* reveals that some interpretive act of explanation and application must occur in the self. This act would likewise have to be underwritten, "authorized," and so we find ourselves in the infinite regress of self-defining or self-reflexive subjectivity. The unity of the Kantian will seems therefore threatened by the introduction of the sign (and signature) that would be necessary to guarantee it.

Viewed in this way, the basic questions of Derrida's preamble are taken up in the body of the talk after all since it, like the response to Gadamer, takes up the problematic unity of the interpreting will. That is, although often only implicit, the knot tying together issues of the law's "underwriting," Nietzsche, the process of interpretation, and a critique of Gadamer, is none other than the dialectic of the will to interpretation, for, Derrida writes, we must grapple with "what he [Nietzsche] has willed in his name" (*OTO,* 7).

Derrida first addresses a mode of interpretation that is different from both typical philosophical and biographical readings. It must "mobilize other sources of power" and offer a new analysis of the proper name and the signature. He describes it as follows:

> Neither "immanent" readings of philosophical systems (whether such readings be structural or not) nor external, empirical-genetic readings have ever in themselves questioned the *dynamis* of that borderline between the "work" and the "life," the system and the subject of the system. This borderline—I call it *dynamis* because of its force, its power, as well as its virtual and mobile potency—is neither active nor passive, neither outside nor inside. It is most especially not a thin line, an invisible or *indivisible* trait lying between the enclosure of philosophemes, on the one hand, and the life of an author already identifiable behind the name, on the other. This divisible borderline traverses two "bodies," the corpus and the body, in accordance with laws that we are only beginning to catch sight of. (*OTO*, 5f)

This passage summarizes in paradoxical yet explicit form the contradictory determinations that have informed the history of the conceptualizations of willing. The best way to envision what Derrida has in mind here, I think, is to recall the model of the will as the intersection of overlapping circles. Based on the Lacanian schema to explain alienation and separation, this model was seen to work for both Kant's and Adorno's dialectical determination of the will. Here we see variations that involve the spheres of "Life" and "Work," or the "Autonomous Spirit" and the "Letter," the "Self" and its "Name(s)."

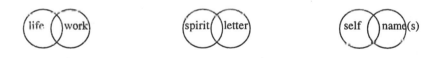

The "middle ground" (or Derridean "borderline") here needs to be conceived of as unstable given its participation in contradictory yet implicated spheres. Derrida marks that central dialectical[38] space that is neither/nor and both/and as the source and object of interpretation: the object, because one can only understand Nietzsche if this is taken into account, indeed for Derrida, "one reads only by taking it into account" (*OTO*, 6); and the source, because it is the constitutive place from which interpretation commences. Let us see how this place is the contradictory site of the will.

Derrida considers a passage at the opening of *Ecce Homo* where Nietzsche addresses the question "Who am I?" ("Wer ich bin") in terms of a "credit" that he has toward himself (*OTO*, 8–11). This means that Nietzsche's identity is formed in two ways: (1) He has no identity except the exchangeability of his name(s), i.e., a credit that is open until he is dead. Only then will the bill come due, but until then life is defined in terms of its open-ended nonidentity. (2) Nietzsche on the other hand feels a "duty" ("Pflicht"), "unwillingly" ("wider Willen"), he says, to call in the debt and to impose an identity onto himself while he is still alive ("Hört mich, denn ich bin der und der. Verwechselt mich vor allem nicht"). Derrida summarizes: "He says this unwillingly, but he has a 'duty' to say so in order to acquit himself of a debt. . . . Forcing himself to say who he is, he goes against his natural *habitus* that prompts him to dissimulate behind masks" (*OTO*, 10). This contradictory "core," which Derrida also sees in Nietzsche's formulation of his life as "gift" (*OTO*, 11–13), is formulated in terms of the contradictory poles of the will— "duty" ("Pflicht") and "drive" ("Trieb"). Hence, it comes as no surprise that this constitutive place of (self-)interpretation is, in fact, a place of willing: "This *place* is to be found neither in the work (it is an exergue) nor in the life of the author. At least it is not there in a simple fashion, but neither is it simply exterior to them. It is in this place that affirmation is repeated: yes, yes, I approve, I sign, I subscribe to this acknowledgment of the debt incurred toward 'myself,' 'my-life'—and I want it to return" (*OTO*, 14). It is the will, the site of wanting, then, as a "contradicting duplicity" (*OTO*, 14) and a "double origin" (*OTO*, 16), what Derrida so aptly calls a "borderline" that underwrites the generation of texts and their interpretations.[39]

Derrida does not stop, however, with bringing this dialectical herme-neutical will into play, but (unfortunately) goes on to collapse the tension into the one side. Concerning the passage cited above, in which Nietzsche sees his self as *both* an empty credit open to future exchange *and* a necessary ("verpflichtet") identity that he would impose upon himself and the world, Derrida wants to place the second possibility into doubt: "On the other hand, however, this auto-presentative exhibition of the '*ich bin der und der*' could well be still a ruse of dissimulation" (*OTO*, 10). This allows Derrida to shift the nature of the duality that would be the transcendental utopia (the non-place)[40] of interpreting anything signed by "F. N." from a simultaneity of identity and fragmentation to a plurality of masks (nonidentities). A hermeneutic of the will (in the sense of a hermeneutic based on Nietzsche's will and a hermeneutic that would see the "identity/nonidentity" of a text as its *vouloir dire*) gives way in Derrida to an antihermeneutic of the splitting textual "machine" (*OTO*, 29). By not taking into account the richness of the tradition of dialectics of willing, Derrida thus misses an opportunity to maintain the radical duality, in willing, of openness and imposed unity.

And yet, the insistence of the dialectic of the will emerges despite Derrida's reductionism when we see in this essay, as we saw before, that Derrida cannot escape the aporia that arises when the "double origin" of unity and disunity is reduced to the one side, in this case disunity. That is, we again see him, against his own pronouncements, at times proposing unity, speaking the language of a unifying will (as had Nietzsche). This occurs both in his own position as reader (as much as he tries to locate himself as playing out a *mise-en-scène,* he is nonetheless aware of his "freedom" to give it its form, e.g., 70) and in his reading of Nietzsche (the number of times he offers a principle of "how to read" him, e.g., *OTO,* 72, 77f, 80). The point here is again not to "catch" Derrida contradicting himself, but to see that in this contradiction lies a powerful hermeneutical principle (even more powerful than Gadamer's own one-sidedness). Derrida is thus quite right when he says, concerning the doubleness that could produce both a fascist and antifascist reading of Nietzsche, "Yet it would still be necessary to account for the possibility of this mimetic inversion and perversion" (*OTO,* 30). But can the notion of a "powerful utterance-producing *machine*" (*OTO,* 29) ever account for the duality of "what [Nietzsche] has *willed*" (*OTO,* 7; my emphasis)? Certainly Derrida is close to the Nietzschean principle of the will that would allow for such inversion, as in the reference to *Ecce Homo* where Nietzsche says "ich bin Dynamit" because his *will,* as unifying force, also splits. But Derrida's reduction of the duality solely to fragmentation blinds him to its positive (unifying) force, a force that *we* can see operating willy-nilly in Derrida's own discourse.

As we turn now to Derrida's reading of Heidegger, we see that one reason for Derrida's misrecognition of the role of the will arises from the fact that he wants to set up the contradiction in a way that he can deconstruct rather than exploit a fruitful dialectic. That is, as we can see in his series of lectures *Of Spirit,* he focuses on oppositions—spirit vs. letter, body, animal, etc.—rather than on the essential mixture of unity and doubleness that inheres in the will. This is a clear choice on Derrida's part, since he stresses at the opening of this lectures that the concept of "spirit" is not a major one in Heidegger, even though it appears at key points and with a contradictory logic. But Derrida has selected it for his analysis because it works for his deconstructive strategy, and not in order to work with other, perhaps more significant or fruitful concepts in Heidegger's thought.[41] This is clear in the very trajectory of the lectures, which follow Heidegger's use of the term *Geist:* After an admonitory mention in *Sein und Zeit* (1926)—i.e., Heidegger says the term should be "avoided"—it appears again in the *Rektoratsrede* of 1933, in different lectures on metaphysics between 1929 and 1935, and then in the 1953 readings of Trakl. One can see the appeal such a trajectory has to Derrida (Why the shift in Heidegger's attitude toward the term? Why is Heidegger's work punctuated in his oeuvre by the term at precisely these historical points?). And yet, it is also a consequence that the accent on *Geist* leads Derrida to circumvent the lectures on Nietzsche from 1935 to 1946. And it is there that *Wille* (*zur Macht*) plays the central role—and, I would add, more fruitfully than *Geist* or its deconstruction in the other texts.[42]

Although Derrida's lectures tend to ramble through various arguments and analyses, a central point emerges in Derrida's deconstruction of the untenable opposition Heidegger (along with the Western metaphysical tradition) sets up between *Geist* and some x, where x changes according to context. This point is clearest in Derrida's discussion of the *Einführung in die Metaphysik* (1935), where Heidegger equates *Geist* with *Welt* and then establishes the trio: stone-animal-human (*Stein-Tier-Mensch*), where "The stone is without world (*weltlos*). . . . The animal is poor in world (*weltarm*) . . . Man is world-forming (*weltbildend*)" (*OS*, 48). What Derrida shows brilliantly is the difficulties of maintaining the opposition *Mensch-Tier*, so that the opposition spirit vs. animal (or life) breaks down, even as it belongs to the foundation of Western thought. We saw a similar kind of argument in the essay on Nietzsche (*OTO*), where the link was explicit between Life and Letter as the binary opposites to spirit/thought.

These binarisms are relevant for the interaction between deconstruction and hermeneutics since Derrida points to the different connections between spirit and hermeneutics. On the one hand, there is a link via the concept of *Gespräch* (conversation or dialogue). Thus, according to Derrida, Heidegger's *Gespräch* with Trakl is intricately linked to the conception of *Geist*. Derrida writes: "The *Gespräch* will be defined as a determinate mode of speech only from what is said of spirit, of the essence of *Geist* as it divides and gathers in conflagration" (*OS*, 83f). Given the central role of the conversation in Gadamer's thought, we can see here how Derrida can implicate hermeneutics in the deconstruction of *Geist*. And more generally, Derrida links his analysis of Heidegger's reading of Trakl, and the problematic role of *Geist* in it, to his investigation of the status of the text in "its relationship with philosophical discourse, with hermeneutics and poetics" (*OS*, 887).

And yet, if we now stand back for a moment and consider why Derrida can deconstruct *Geist* in Heidegger, we see that he is demonstrating the failure of this nondialectical concept to account for a dialectic—even though Derrida himself offers no alternative. Derrida shows how *Geist* is "unavoidable"—Heidegger calls for its avoidance in *Sein und Zeit*, then uses it "in quotations," only to drop the diacritical marks later. Furthermore, Derrida shows the difficulty in answering the question: What is *Geist?* precisely because Heidegger moves towards an increasingly "dialectical" conception, culminating in the inherently contradictory and yet unifying notion of spirit as "flame" ("Flamme," especially *OS*, 884–86, where Derrida shows the difficulty in translating Heidegger; also *OS*, 79f, *Geist* as "bei sich" and "in Bewegung"). The sentence quoted above linking *Geist* and *Gespräch* concludes, after all, with a dialectical description of the "the essence of *Geist* as it *divides* and *gathers* in conflagration" (*OS*, 884; my emphasis).

Thus, it should come as no surprise that an exclusionary and one-sided conception of *Geist* should lend itself to deconstruction. To what concept could Derrida turn, which would *embrace* the contradictions that *Geist* so uneasily contains yet tends to reduce? A hint comes in Derrida's one brief citation from Heidegger's *Nietzsche,* where the "will to power" appears as a different means of conceiving the opposition between "life" and "spirit": "This has nothing 'vital' or 'spiritual' about it: to the contrary, the 'vital' (the 'living') and the 'spiritual' are, as belonging to entities, determined by Being in the sense of the Will to power" (*OS,* 74). The aporias and oppositions in Heidegger, the quote implies, arise from isolating the components that are contradictorily united in the Being conceived of as will to power. The same is true of Derrida. Thus, although Derrida (often correctly) criticizes Heidegger's interpretive "gesture" that would "sav[e] a body of thought by damning it" (*OS,* 73), i.e., that would "save" Nietzsche by reducing him uniformly to the last thinker of metaphysics instead of seeing the plurality inherent in his thought, Derrida does the same by accepting the reduction of the will to "a metaphysics of absolute subjectivity" (*OS,* 73) instead of seeing its more complex dialectic.

Another way to get at this is to look at Derrida's failure to examine Schelling. Derrida knows that Schelling's essay on the essence of human freedom (*Philosophische Untersuchungen über das Wesen der menschlichen Freiheit*), left its trace on Heidegger.[43] And in Schelling's essay, *Geist* fulfills the function of unifying force, as we would expect (*OS,* 77). But there is *more* to Schelling than this attention to *Geist* and unity, namely his attention to will, as a radically dialectical *Ursein* (as we saw in the introduction) and that is why his presence in Heidegger is ambivalent and "disconcerting."[44] Derrida immediately takes up a Heideggerian stance in downplaying the significance of Schelling's analyses since they supposedly belong to a "metaphysics of the will" that Heidegger supposedly overcame. Given this stance, the presence of Schelling/the will in Heidegger *would* be "disconcerting." But all this presumes on the part of Derrida (and as we shall see on the part of Heidegger as well) an ambivalent relation to the concept of the will, since in deconstructing the role of unifying *Geist* he breaks down oppositions between *humanitas* and *animalitas* (*OS,* 102), but cannot consider how the will mediates these spheres dialectically. The will, therefore, is as much a disconcerting absent-presence in Derrida as Schelling is in Heidegger.

What we have seen, then, is that Derrida, from the opposite direction of Gadamer, approaches and yet shortchanges the dynamic dialectic of the will to interpretation. He either reduces Heidegger's interpretation of Nietzsche to a simple, imposed unity of thought (spirit), against which he can play the disseminating force of the name (letter); or he circumvents the interpretations of willing by Nietzsche and Schelling to deconstruct directly the concept of *Geist*. In both cases, he points to aporias in a hermeneutic of Spirit but gets into his own because he never unfolds the dialectic of the will. Thus, I shall now turn to Heidegger because he provides, I think, the common ground out of which the two positions—Derrida's and Gadamer's—grow. He occupies this place because he grappled with and understood the dialectic of the will as a totalizing contradiction that cannot be avoided but only worked through. But it is from him, albeit in different ways, that both Gadamer and Derrida *also* got the idea that nonetheless some other principle beyond the will is operating. That is, *Sein* and *Denken* displace *Wille* in Heidegger, and these concepts lead to the primacy of an identity-creating tradition for Gadamer and the insistence on *différance* for Derrida. The inherent connection of these sides in the will is thus suppressed.

Heidegger: Willing/Being/Thinking

Derrida's "deconstruction" of Heidegger revolved around the effort to expose the metaphysics of *Einheit* in Heidegger's *Nietzsche*. This critique of Heidegger was Derrida's way of answering Gadamer. Derrida took exception with Gadamerian hermeneutics for relying on a metaphysics of the subject that would ground understanding in an identity of meanings. And yet, as we have seen, Derrida falsely reduces the role of the (good) will in understanding to a kind of unity of spirit. Moreover, the Derridean fragmentation of the name itself feeds off moments of posited unity. In Heidegger, all these issues—*Einheit,* metaphysics, subjectivity, fragmentation (*Zerstreuung*)—are knotted together by the concept of the will (in Nietzsche). All of metaphysics culminates in Nietzsche's formulation of the will to power, according to Heidegger, because "in its essence" all of western metaphysics was driven by the motor of the will which it had "not yet comprehended" (*N* 11, 114). By placing this concept at the center of his analysis of Nietzsche as the culmination of Western metaphysics, Heidegger introduces the potential for a productive dialectical tension into his interpretation, indeed into the very process of interpretation itself. It is that dialectic around the will to interpretation, and Heidegger's own problematic reduction of it to its exclusive poles, that I shall analyze.[45] What I want to show, then, is that both Gadamer and Derrida are right (and wrong) in respectively stressing and attacking the centrality of *Einheit* in Heidegger's interpretation of Nietzsche as the *Vollendung* of metaphysics. The reason is that Heidegger, in his pivotal lectures on Nietzsche, emphasizes the will and therefore, so to speak, cannot help but take up both sides of the debate over unity or fragmentation (since both positions are inherent in the will's dialectic). Indeed, Heidegger's dialectic of *Einheit* and *Unterschied* in the will can reveal why interpretation and understanding always involve both. We will furthermore see how Heidegger's particular formulation of the dialectic of the will, which gradually takes a turn *from* willing to Thinking and Being,[46] also contains the seeds of reductive readings (one-sided and thus contradictory, either metaphysical or "antimetaphysical").[47]

I shall approach in three ways the centrality of the will (to power) for Heidegger's history of metaphysics. The goal here is to show how throughout the years of his Nietzsche lectures, Heidegger reconceptualized Western thought time and again in terms of the will (to power). He explored key philosophical concepts as inherently linked to the will; he interpreted the eclipsing of the question of Being as the result of a fixation on human willing—an eclipse that culminated in modernity; and he, modifying Nietzsche's notion, identified this culmination with nihilism. Although in all these cases the concept of the will (to power) is central to Heidegger's emerging sense of a uniform *Seinsgeschichte*, it plays a negative role vis-à-vis the "thinking of Being" that he would see as the "overcoming of metaphysics." And yet, we shall see that precisely the dialectic inherent in the will seems to drive this history forward and makes possible its (constant) self-overcoming. In a somewhat extreme formulation, I would say that it is a shame Heidegger's turn to *Seinsgeschichte* eclipses the dialectic of willing, not (as Heidegger himself argued) vice versa.

First, Heidegger argues that the will to power is contained essentially, even if implicitly, in the concepts that form the moments in Western metaphysics. As he says, the conception of being as fundamentally will is a part of the unfolding history of the interpretation of the world (in the West): "It has not been the view of particular thinkers to understand being fundamentally as will; rather this is a necessity of the history of human existence that they are grounding" ("Das Sciende nach seinem Grundcharakter als Willen begreifen, ist keine Ansicht von einzelnen Denkern, sondern eine Notwendigkeit der Geschichte des Daseins, das sie begründen"; *N* I, 46). Over the course of the six years of his Nietzsche lectures, Heidegger comes to emphasize the historical component more and more. Heidegger works from three assumptions: (1) that the will to power is the central idea in Nietzsche's thought (or, as he says, it is *the* thought in Nietzsche's philosophy, since all philosophers have *one* thought—we will explore the hermeneutic consequences of having the will to power as the unifying thought below); (2) that the will to power is to be grasped as the "positing of values" ("Wert-Setzung"; "will to power and positing value are the same" ["Wille zur Macht und Wert-setzung sind *dasselbe*"]; *N* II, 108), i.e., the imposing of being onto becoming, as Nietzsche says; and (3) that will to power is the *Vollendung* of Western metaphysics. These three assumptions are contained in the statement: "The metaphysics of the will to power interprets all prior fundamental metaphysical positions in light of the idea of value" ("Die Metaphysik des Willens zur Macht deutet alle ihr voraufgegangenen metaphysischen Grundstellungen im Lichte des

Wertgedankens"; *N* II, 272). Thus, he must answer the question: How can Western metaphysics be interpreted in such a way that it culminates, i.e., comes fully to itself, as absolute *Wert-setzung?*

Heidegger answers this question by positing two strands in metaphysics, both of which define the essence of being in its totality as *Wirklichkeit,* whereby one should hear in this the notion of *wirken,* the effective force of will. From Plato emerges the view of the essence of the world as *idea,* which means that the mode of relating to the world is one of *Vor-stellen* (re-presentation). This culminates in a split between the subject and the object, the re-presenting (*Vor-stellendes*) and the represented (*Vorgestelltes*), a split that must be bridged. The bridge comes in the form of the effective relationship between the two, i.e., subject and object are linked by the same *Wirklichkeit,* whereby all that is is that which has an effect (or even which the subject has produced, made real). This is an unstated form of will to power.[48]

The second strand that would see being as will proceeds from Aristotle on a conceptual path from the primacy of *energeia.*[49] The point for Heidegger is not to link "energy" and "power" but, rather, to show that the modern, post-Leibnizian, reception of Aristotle's *energeia* "subjectivizes" reality itself. This paves the way to Schopenhauer and Nietzsche. Given this line, according to Heidegger's hermeneutic principle, what is at issue is *not* that Nietzsche so developed (his *Bildungsgang,* the fact that he read Aristotle, Leibniz, Schopenhauer) but that the *essential* connection between *energeia* and will to power comes to the fore at its utmost in Nietzsche.

By highlighting both these strands, Heidegger can show how the will to power, as an effective and imposing *Wert-setzung,* is inherent (though unquestioned) in the main ideas of Western metaphysics (the Platonic Idea, Descartes's self-certain subject, Kant's view of man in the world of objects-of-experience, Hegel's absolute Spirit, etc.). This means that the very history of Western thought is the history of the domination of the will and the sphere of the will, what Heidegger calls "beings" (*Seiendes*), over the thought of Being. That is, metaphysics is the very history of the differentiation between beings and Being, whereby the focus on the former leads to the blindness toward both the latter and the differentiation between them. Heidegger says that we must keep as part of our "thought"

> the way that Being as will to power arises out of the essential determination of *idea* and thus bears within itself the differentiation between Being and beings, such that the differentiation, unquestioned as such, forms the fundamental structure of metaphysics.

> wie das Sein als Wille zur Macht aus der Wesensbestimmtheit der *idea* entspringt und daher in sich die Unterscheidung von Sein und Seiendem

mitbringt, dieses aber so, daß die Unterscheidung, als solche unbefragt, das Grundgefüge der Metaphysik bildet. (*N* II, 240)

The will to power has been operative *in essence* from the beginning of the history of Being. It has been there since the Greeks developed a metaphysics around the concept of *idea* and *energeia*. It has been responsible for both the differentiation between beings and Being, and, because of its totalizing emphasis on the former, even for the blindness to that difference. We can already see how the will to power acts in Heidegger's hermeneutics of Being as both unifying and differentiating force: namely, the will to power is *the* thought of Western metaphysics, but this one thought has a fundamentally disuniting effect.

Now to the second approach to the centralitiy of the will in Heidegger. If Heidegger sees the metaphysics of will to power in terms of the history of Being, whereby the former comes to eclipse the very thought of Being, the will (to power) occupies a unique historico-conceptual position as the culminating point/force of *Seinsvergessenheit*. What, then, is the dynamic relationship between conceptions of being and Being (the sphere of willing)? Once that relationship is established, we can use the argument above: Being relates to being/metaphysics in a certain historical way for Heidegger, leading to the eclipsing of Being; and we saw above that all metaphysics can be comprehended (*begriffen*) in the concept of the will; therefore, the will, as the conceptual core (*Inbegriff*) of metaphysics is the high point of *Seinsvergessenheit*.

Heidegger compresses the essence of this development in a comparison between Protagoras and Descartes (as in the way two points are needed to make a line). Taking the statement of Protagoras that man is the measure of all things, Heidegger offers two readings. The one, an "originary" reading that captures the early Greek appreciation for Being, opposes a modern reading that emphasizes subjectivity. The first reading begins with a sense that the "all things," of which man would be the measure, mean all beings (*Seiendes*) but only as they exist (*anwest*) in a state of openness (unconcealedness, *Unverborgenheit*) within the "larger" sphere of Being. Man is the "measure" (*Maß*) to the extent that he carves out within this sphere a space of things that are opened to him thanks to a horizon that is greater than both him and them. Man is the measure to the extent that he defines through his limiting, controlled existence (*Mäßigung, Einschränkung*) a sphere of experienced being within the revealed openness of beings presented to him (thanks to Being). In Heidegger's terms:

> The way that Protagoras determines the relation of man to being is only an emphatic limitation of the unconcealedness of beings to the particular circle of man's experience of the world. This limitation *presupposes* that this

unconcealedness presides over that experience, or more significantly, that this unconcealedness as such was once experienced and was raised to the level of knowledge as the fundamental character of being.

Die Art, wie Protagoras das Verhältnis des Menschen zum Seienden bestimmt, ist nur eine betonte Einschränkung der Unverborgenheit des Seienden auf den jeweiligen Umkreis der Welterfahrung. Diese Einschränkung *setzt voraus,* daß diese Unverborgenheit des Seienden waltet, noch mehr, daß diese Unverborgenheit bereits als solche schon einmal erfahren und als Grundcharakter des Seienden selbst ins Wissen gehoben wurde. (*N* II, 139).

Graphically one could depict this fundamental relation as an originary horizon of Being, within which a sphere of beings is opened up:

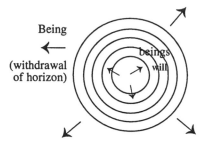

We have here a smaller, *willfully* expanding circle that is *determined* by the limited/limiting perspective of man's measuring will. But this area of man's driving expansion is *given* or opened up thanks to the more fundamental "unconcealedness."[50] Man can be the measure of all things only if we presuppose a "more originary" revealing that is *not* dependent on man's will.[51]

In the modern interpretation, however, the subject is assumed to be there from the start.[52] That is, the originary position is not one of a sphere of being opened up to or for a "measuring" man but two conflicting spheres, i.e., some sphere independent of the subject's domain would now stand problematically in opposition to it (the subject's *Gegenstand*), while the subject stands "free" from the domination of objects or Nature. This raises a major problem of how the subjects and objects will then relate to each other. The will supposedly bridges the gap. Graphically:

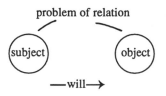

The question for modern (post-Cartesian) philosophy becomes then not "What is being?" but "How can the subject be *certain* of its experience?" This search for a self-grounded certainty of human knowledge is, of course, a form of liberation (from the tutelage of Nature, or authority), as Kant defines the will of the Enlightenment. But this liberation also changes the conception of freedom (*N* II, 142f) such that it no longer means the openness of being within the horizon of Being, and thus an openness to Being, but instead the demand that the subject become the sole object of philosophy in the search for certainty. Man, in the modern sense of the measure of all things, cannot allow any other perspective besides that which he can, in his frantic search for certainty, impose on the world.

We can see at this point the way Heidegger identifies metaphysics as the history of the eclipsing of Being by being, i.e., the totalizing focus on being, and the development of the will as ground of the subject from which it can impose itself on the world, indeed posit it ultimately in Nietzsche's terms as *Wert-setzung*. That is, Heidegger's conception of the history of Being would be inconceivable were it not for the centrality of the concept of will, since the will defined in a certain way as active, controlling, unifying, rationalist, and individualistic, is the motor behind the Western history of Being. Heidegger thus places the will both at the center of the unfolding of Being *and* opposed to Being in its essence. Precisely this tension will be crucial and will point the way to a broader definition of the will.

But before we can open the will up to a richer interpretation, we need to see how Heidegger came to this historical interpretation through an analysis of Nietzsche's concept of nihilism. This is our third approach to the centrality of the will in Heidegger. The history of nihilism contains the essential moves of the history of Being, but it is seen from the perspective of values. Once the will to power eclipses Being (the more primary ground of unconcealedness), there are no values anymore outside of the sphere of the will to power as that which posits values. Even *Sein* is nothing but a posited value of the will to power (according to Nietzsche). Nihilism is the sense of loss—both psychological and metaphysical—that comes with the totalizing *Wert-Setzung* of the will to power, or, in Heidegger's terms, the eclipsing of Being by being. This connection occurs thanks to a basic hermeneutic principle. The *thought* of Nietzsche's nihilism is part of *Weltgeschichte*. Heidegger writes:

> We can experience the full weight of what the title [nihilism] means in *Nietzsche's* sense. It means: the history of Western metaphysics as the ground of our own history, i.e., our future decisions

> Wir können aber auch das volle Schwergewicht dessen erfahren, was der Titel im Sinne *Nietzsches* sagt. Dies bedeutet dann: die Geschichte der abendlän-

dischen Metaphysik als den Grund unserer eigenen Geschichte und d.h. der
zukünftigen Entscheidungen denken. (*N* II, 42)

That is, nihilism, according to Heidegger's Nietzsche, is not a limited
phenomenon of a few late nineteenth-century intellectuals. And the thought
of nihilism is not just "Nietzsche's idea." Rather, both the phenomenon
and the thought of nihilism culminate a historical development.[53] And since
this thought centers on the will, a tension has been generated that we can
exploit below.

But what is the historical development that Nietzsche's thought captures? The culminating statement for Heidegger is bold and clear: "Metaphysics, as metaphysics, is actual nihilism" ("Die Metaphysik ist als Metaphysik der eigentliche Nihilismus"; *N* II, 343). The reason for this is contained in the answer to the question he poses: "Does metaphysics think
Being itself? No and never. It thinks only being(s) with regard to their
Being" ("Denkt die Metaphysik das Sein selbst? Nein und niemals. Sie
denkt *das Seiende* hinsichtlich des Seins"; *N* II, 345f). The absolute negative
answer to this question is the negation that is nihilism—the inability to
pose the question of Being. If metaphysics (in the manner of Leibniz)
poses the question instead: "Why are there beings at all, and not rather
nothing" ("Warum ist überhaupt Seiendes und nicht vielmehr nichts?"; *N*
II, 347), there is often the need to go beyond being by positing some
transcendentally existing realm so that the realm of being can be thought. But
this "transcendental-transcendent beyond" ("transzendental-transzendenten
Überstieg"; *N* II, 350) in fact leaves the thought of Being empty, since its goal
is the explanation of the realm of being. It comes as no surprise, then, that
from the perspective of being/metaphysics even the "transcendental" option
should eventually be rejected, or rather turned explicitly into what it was
(e.g., by a Feuerbach): the imposition of values from the immediate world
of being onto some higher order of "Being." Metaphysics undermines itself
in the sense that its own view of Being leads to the conclusion that Being
is, as a projected value from the realm of being, "worthless," i.e., nothing.
Nihilism, the victory of nothingness over Being, is thus the inherently logical
conclusion of metaphysics and its focus on being.[54]

This reified history seems patently absurd in these terms (as if Being
and being were actors on the stage of world history). But it gains significance
when the motor is seen as the human, all too human, will to power. Heidegger
works from Nietzsche's statement: "It is the highest will to power to impose
Being on becoming" ("Dem Werden das Sein aufzuprägen ist der höchste
Wille zur Macht"; *Nachlaß, Werke* III, 895). Since one of the essential
characteristics of the will to power, as we have seen, is that it posits value, this
claim by Nietzsche makes the will to power the key to metaphysics since the

latter is defined as the study of the "constancy of presence" ("Beständigkeit des Anwesens"; *N,* I, 648ff). That is, the rhetoric that permeates Heidegger about "metaphysics doing this or that" needs to be understood in terms of the *will* doing this or that. (Even this can be reformulated in terms of "humans willing," a formulation that avoids the reification of the will as entity.) And in fact, it makes much more sense to define the will (as it has been for centuries) as the human ability that posits/imposes value, consistency, and change. Thus, the abstract Heideggerian notion of the "determination of nihilism in terms of the history of Being" ("seinsgeschichtliche Bestimmung des Nihilismus"; *N* II, 44) gains in significance and dialectical movement when seen in terms of the activity of the human will.

So, once again, what relations does Heidegger establish among the will, nihilism, values, and metaphysics?[55] Values are posited by the will as existing, and yet they are revealed to be "only posited." The condition of nihilism is summarized in a fragment by Nietzsche (quoted by Heidegger): "In brief: the categories 'purpose,' 'unity,' 'being,' with which we have interjected value into the world, are *withdrawn* again by us—and now the world appears *worthless*" ("Kurz: die Kategorien 'Zweck,' 'Einheit,' 'Sein,' mit denen wir der Welt einen Wert eingelegt haben, werden wieder von uns *herausgezogen*—und nun sieht die Welt *wertlos aus*"; *N* II, 70f). The reason why this is not an "arbitrary" (i.e., individual or period-specific) development but rather a development in the very history of Being is that Being owes its development (history, *Geschehen*) to man (*Dasein*) and man is essentially will, and that will is, in its essence, the positing of values. Will, without such positing, would not be will. Thus, the key categories that are at the heart of the debate between deconstruction and hermeneutics are seen in Heidegger's reading of Nietzsche as necessary positings (*Ansetzen* or *Wert-Setzungen*) that simultaneously (co-originally) miss the point and undermine the very meaning and value they would grant.[56] In short, at the heart of Heidegger's "history of Being" is a self-sublating process of human willing.

These arguments show that it is in fact inaccurate to speak of a "metaphysics *of* the will" (although Heidegger himself does) because for Heidegger *all* metaphysics is contained in the conception of the will to power as the ground of being, and conversely the notion of the will is the fulfillment of the history of metaphysics (history of Being) itself (it "fills in" or eclipses Being with the totality of being). The will, therefore, is not just one "metaphysical" concept among many but the "name" for a crucial development in the history of Western thought. Although it might seem as if Nietzsche and the will play a sharply circumscribed role in the formation of Heidegger's later thought, they permeate his entire philosophical enterprise. Nietzsche and the will are at the center of the *Kehre,* for they bring together essential moments in Western metaphysics and a conception of the domination/eclipsing of Being. (Not by chance, the vision of this domination grew increasingly negative in Heidegger's thought between 1935 and 1946 as he witnessed the fascist "triumph of the will." More on that below.) Thus, the will exposes the "essential unity" (*Wesenseinheit*) of nihilism and, by extension, not just of Nietzsche's thought but also of the history of Western thought in general.

Moreover, Heidegger brings out something crucial that we saw in Nietzsche, namely the ambivalent relationship between the will and the metaphysics of subjectivity. On the one hand, the will is clearly the culminating point of an entire metaphysical tradition that, in separating "being in its totality" ("Seiendes als Ganzes") from Being, was moving toward an ever more radical subjectivity ("radical" in the sense of isolated from and defined in opposition to an objectified world [*Gegenständlichkeit*]). The will in this reading represents the point of the subject's "domination." And yet, on the other hand, because the will is the *Grundcharakter* of Western metaphysics and because metaphysics is for Heidegger not just a loose collection of individual philosophers' ruminations but an unfolding of man's relation to Being, the will is given trans-subjective status. It is not "transcendental" in the sense of standing outside the movement of history; rather, it is that very movement in its conceptual essence and unity. Given these two modes of reading the will, it is clear why both Gadamer and Derrida are "right" in their use and criticism of the category of will. To refer to the will is to use *the* essential language of the history of subjectivity, but it is not enough merely to criticize this use, since the will also makes possible the understanding of that history as more than a subjective process. Moreover, to refer to Heidegger and the will is to refer to both a differentiating and unifying force in human existence.

And now, once we have seen the will as the fulfillment of metaphysics, as the totality of being (i.e., the total eclipse of Being), as the culmination of nihilism, we need to look at the inherent dynamism of the will itself. It is not enough to stop at the point where one sees a problematic insistence on "unity" in Heidegger's argument since the *Wesenseinheit* is associated essentially with the concept of the will that is itself dynamically dialectical. This is the way we can move beyond criticisms of the "metaphysics of the will" (as they often appear unanalyzed in Derrida), since indeed for Heidegger there is an identity between metaphysics and the will, but because willing is inherently dialectical, the self-overcoming in willing applies to metaphysics as well. Heidegger analyzes the splitness in the will, and hence in the center of the history of Western thought, at many points in his reading of Nietzsche. Let us consider a few formulations of this splitness.

The dialectical *Bestimmung* of the will (to power) was the first and central object of Heidegger's lectures on Nietzsche. Relatively unaffected (uninfected) by Heidegger's own philosophical language about *Seinsge-schichte,* metaphysics, *Seiendes als Ganzes,* etc., these analyses offer in-sightful reworkings of the definitions of the will in the Western tradition and in Nietzsche. Heidegger stresses to begin with the fact that the phrase "Wille zur Macht" must not be misunderstood as meaning that there is such a thing as a vague and pure willing that in this particular case happens to have power as its object. Rather, the identity of will and power is fundamental because of their respective dual characters: Will includes both the one willing (*Wollender*) and the thing willed (*Gewolltes*) (*N* I, 51), which means that will is both its own ground and something beyond itself; and likewise, power is not some one stable thing but a movement for more power, since it stops being power once it is no longer "over" something (*N* I, 36). Thus they are the same (*N* I, 52) and in this sense we can understand Nietzsche's statement: "Willing appears to me, above all, to be something *complicated,* something that is a unity in word alone" ("Wollen scheint mir vor Allem etwas *Kompliziertes,* Etwas, das nur als Wort eine Einheit ist"; *N* I, 48f; *Jenseits Von Gut und Böse,* §19).

Likewise, in his analysis of Nietzsche's association of will as both affect and feeling, Heidegger finds different modes of doubleness. Will, Nietzsche claims at different points, is affect, passion, and feeling. All these three words, however, have different connotations, as Heidegger points out in an insightful argument or phenomenological description. Affect is related to an explosion of feeling. In the notion of will as affect, Heidegger emphasizes the simultaneity of activity and passivity that inheres in the act of self-overcoming. Any time one goes beyond oneself, as in the basic act of "über sich hinaus Wollen" (*N* I, 56f), one is *both* in control of the movement *and* one is in the act of losing oneself. Like affect, the will is something that befalls us as in an "attack" ("Anfall"), but like passion, it is something we have, something that contributes to defining our relation to the world.[57] The will contains the doubleness of loss and collection, the finding of the self in the process of self-loss and vice versa.

> Willing is always a bringing-the-self-to-itself and thereby a finding-oneself in going-beyond-oneself; it is a self-relating in the pushing of something away and to something else.
>
> Wollen ist immer ein Sich-zu-sich-selbst bringen und damit ein Sich-befinden in dem Über-sich-hinweg, ein Sich-halten in dem Drängen von etwas weg zu etwas hin. (*N* I, 63; or: "a feeling of bringing-us-back-to-ourselves in a mode of being-beyond-ourselves" ["ein fühlendes Uns-zu-uns-selbst-bringen, in der Weise eines Über-uns-weg"]; *N* I, 65).

This dialectical form is essential to Nietzsche, according to Heidegger: "That Nietzsche characterizes the will as affect, as passion, as feeling, means that

Nietzsche sees something more unitary, more originary, and at the same time more complicated, behind the mere word 'will' " ("Daß Nietzsche den Willen bald als Affekt, bald als Leidenschaft, bald als Gefühl bezeichnet, soll sagen: Nietzsche sieht etwas Einheitlicheres, Ursprünglicheres und zugleich Reicheres hinter dem einen groben Wort 'Wille' "; *N* II, 64f).

Recalling the key position the will plays in Heidegger's ontic-ontological differentiation between being and Being, i.e., the role we saw above for the will in Heidegger's history of Being as the history of the will to power and *Wertsetzung,* we find again a fundamental doubleness in terms of the will's imposition of stability and constancy onto the chaos/*Werden.* According to Nietzsche, the *Grundcharakter* of all being is *Werden.* It is the will to power that "imprints" ("aufprägen") Being (*Sein*) onto becoming. This means that the will to power occupies a peculiar position between being and becoming, movement and stasis, a position that also is simultaneously both. Heidegger says:

> The thought of the will to power is supposed to think that which is most properly becoming and movement (namely life itself) in its constancy. Certainly Nietzsche wants becoming, and that which becomes, to be understood as the basic character of beings in their totality; but he wants to see becoming precisely and above all as *the constant*—as actual 'being'—namely in the sense of Greek thinkers.

> Im Gedanken des Willens zur Macht soll das im höchsten und eigentlichsten Sinne Werdende und Bewegte—das Leben selbst—in *seiner* Beständigkeit gedacht werden. Gewiß will Nietzsche das Werden und das Werdende als den Grundcharakter des Seienden im Ganzen; aber er will das Werden gerade und allem zuvor als *das Bleibende*—als das eigentlich "Seiende"; seiend nämlich im Sinne der griechischen Denker. (*N* I, 656)

Here we can see that the doubleness of this conception of will as "Beständigung," i.e., as a movement that relies on stasis and a stasis that gives way to new movement, corresponds to Nietzsche's contradictory relation to the tradition of metaphysics. For here Nietzsche, according to Heidegger, formulates the Greek conception of being in terms from the modern subjectivist tradition, thereby "completing" them both, taking them to their extreme. (This also leads him to the identity of will to power and eternal recurrence by means of the notion of "*ein ständiges Werden*"; *N* II, 37f.)[58]

We can approach the doubleness inherent in the concept of the will, finally, from yet another perspective, namely the way will and power as *Wert-Setzung* are identified. Heidegger develops the two sides—preservation and intensification (*Erhaltung und Steigerung*)—on the basis of Nietzsche's fragment: "The perspective of 'value' is the perspective of the *conditions of preservation or intensification* within becoming" ("Der Gesichtspunkt des

'Werts' ist der Gesichtspunkt von *Erhaltungs-, Steigerungs-Bedingungen* innerhalb des Werdens"; see e.g., *N* II, 103). Since will, value, and becoming are identified, Heidegger can work out a common structure, a structure he derives from the very principle of "overpowering" ("Übermächtigung"):

> In whatever is real both preservation *and* intensification are simultaneously necessary, since in order for the will to power, as overpowering, to move beyond a particular stage, this stage must not only be achieved but also be established and maintained with power; otherwise the *over*powering could not be an over*powering.* Only what already has a firm state and stance can "think" about intensification. A stage must first become firm in order to be a staging ground for another.

> Im Wirklichen handelt es sich gleichnotwendig um Erhaltung *und* Steigerung; denn damit der Wille zur Macht als Übermächtigung eine Stufe ubersteigen kann, muß diese Stufe nicht nur erreicht, sie muß auch inne-ja sogar *machtend* festgehalten werden, anders könnte die *Über*mächtigung keine *Über*mächtigung sein. Nur was in sich bereits einen festen Bestand und Stand hat, kann an Steigerung "denken." Eine Stufe muß zuerts in sich fest geworden sein, damit auf ihr aufgestuft werden kann. (*N* II, 103)

Heidegger rephrases this many times (*N* II, 105f; also *N* II, 324), each time reformulating the fundamental idea that the will to power is in its essence a complex knot:

> The reality that is determined as real by the will to power is precisely an interweaving of perspectives and value-positings, a formation "of a complex nature", the reason is that the will to power is itself essentially complex

> Das durch den Willen zur Macht in seiner Wirklichkeit bestimmte Wirkliche ist jeweils eine Verflechtung von Perspektiven und Wertsetzungen, ein Gebilde "komplexer Art"; dies aber deshalb, weil der Wille zur Macht selbst komplexen Wesens ist. (*N* II, 105).

The essense of the will to power is a "komplexe Einheit" or "ein Verflochtenes" (*N* II, 105f).

This dialectic within the will is important since the model that Heidegger proposes for understanding the history of Being and thinking, which I sketched as concentric circles, had posited an *un*dialectical opposition between the will and Being (thinking). A more valuable movement is now guaranteed, however, by reintroducing the internal dialectic of the will, the simultaneity of self-maintenance and self-overcoming, of heightening the self's character by going beyond the self affectively, etc. One way of seeing why this dialectical view is necessary is to wonder why the high point of the will (Nietzsche), as *Seinsvergessenheit,* can lead to anything positive? We can approach this by asking with Heidegger whether metaphysics/nihilism can be overcome. Here too we encounter the reified rhetoric of the history of Being. But a clearer answer lies in the concept of the will that carries this history. Heidegger considers the phenomenon of the "Überwindung der Metaphysik" (or "des Nihilismus") with greatest force in the lectures from 1945–46. Given the self-destructive, disastrous "triumph of the will" in those years his descriptions have a special power that captures the only kind of hope one could generate, namely the thought that perhaps the darkest hour contains the possibility of a radical alternative (or openness to a new question). In terms of metaphysics, the high point (low point) is familiar: "The positing of Being as a value posited by the will to power is only the last step of modern metaphysics, according to which Being only comes into appearance as will" ("Die Vorsetzung des Seins als eines vom Willen zur Macht gesetzten Wertes ist nur der letzte Schritt der neuzeitlichen Metaphysik, in der das Sein als der Wille zur Erscheinung kommt"; *N* II, 379). The effect is that all being is objectified (through *Vergegenständlichung*) vis-à-vis "the exclusive self-willing of the will" ("das ausschließliche Sichwollen seines Willens"; *N* II, 378) and man enters into a literally mad race to ensure himself of the certainty of his knowledge—mad, because the very tools he would use undermine his effort. Indeed, in this effort man—often in the most brutal and horrifying ways—becomes objectified. Being, as the openness within which this domination of being occurs, is "left out" as openness. Nietzsche, then, as the supposed overcomer of nihilism, is at the same time its high point:

> The supposed overcoming of nihilism erects first the domination of the absolute omission of the non-appearance of Being itself for the sake of being in the manner of a value-positing will to power. By its withdrawal, which is at the same time the relation to being, as the appearance of "Being," Being itself gives itself over to the will to power, as which being appears to reign before and over all Being.

> Die vermeintliche Überwindung des Nihilismus errichtet allererst die Herrschaft der unbedingten Auslassung des Ausbleibens des Seins selbst zugunsten des Seienden von der Art des wertsetzenden Willens zur Macht. Durch seinen Entzug, der gleichwohl der Bezug zum Seienden bleibt, als welches "das Sein" erscheint, läßt sich das Sein selbst in den Willen zur Macht los, als welcher das Seiende vor und über allem Sein zu walten scheint. (*N* II, 375f)

Thanks to the inherent dialectic within willing, the absolutization of the reality of the will (i.e., the domination of "reality" as the *Wirklichkeit* of the interaction of subject and object) is the "essential unity of nihilism" ("Wesenseinheit des Nihilismus"; *N* II, 376) that is governed by a basic "Unterschied"—and this internal differentiation makes for the continuation of history and the potential end to the domination of metaphysics. In terms of the history of nihilism, i.e., the history which *is* nihilism, the difference in the will is essential, for if that is lost, then there is no hope for *Überwindung*. The high point of nihilism is, we have seen, the eclipsing of Being by being. This is the point where the *Wesenseinheit* of nihilism is reached. But this point will only be overcome in turn thanks to the difference that reigns within the unity of nihilism: "the difference between the proper and the im-proper that reigns within the essential unity of nihilism" ("der in der Wesenseinheit des Nihilismus waltende Unterschied des Uneigentlichen und Eigentlichen"; *N* II, 377). This difference exists because the unity of nihilism is, as we have seen, the unity of metaphysics, which is the unity of the history of Being as the will to power—and the unity of the will is dialectically split. That is, the end of Nihilismus is the *Wesenseinheit* of the domination of the will, and yet the will is *not* fundamentally *einheitlich,* and so its domination "overcomes itself"—essentially. Thus, the extreme unity of nihilism must be passed through, i.e., this will to power experienced, as a *Zwischenzustand* (*N* II, 81). It is because the will goes beyond itself that the unity it has attained is also overcome.

What all this shows is that a fragile dialectic revolving around the activity of willing permeated Heidegger's thought during the years he dealt with Nietzsche. The dialectic maintained a simultaneity of *Einheit* and *Unterschied.* The dialectic seems so "fragile" because there is a consistent foregrounding of *Einheit* (which Derrida points out), and it is only by uncovering what that unity is based on (the will) that we can maintain the dialectical tension.[59]

The *Gleichursprünglichkeit* (or in the terms from Derrida's *Of Spirit,* the "origin-heterogeneous") of unity and fragmentation, self-willing and self-overcoming, in the will has major hermeneutic implications. After all, Heidegger is (as we all are) striving to understand someone's (Nietzsche's) "Denkwillen" and so just as there are tensions between Being and Will (ontology and metaphysics), so too for Heidegger's hermeneutic there are tensions between thinking and willing. The goal now, in conclusion, is to return to the conception of understanding/interpretation with which we began. Gadamer uses Heidegger as a point of departure by stressing the nature of man's *Dasein* as the unfolding of understanding. But for Heidegger, that process is linked with willing and its dialectic. Therefore, understanding must be grasped in essence as *dialectical,* like willing. What we need to consider is the relationship between thought and will to see if we can work around the impasse of oppositions like thought (spirit) and letter by focusing on the dialectic within thought conceived of as willing. The problem with Heidegger will be that he conceives this dialectic and then still wants to leave will behind for thought and Being. Gadamer suffers from this, as does Derrida from its deconstruction.

We can approach this question of a complex willing by turning to the dialogue by Heidegger on *Gelassenheit,* which was written 1944–45.

This exchange between a "seeker/researcher" ("Forscher"), a "scholar" ("Gelehrter"), and a "teacher" ("Lehrer") reworks much of the interpretation of Nietzsche in yet a different set of Heideggerian terms. What we see in it is both the powerful ambiguity (dialectic) Heidegger can get from the concept of the will, and his resistance to that ambiguity for the sake of "Thought." It opens with reflections on a paradox, namely how could one best understand the *essence* of man by turning away from man? The unraveling of the paradox involves the distinction between thinking and willing. If man's essence, and the understanding of it, both involve thinking, but man has traditionally defined himself and his thought in terms of willing (as we saw above, the connection between willing and *vor-stellen*), then a tension has been set up between thinking and willing.[60] Heidegger formulates this tension by seeing thinking as the willing of nonwilling: "ich will das Nicht-Wollen" (*G,* 30). Inhering in this statement is an ambiguity: on the one hand the entire statement is permeated with willing (either "positive" or "negative"), while on the other, nonwilling can be seen as that "which simply remains beyond the sphere of any kind of willing" ("was schlechthin außerhalb jeder Art von Willen bleibt"; *G,* 30).

Here Heidegger makes a crucial turn that has consequences for his ontology and hermeneutics. In order to provide an example of what this paradoxical thinking would be like, the conversationalists discuss briefly both the effects of the oncoming night, "which presses them to gather themselves, without applying force" ("die zur Sammlung zwingt, ohne Gewalt anzuwenden") and the sense of following "the unassuming lead that takes us, in this conversation, by the hand, or more properly speaking, by the word" ("dem unscheinbaren Geleit, das uns in diesem Gespräch an die Hand, oder richtiger gesagt, beim Wort nimmt"; *G,* 31f).[61] What is so important here is that Heidegger begins by seeing these peculiar activities as part of the ambiguity of the will—e.g., the fact that the will could will its own dissolution, whereby it also maintains itself in its self-negating willing—but then shifts the ground to the term "Gelassenheit" (calmness, composure). The goal of the thinker, for Heidegger, is to establish an openness, to be "gelassen," whereby one is beyond even the desire "to actively abandon the will" ("sich des Willens zu entwöhnen"; *G,* 32), because *Gelassenheit does not* belong to the sphere of the will" ("*nicht* in den Bereich des Willens gehört"; *G,* 33). To the extent that *Gelassenheit* is thought within the sphere of the will it becomes mere "mysticism," i.e., the individual will is replaced by a giving oneself over to the divine will.

Heidegger is now in a fundamental bind. The relationship between willing and thinking has been mapped out in a brilliant way that takes into account the contradictory tradition culminating in Nietzsche. That is, the will can maintain a dialectical duality that opens it up to other forms of experience, that makes it the moving ground of experience. And yet, Heidegger at the same time wants to move beyond the dialectical interpretation of the will. When the *Forscher* says: "I can't imagine, with the best of wills, this essence of thinking (as *Gelassenheit*)" ("Ich kann mir dieses Wesens des Denkens [als Gelassenheit] mit dem besten Willen nicht vorstellen"), the *Lehrer* responds: "Precisely because this best of wills and your mode of thinking by imagination prevent you" ("Weil gerade dieser beste Wille und die Art Ihres Denkens als Vorstellen Sie daran hindern"; *G,* 34). In this way there is no possibility of the "good will" (indeed even the "best will") as the force that provides the condition for understanding. Here we see how Heidegger (problematically) would leave behind even the best interpretation of will for another kind of thinking.

The middle third of the dialogue is the attempt to give names to the essence of this thinking.[62] Spatial imagery dominates the dialogue as Heidegger attempts to characterize the openness *within which* the experience of objects as objects could even occur. Using the phenomenological subject (which could also be the will to power) as the starting point, he shows how the construction of a world outwards to the horizons of our perception still does not grasp the "other side" of experience, i.e., the way the horizon has a "beyond" that continually opens up or withdraws in order to "make the space" of our world possible. The movement is what he here calls the *Gegnet,* which we might consider a kind of encounter (*Entgegenkommen*) that opens up a space (*Gegend*). This is a reworking of the history of nihilism and subjectivity we saw in the Nietzsche essays and can be represented graphically:

subject Being the *Gegnet*

subject Being the *Gegnet*

encounter at horizon:
"toward subject" "toward Being"
willing unwilling

This ontological analysis has great power and yet we must return, as Heidegger does, to the problem raised by the *Forscher:* "The transition from willing to *Gelassenheit* appears to me to be the difficult point" ("Der Übergang aus dem Wollen in die Gelassenheit scheint mir das Schwierige zu sein"; *G,* 33). The *Lehrer* characterizes the relation of man to the openness of Being in the paradoxical terms that opened the essay: "Whenever we let ourselves in to a *Gelassenheit* vis-à-vis the encounter, we are wanting not to will or willing non-willing" ("Wenn wir uns auf die Gelassenheit zur Gegnet einlassen, wollen wir das Nicht-Wollen"; *G,* 57). The *Forscher* gives this an interpretation that is ripe for deconstructive analysis. He implies that the will might indeed then be necessary to initiate *Gelassenheit,* but once there it is removed *without a trace.* He says:

> *Gelassenheit* is indeed a letting oneself loose from the mode of transcendental representation and thus a turning away from willing the horizon. This turning away does not come from a willing, although the impulse to this letting oneself into the belonging to the encounter requires a trace of willing, a trace that disappears however in giving oneself over to it and is fully erased in one's *Gelassenheit.*

> Die Gelassenheit ist in der Tat das Sichloslassen aus dem transzendentalen Vorstellen und so ein Absehen vom Wollen des Horizontes. Dieses Absehen kommt nicht mehr aus einem Wollen, es sei denn, der Anlaß zum Sicheinlassen in die Zugehörigkeit zur Gegnet bedürfe einer Spur des Wollens, welche Spur jedoch im Sicheinlassen verschwindet und vollends in der Gelassenheit ausgelöscht ist. (*G,* 57)

The opposition would of course be impossible to maintain and one has to wonder whether Heidegger cannot hear his own failed oppositions in the words of this younger partner. The question is, does/can Heidegger also offer another interpretation?

I think the notion of *Gelassenheit* as the willing of nonwilling can be read differently, and that even Heidegger attempts this. This *could* mean, from a fully dialectical interpretation of the will, that the will contains that unique ability to turn against itself and maintain itself at the same time. The will, as the condition of the individual to be both present to itself and engaged constantly in the movement of self-overcoming, allows us to begin with the point of phenomenological experience even as it reminds us that this experience always involves an openness to otherness. We could see this, as Heidegger implies, in the term *Entschlossenheit,* which has both the decisiveness of the will and its necessary openness, without which decisiveness would be impossible. The concept of *Entschlossenheit* is linked by the *Lehrer* to that of "stamina" ("Ausdauer"), which, as we have also seen in Nietzsche, does not just mean the insistence of the will to persist actively in its execution but also the temporal openness and calm to see something through to its end. In this reading, the "good will" would be the essential condition for all thinking, understanding, and *Welterschließung.* It would not be a will reduced to the metaphysics of the subject because its very definition brings an openness to otherness, for its self-presence is guaranteed only by constant movements of self-negation. Thus, the *Forscher* reformulates

Gelassenheit as that "which could correspond to the highest will and yet may not" ("was dem höchsten Willen entsprechen könnte und es doch nicht dürfte"; *G*, 59).[63]

The problem comes in, as Derrida has pointed out, when Heidegger takes the ontological difference to mean that there is something else *besides* (or beyond) the back and forth between unity and fragmentation, between the opening and closing of interpretation. In Heidegger's hermeneutics, this something else besides the dialectical movement of willing would be "thinking." Here, then, we could agree with Derrida that Nietzsche does "go beyond" Heidegger—but for different reasons than Derrida says. The opposition is not between Heidegger's unity (*Geist*) and Nietzsche's dissemination (name, letter), but between Heidegger's desire to escape the dialectic of unity and fragmentation (by means of "thinking Being") and Nietzsche's insistence on the (good/bad) will to interpretation.[64] The problems raised at the end of *Gelassenheit* all have to do with Heidegger's desire to remove the will, even the trace of the will, from the realm of thought. Gadamer is therefore not to be criticized for bringing the will back into the process of interpretation. And hermeneutics should not shy away from stressing the richness of that category. On the contrary: its dialectic prevents the collapse of hermeneutics into a metaphysics of "unity of meaning" (*Sinneseinheit*). Derrida is right to point out that the "good will" is not so "gelassen" as Heidegger and Gadamer would imply. But he certainly can and should not criticize the reintroduction of will *as such*, as if introducing the will meant a reduction to the metaphysics of subjectivity. Precisely the refusal to eliminate the trace of the will in thought and interpretation is what keeps the dialectic of understanding going. Like Heidegger, *both* Gadamer *and* Derrida, in different ways, work with but do not fulfill the dialectic of the will to interpretation. By reading their work together, we can reconstruct the dialectic of the will.

Conclusion

A Dialectical Model of Agency and the Will of Theory

(Feminism, Queer Theory, Nationalism)

I begin this conclusion with a brief but important statement of what the preceding book was *not* meant to be, namely a grounding or a theory of the will as a necessary propedeutic to any future discussions on freedom, power, or understanding. That is, I do not think that before one can do any work in areas of, say, political or literary theory, one must first have a "foundation" in the theory of the will, which I would claim to have provided. Rather, I would hope that my book would be read in a more "late-Wittgensteinian" spirit. By this I mean that the analyses of the dialectics of the will that I have presented are intended more as a clarification of the way I think the word has been used in a very long philosophical tradition so that, to the extent that anyone continues thinking in this tradition (and who of us cannot at least to some extent?), we can see how such thinking unfolds in the patterns carved out already. To see those patterns as inherently dialectical might help us avoid blind alleys, which for me take the form of metaphysical interpretations, i.e., attempts to "solve" some complex issue by coming down definitively on one side or the other (or in Hegelian terms, by fixing upon a partial determination). My hope would be that as readers turn to past and contemporary works that raise questions concerning human agency (especially in relation to freedom, power, and understanding), the analyses I have presented of the oppositions contained within willing can show the lasting and beneficial effects of dialectical thinking. In the readings of passages from contemporary theory that I offer below, I use the dialectics of the will to make explicit and more effective arguments about agency in work on feminism, queer theory, and nationalism.

One model of the kind of work I have in mind here is Eve Kosofsky Sedgwick's brilliant analyses of the binarisms that inform the discourse of modernity. She argues that as we look at discourses around sexuality, we see that from the nineteenth century on they are organized around basic binarisms: homo- vs. hetero-, universalizing vs. minoritizing, etc. Her point is not to provide a new theory, nor to "decide" the issue (the way constructionists and essentialists attempt to do), but, rather, to reveal the many places in which these binarisms have structured our discourses of the past so that we understand their continued effects in the present. It is also not by chance that she has done recent work on the will.[1]

I have argued that the dialectical structure of willing, which takes many forms throughout the history of Western theories of agency, is central to the philosophies of major German thinkers—Kant, Nietzsche, Heidegger. Moreover, I argued that more recent responses to these philosophies engage in often polemical debates because each respondent pursues only partial determinants of the dialectic, i.e., isolated poles, rather than the mutual interdependency of the oppositions. In the case of the role of willing in the conception of freedom, we saw that the later thought of Adorno and Lacan, from different perspectives, brought out dialectical possibilities inherent in Kant's ethics. More precisely, we saw how despite a tendency on the part of Adorno (and Horkheimer) and Lacan to offer a blanket critique of Kant because of a purported rationalist one-sidedness, they develop richer readings of the will as the "cause" of desire and freedom. That cause does guarantee the autonomy of human agency, but not because it exists like a metaphysical entity, a "little agent within the agent." Rather, the cause or special "thing" that makes human willing possible is precisely a non-thing, an "empty place" (*ein leerer Platz*), a moment of negativity in the self that makes the self irreducible to any chain of external causes.

In chapter 2, I was able to demonstrate a dialectical understanding of power in the concept of the *will* to power formulated by Nietzsche, a dialectic that came more clearly into focus in contrast to Foucault's and Habermas's failure to work it out. Contemporary thought in many disciplines has been obsessed with analyzing, unmasking, and criticizing "power" in all areas of social and private life. And Foucault has contributed more than most to this significant and politically charged enterprise. But as Habermas has argued, it becomes ultimately self-defeating (politically and conceptually) to develop an understanding of power that stresses supraindividual forces at the expense of individual agency, the irrational at the expense of the rational, the empirical (positivistic) at the expense of the transcendental, or the metaphysical at the expense of the concrete.[2] Although Habermas's argument is in principle absolutely right in my view, he mistakenly traces that self-defeating position back to Nietzsche. I have presented a different reading of Nietzsche according to which his concept of the "will to power" insistently strives to maintain the dialectical tensions between the supraindividual and the individual, the irrational and the rational, the empirical and the transcendental. Nietzsche saw that willing, unique among human activities, thrives on the dialectic that he often summarized in the concept of "self-overcoming." By insisting on the *will* in the "will to power," Nietzsche drew on the historical dialectics we traced out in chapter 1. And by reading this dialectic back through Nietzsche into Foucault, we see how he avoids the "aporias of theories of power" that Habermas attributes to him and in fact approaches a "critical theory" of the will.

Finally, we have seen how the will is indispensable to a rich conception of understanding and interpretation. Derrida brings this out polemically in his response to Gadamer in Paris, drawing attention to what might seem to be a passing reference to the "good will" necessary, according to hermeneutics, for the success of any act of understanding. And Gadamer, far from rejecting Derrida's focus on this "detail," agrees with the fundamental significance of good will to interpretation. But what makes the "dialogue" between Derrida and Gadamer so tantalizing and yet "impossible" is the fact that they approach this central place of the will in/to understanding from opposite directions, never seeing the necessity to think these opposites *together.* In particular, Derrida, drawing on Nietzsche in contrast to Heidegger, brings out the fragmentary and fragmenting force of the will (to power). Gadamer, on the contrary, relies on Heidegger for his irrefutable argument concerning the basic unity and unifying force of one's will to understand, and to make oneself understood by, another human being. By going a step beyond Derrida's and Gadamer's readings of Heidegger, however, we can arrive at not an either/or-structure (either fragmentary or unifying) but the *coincidentia oppositorum* that lies at the heart of the will.

These readings have striven therefore to illuminate conceptions of agency in theories that form the foundations of much contemporary thought. I hope that a clearer image of the conceptions of agency has emerged at the heart of these thinkers. One gains a fuller and more direct understanding of both Adorno and Lacan, for example, when one sees them searching for a "dialectical determination of the will." Certainly both have rejected the Cartesian subject, but not a concept of the individual agent at whose center we find a paradoxically active lack or negativity. Likewise, Foucault and Habermas seem to speak to each other more directly once the rattling of the sabers over "power" gives way to the quieter, less developed concept of the social, willing, agent. And Derrida and Gadamer might never in reality come closer to each other than their "impossible debate"; and yet, we can see them approaching the same dialectical phenomenon—the will to understand, the *vouloir dire*—from the opposing directions of the fragmenting letter and the unifying spirit. In addition, I hope to have shown the reasons why in some cases those conceptions were handicapped by a lack of dialectical rigor.

Out of these interactions, a model of willing emerges that can be abstracted into general terms before it is applied to a limited set of theoretical positions on feminism, queer theory, and nationalism. Our willing draws us in two directions: toward a radical individuality of self-relation and toward some Other that "establishes" us. As opposed to philosophies of subjectivity and self-reflection, a theory of willing accounts for the duality of our being, our "wanting" that says so much about ourselves by indicating how our inner desire is connected to what is outside of us. To say that "I am what I want" captures our deep sense that we are unique and possess a kind of autonomy, but an odd autonomy that necessarily thrusts us on otherness in ways that characterize us as individuals. Kierkegaard writes of this dual basis of our ethical being: "The human self is such a derived, established relation, a relation that relates itself to itself and in relating itself to itself relates itself to another."[3] He furthermore shows how each mode of willing (viz. self-relation and relating to another) is in a sense radically incomplete vis-à-vis the possibility of the other (i.e., each stands in a dialectical relation to the other), so that insistence on either one alone (on either the self or dependence on another) leads a person to a different form of despair. That is, given our individuality (my wanting is what *I* want), despair can arise from "not willing to be oneself," i.e., "to will to do away with oneself"; and conversely, because we ultimately are not our own ground, despair can also arise from "will[ing] [only] to be oneself," i.e., from failing to give over one's willing to the relation *in which* one is established and instead feeling driven to chase without rest after one's individual self (à la Kant and Sade). An ethics that accounts for our willing, then, is neither egoistical (based on a driving, self-sustaining ego) nor objectivist (based on the power of objects), since the will occupies the space where, at the limits of ourselves, these two spheres intersect.

I turn now to some contemporary theoretical debates in which a more nuanced, historically grounded, and dialectical concept of willing would be useful in developing an approach to agency. My aim here is merely to point the way to more extensive research projects that would unearth and develop the role of willing in these theoretical directions.

First, let us consider feminism. I begin with two quotations from an essay written in 1989 by the feminist political scientist and philosopher Alison Jaggar. The fact that the essay was reprinted unchanged in 1994 leads me to believe that the project she lays out for feminist thinkers of the 1990s has still not been completed—even at the end of the decade. She writes:

> It is evident that a central concern for feminist ethics in the nineties must be to develop ways of thinking about moral subjects that are sensitive both to their concreteness, inevitable particularity and unique specificity, expressed in part through their relations with specific historical communities, and to their intrinsic and common value, the ideal expressed in Enlightenment claims about common humanity, equality and impartiality.

And she continues: "Feminist ethics in the nineties must find ways of conceptualizing moral agency, choice and consent that are compatible with the feminist recognition of the gradual process of moral development, the gendered social construction of the psyche, and the historical constraints on our options."[4] I would reformulate Jaggar's statements to read: "Feminism needs a will of its own, one based on a reformulation of traditional concepts. Feminism need not abandon those concepts because, read through feminism, they emerge as dialectical and hence useful for feminism."

In this undertaking I join others working in the area of feminist ethics. For example, Jean Grimshaw who sees the need to criticize the "humanist paradigm" of selfhood for the sake of a new "dialectic": "There is no authentic or unified 'original' self which can simply be recovered or discovered as the source of 'autonomous' actions. But we are often faced with the experienced need to make 'sense' of our lives and our feelings and goals, to relate confused fragments of ourselves into something that seems more coherent and of which we feel more in control."[5] However, whereas she turns to psychoanalysis to get a handle on this dialectic—a reasonable choice given the interplay of reason and desire, self-knowledge and self-deception, fantasy and social reality that permeates both psychoanalysis and Grimshaw's conception of selfhood—I would stress the productiveness of considering a wider range of theories of human willing. The dialectic inherent in willing has the advantage of addressing fundamental issues of human experience, from ethics and politics to phenomena of creativity.[6]

A likely objection that might arise at this point would be the following: But is the will not a hopelessly masculinist concept—if not burdened by downright *machismo*—and thus the very opposite of what feminist ethics has or needs? This impression gains strength from various quarters. For those who espouse some variation of the "ethic of care," for example, the great contribution that women and feminists have made and can make to the formulation of an alternative moral reasoning depends on turning away from a model of the independently willing person (man).[7] One could think of Gilligan and others implicitly formulating their views of care and connectedness as a response to traditional views according to which the goal of moral development is a firmer, more autonomous, principle-oriented will. And even if one does not embrace the controversial views that have grown out of Gilligan, one will find over and over again, wherever the concept of the will is mentioned, a clear association with notions long since discarded as "phallogocentric." Judith Butler, for example, clearly associates the will with the false view of a kind of "self-within-or-beneath-the-self," an independent entity that both is me at the deepest level and *chooses* for me my courses of action.[8] This is why one of the more common critical epithets one finds connected to the will is the implicitly male-oriented "metaphysics of subjectivity," always played off against a feminist deconstruction of autonomous agency.

My point is not to dismiss those critiques of traditional theories of agency. On the contrary, my work is certainly a part of this movement of critique. However, they emerge from a *limited* reading of the tradition and they could be made stronger by working out dialectical possibilities rather than by merely rejecting a position as masculinist. We see an example of this in Paul Benson's essay, "Feminist Second Thoughts About Free Agency," which correctly stresses that feminism has not been interested in "liberal" notions of agency that are nonrelational, non-normative, and overly hierarchical,[9] and yet problematically identifies these positions with a view of the will (probably by association with that problematic side of Kant we explored in chapter 2) rather than considering that the legacy of the long history of Western theorizing on the will is conflicted, split, rich, and hybridized precisely in the way that feminism calls for.[10] This can be read two ways: On the one hand, it means that feminism can appropriate such a view; but on the other, it also means that the tradition of philosophizing the will has *always already* been "feminized" in the way that nonfeminists (and many feminists) have not recognized. What, then, are some consequences for feminist theory and practice of introducing such a dialectial conception of willing? Let us consider some issues facing feminist theory.

Feminist ethics and legal theory cannot do without reflections on the will. Because the will has been at the center of discussions on ethics, law, and even politics throughout the Western tradition, it is hard to imagine analyzing notions of responsibility, freedom, action, or accountability without an implicit or explicit sense of willing agency. Nonetheless, contemporary theories commonly attempt to think through these issues while circumventing a concrete and traditional notion of willing. Drucilla Cornell serves as one example among many. Her argument in *Beyond Accommodation: Ethical Feminism, Deconstruction, and the Law* delineates an "ethical feminism" that accounts for the paradoxes of agency. Near the end of the book, she summarizes the call for a mimetic agency that would be responsible for the process of redefining gender identities:

> Gender identity is a prison for both sexes, but given "the reality" of masculine privilege, the two genders do not suffer the same entrapment. As a result, *mimesis* tells us how to re-evolve with the definitions of the feminine. In that sense, it is explicitly ethical. The feminine is not an established set of properties of the female. The feminine, as continually remetaphorized, does not demand that we reinstate a unified, identifiable subject, Woman. The feminine, through *mimesis,* is an affirmation, a valuation, but even so, is not a traditional, ethical concept that would identify the good of Woman with her fundamental properties. This approach to the truth of Woman . . . is ethical.

> Yet the affirmation I offer, as an affirmation, as valuation, is also ethical in that
> it recognizes the value of the Other of sexual difference. This is why I have
> adopted the expression "ethical feminism."[11]

This complicated passage could, with the aid of the conceptual tools I have
elaborated, be translated as follows: Feminism is ethical because it has a will
that is capable of initiating a new series of values out of the very real (and
constraining) ones that come before. This new series is open to the future
and open to others. Such a will is not in pursuit of (or determined by) some
abstract "Good" but is nonetheless essentially a "good will" because of this
openness. Thus, it gains a normative status, since, as Kant said, "good will"
is the only thing that there can never be too much of. "Ethical feminism,"
therefore, plays out the dialectics of willing.

Another brief example of a place where feminist ethics, striving
for liberation from or subversion of limiting gender identities, calls forth
(generally by circumlocution) a rich concept of willing is Luce Irigaray's
An Ethics of Sexual Difference. In particular, her discussion of Spinoza's
analysis of a special kind of "causality" in humanity is couched in the
paradoxical terms of passivity and activity, perception *and* conception,
freedom *and* necessity. She writes:

> What would man and woman have in common? Both conception and percep-
> tion. *Both*. And without any hierarchy between the two. Both would have the
> capacity to perceive and conceive. *To suffer and to be active*. To suffer the
> self and to understand the self. To receive the self and to envelop the self.
> Becoming more open because of the freedom of each, male and female. Since
> freedom and necessity are correlated. With each giving the other necessity and
> freedom. In self, for self, and for the other.[12]

The will, as we have seen, traditionally plays the role of this common
element. It is gender neutral, internally split (in both men and women), and
historically grounded (with its vicissitudes of individual and supraindividual,
genderized developments).[13]

This appeal to the will has the benefit of allowing us to use a term
that is very much part of our common way of viewing ourselves as agents.
We thereby avoid the danger that, in Rosi Braidotti's words, "the question
of the deconstruction of phallo-logocentrism could be disconnected from
the concrete changes taking place in women's lives."[14] We can reconnect
feminist deconstructions with how women (and men) *talk* about their lives.
People typically express a strong sense that they are both free and not-free,
that they want and do not want things, that they are fundamentally split in
their desires even as they are consistent in character, and that they expect
themselves and others to express specific acts of (relatively autonomous)
will precisely in the midst of (and against) recognized determining forces.

That is, although I am convinced of the power of "high theory" to illuminate phenomena, the tradition of theorizing the will gets at many of the same things more accessibly by echoing the formulations we commonly use. Perhaps the most obvious example is the necessary appeal made in so many feminist discussions (especially around rape and abortion) to the notion of not being forced to do something "against one's will."[15] Although most feminists would reject the notion of the "autonomous subject," the appeal to the will appears time and again. I think we can accept its fundamental role once we recognize the "will" that needs to be protected can be collapsed neither into a "subject" nor into the objectivized body, but, rather, is the discursively and relationally embedded agent. Thus, the will against which power cannot be illegitimately asserted is complicated by its own desires and heteronomy.

Finally, recalling the quotes from Jaggar that introduced this section, I would stress that feminism needs to account for agency generally, and the will helps us do so in a way that makes the approach to a feminist agency less of a choice between a "touchy-feely" notion of care (maternal) versus a concept of aggressive, autonomous, male-oriented action. Consider, for example, the effect that a more dialectical notion of willing could have on Simone de Beauvoir's powerful, yet flawed "manifesto," *The Second Sex*. By focusing on a conception of *consciousness* (as opposed to willing), which she sets up synecdochically to stand for the entire human being, Beauvoir posits a choice between immanence as the present state of woman and transcendence as the present possibility for men and the hopeful future of women. She writes:

> The world does not seem to woman "an assemblage of implements" inter-mediate between her will and her goals . . . it is something obstinately resis-tant, unconquerable. . . . Woman's mentality perpetuates that of agricultural civilizations which worshipped the magic powers of the land: she believes in magic. Her passive eroticism makes desire seem to her not will and aggression but an attraction akin to that which causes the divining rod to dip. . . . [S]he [is] ignorant of what constitutes a true action, capable of changing the face of the world.[16]

The contrast is radical: active vs. passive, consciousness vs. objects, man vs. woman. In her words: "A free individual blames only himself for his failures, he assumes responsibility for them; but everything happens to women through the agency of others, and therefore these others are responsible for her woes" (674). Beauvoir's mistake is to view as opposition and choice—immanence *or* transcendence, passivity *or* activity, objecthood *or* consciousness—what in terms of human willing is inherently dialectical. Even worse, she tends to put "will" on the one side (male, aggressive, active). Her moving call—"Let but the future be open to her, and she will no longer be compelled to linger in the present" (672)—plays out a temporality that marks human willing in all its contradiction, and her dichotomous thinking would benefit from an interpretation that highlights the inherent dialectic of the will.[17]

To reintroduce a concept of will into feminism—and I stress *reintro-*duce since it is already there as an unexploited legacy of a dead masculinist tradition—would make it possible develop a richer dialectic of agency and freedom.

Concerning the role that a dialectical conception of willing could play in queer theory, I begin with a quote from Michael Warner: "Queerness . . . bears a different relation to liberal logics of choice and will, as well as to moral languages of leadership and community, in ways that continually pose problems both in everyday life and in contexts of civil rights."[18] I could not agree more that the "queering of the will" Warner points to here can be useful in reconceptualizing the subject of ethics and politics for a postmodernist feminism and antihomophobic praxis. Because modern and postmodern debates about sexuality, especially male homosexual identity, have been inseparable from debates about the will, and because those debates are thoroughly permeated by the radical ambivalence inherent in the traditional concept of the will, by passing through these debates we could see how the concept of the will is, in fact, "queerer" than we had thought and in that way more useful than we had thought as the basis of a liberatory conception of sexual agency.[19]

To develop a richer understanding of the interrelationship between sexuality and agency around the will, we would have to tie together three argumentative strands, each one involving conflicting historical and concep-tual phenomena: (1) the double configuration of same-sex desire as either "perverse" or merely a "diverse" form of desire as such (rhyme borrowed from a recent paper by Gayle Rubin);[20] (2) the tensions that exist between lesbian and gay studies as a kind of "identity politics" and queer theory as a radical questioning of "normal," indeed all, identity and politics; and (3) the two modes of agency, commonly thought of as modernist (or Enlightenment) and postmodernist (deconstructive), that have conceived of human freedom very differently in terms of either autonomy or heteronomy.

My point is that these three strands are tied together by the concept of the will. The will lies on the line of each of the three argumentative strands, thereby forming the common point of intersection as follows: (1) It played a major role in the history of (homo)sexuality as that which, in the nineteenth century, bore sexual desire, that is, it is what was thought to have taken a "turn" for the worse in "perversity"; but it also contains a radical ambivalence—as good and bad will, as control or choice and impulsive drive, as unifying character and fragmenting senses—which lays the foundation for a richer, more "diverse" understanding of desire. The will helps us understand how the very notion of "perverse" sexuality arose and how human desire is inherently "diverse." (2) Lesbian/Gay studies and queer theory can be said to have their roots in these two differing conceptions of sexual will and desire. Where the former tends to be organized around a notion of "identity," the latter has challenged the stability of all identity—and in both cases, that "identity" rests on the generally implicit understanding of willing and/or unwilling sex. Each of these directions in theory and institutional politics appeals, implicitly, to a different facet of willing—its unifying, identity-granting or its disseminating, coalitional force. (3) If the Enlightenment introduced an ethics and politics based on the autonomous subject and its critics, beginning perhaps with Schelling and Hegel and culminating with Nietzsche, strove to embed that subject within structures of signification and power (that is, unmask it as subjected), the question still remains how to redefine agency such that a different ethics and politics will be possible. The concept of the will, much maligned and read reductively by both its Enlightenment proponents and postmodern debunkers, can be resuscitated if embraced dialectically and often read against the grain in all its ambivalence and contradictoriness. A (gay) liberation politics can thus appeal to an Enlightenment legacy on the will that avoids both voluntarism and determinism.

Putting these three strands together permits us to relate theoretical movements (like lesbian/gay studies, queer theory, and feminism) dialectically and to show the inherent (and "productive") sexual ambivalence within the will as the key concept of ethical and political agency. To demonstrate in this way that the will is and has been "queer" is to "think sexuality" (to echo Gayle Rubin's essay, "Thinking Sex") in terms of the will, and to think the will in terms of the history of sexuality. We thereby "do justice" to the historical formations of a major concept concerning agency and to its dialectical richness. With this reformulated concept of the will, in all its queerness, we can approach agency, ethics, and politics anew, at the same time creating bridges between feminism and the study of sexuality (a gap of varying size since the early 1980s).

Turning to a third area of contemporary theory where a richer understanding of the will could provide a useful analytical tool, I will briefly address two approaches to nationalism. In the first, I offer just one way of using the will, through a contrast between Hegel and Nietzsche, to rethink the concept of the nation itself;[21] in the second, I mention one discussion that revolves around the "subject" of the nation.

For centuries, Western thought has modeled collective politics on conceptions of the individual. The link between the individual and the collective generally has occurred at the nodal point of the concept of the "will." This occurs to the present day, as can be seen in such notions as the "political will" of the people, nation, etc.[22] In particular, Hegel's *Philosophie der Rechts,* in locating the will at the center of his analysis and in placing the nation-state as the culmination of the political or social development of the will, explicitly conceived of the state in terms of a will engaged, like the individual self-consciousness, in a master/slave relation struggling for recognition with other nations. Nietzsche, however, strove, as we have seen, throughout his entire philosophical oeuvre to reconceptualize the traditional will in terms of his own notion of "will to power." In so doing, he simultaneously redefined the terms of political agency, since the will to power is *not* an individualized, self-identical entity modeled on a self-consciousness that engages in struggles with some other likewise self-contained individuals, but, rather, an internally self-differentiating force always experiencing affective interactions and hence implicated by otherness.[23] A different conception of the state and nation follows from this view. Nietzsche's attacks against the new German nation-state are thus central to his thought and can be best understood in terms of his philosophy of the will to power as an alternative way of conceiving unstable individual and collective identity (which nonetheless has agency). He therefore can offer us a model for a politics beyond the formation of nation states out of wars for recognition, a politics that can account better for social structures that accept *within* themselves radical diversity.[24]

In claiming that we can understand the formation of nations around a notion of the common "will," I need to make clear that I do not see this as celebrating a "triumph of the will" in a protofascist way. On the contrary. Since, as I have argued, the will contains within it a vital tension between the individual and the supraindividual, the "will of a nation" ought likewise to be understood in its dialectical richness. For all the forces that both historically and conceptually grant that will a unifying effect, there are at the same time counterforces in that very will that work to fragment and diversify this "agent's" energies. Attempts to impose the one side or the other, i.e., in the name of the "will of the people" to solidify unity or radicalize fragmentation, are thus doomed to fail. Instead, politics needs to navigate the unpredictable interactions of these conflicting directions.

In considering the formation of the individual subject of a nation, I turn briefly to the insightful analyses of Etienne Balibar to show how the dialectics of the will unfolds in theories of radical democracy. He argues that with the French Revolution, "the time of man-the-subject (empirical and transcendental) can begin,"[25] a citizen subject, imbued with the political. He sees this subject as radically split, not only by the principle of its constitution as speaking but by the "antinomies" of the individual and universal, the representable and the unrepresentable, activity and passivity, above and under the law. These are embedded in the subject—we could say developing Balibar's position—because this modern subject is conceived as a *will,* a concept only implicit in Balibar's discussion. Thus, I would embrace and provide a slightly different reason for Balibar's conclusion. This new citizen subject, constituted fundamentally as a *will* in a complex way, provides the "ground" for a continual radical politics—here I agree. But the reason or source of this radical political potential is not given solely by deconstructing the firm substance (*subjectum*) underlying all claims to the political. Rather, we need to stress this subject's constitution through a radically splitting process of willing that is open to and opens up new possibilities for political activity.

In these two spheres—the analysis of the nation and of the subject of the nation—theories of the will, with all their historical and conceptual richness, allow us to begin to reconceive political structures and potentials for political agency. Political organization involves an act that coalesces disparate forces, draws them together to respond in a unified way, with a "common will," to pursue a represented goal. Such a union responds to historical circumstances and is therefore in part shaped by them; but it is also a *response,* an innovative conception that raises the possibility of a new articulation of those circumstances. At the same time, that union, as "will," contains necessarily a plurality that gives it life, since if it were self-contained it would have no drive or "wanting."[26] Hence, I would argue that the "will" has a central place in theorizing politics. It should be neither falsely celebrated nor debunked. Rather we need to pursue its dialectical vicissitudes that make up the very space of the political.

In sum, we may be able to say, as is commonly proclaimed in areas of contemporary theory, that the "subject is dead." It has, in fact, been critically ill since Hegel. But the fears that accompany such a declaration can be allayed by introducing a dialectical concept of the will. The will offers us the tool for understanding agency in a way that speaks to both our pretheoretical self-conceptions and the ethico-political theories of Western culture. But it is crucial that the will be conceived in its antithetical richness, which it derives from its long history, so that it not be mistaken for a metaphysical entity or reduced to a mere empirical phenomenon. Once the will is conceived dialectically, it offers us a model of agency that has great effectiveness for a liberatory ethics, politics, and hermeneutics.

Abbreviations

Unless otherwise noted, all translations are my own. I have therefore generally provided the titles and bibliographical information of the German editions.

AF: Aktualität der Frühromantik. Edited by Ernst Behler and Jochen Hörisch.

DA: Dialektik der Aufklärung: Philosophische Fragmente. By Theodor Adorno and Max Horkheimer.

DD: Dialogue and Deconstruction: The Gadamer-Derrida Encounter. Edited by Diane P. Michelfelder and Richard E. Palmer.

DP: Discipline and Punish: The Birth of the Prison. By Michel Foucault.

EI: Erkenntnis und Interesse. By Jürgen Habermas.

FFC: The Four Fundamental Concepts of Psycho-Analysis. Edited by Jacques-Alain Miller. Translated by Alan Sheridan.

G: Gelassenheit. By Martin Heidegger.

GzMdS: Grundlegung zur Metaphysik der Sitten. By Immanuel Kant.

Hermeneutik II: *Gesammelte Werke. Hermeneutik II. Wahrheit und Methode. Ergänzungen.* By Hans-Georg Gadamer.

IS: "Interpreting Signatures (Nietzsche/Heidegger): Two Questions" in *DD*. By Jacques Derrida.

KpV: Kritik der praktischen Vernunft. Vol. 5, "Akademie-Textausgabe." By Immanuel Kant.

KrV: Kritik der reinen Vernunft (Nach der ersten und zweiten Original-Ausgabe). By Immanuel Kant.

KS: "Kant with Sade." By Jacques Lacan. Translated by James B. Swenson, Jr.

LCMP: Language, Counter-Memory, Practice. Selected Essays and Interviews. By Michel Foucault. Edited by Donald F. Bouchard.

N: Nietzsche. Vols. I and II. By Martin Heidegger.

ND: Negative Dialektik. By Theodor Adorno

OS: Of Spirit: Heidegger and the Question. By Jacques Derrida. Translated by Geoffrey Bennington and Rachel Bowlby.

OTO: "Otobiographies: The Teaching of Nietzsche and the Politics of the Proper Name." By Jacques Derrida.

PDM: Der philosophische Diskurs der Moderne. By Jürgen Habermas.

PPC: Politics, Philosophy, Culture. Interviews and Other Writings, 1977–1984. By Michel Foucault. Edited by Lawrence D. Kritzman.

Seminar VII: The Seminar of Jacques Lacan: Book VII. The Ethics of Psychoanalysis 1959–1960. Edited by Jacques-Alain Miller. Translated by Dennis Porter.

TI: Text und Interpretation: Deutsch-französische Debatte. Edited by Philippe Forget.

UP: The Use of Pleasure. Vol. 2, *The History of Sexuality.* By Michel Foucault.

WM: Wahrheit und Methode: Grundzüge einer philosophischen Hermeneutik, 2d ed. By Hans-Georg Gadamer.

Notes

INTRODUCTION

1. As David Hume said in *An Enquiry Concerning Human Understanding*, the subject of free will has been contested by philosophers for centuries, and it is worth looking for the common elements uniting the opposing viewpoints (*Enquiries Concerning Human Understanding and the Principles of Morals* [Oxford: Clarendon Press, 1975], 80–81).

2. For general reference works discussing the will, see Rudolf Eisler, *Wörterbuch der philosophischen Begriffe*, 4th ed. (Berlin: Mittler und Sohn, 1930 [1st ed. 1902]). Other useful encyclopedia articles are: Hermann Krings, Hans Michael Baumgartner, and Christoph Wild, eds., *Handbuch philosophischer Grundbegriffe* (Munich: Kösel-Verlag, 1974); entry on "Der Wille" by Hans Oberdiek, in *An Encyclopedia of Philosophy*, ed. G. H. R. Parkinson (London: Routledge, 1988).

3. B. A. O. Williams notes: "the problem of freewill makes its first large-scale appearance in a religious context, when men had come to believe that there was one God, omnipotent, omniscient, and concerned with human action. The problem of freewill was first definitely stated as a problem of Christian theology. The problem arose, in fact, from a number of different roots in Christian belief: Christianity asserts on the one hand that man does freely choose his actions, but also asserts on the other hand statements not evidently compatible with this, for instance that God being omniscient knows from all eternity what actions a man will in fact perform" ("Freedom and the Will," in D. F. Pears, *Freedom and the Will* [London: MacMillan, 1965], 4f).

4. I will be largely focusing my arguments on the modern continental tradition and merely refer here to some recent studies by Anglo-American analytic philosophers. Donald Davidson's theories of action, *Decision Making: An Experimental Approach* (Westport, Conn.: Greenwood Press, 1977) and *Essays on Actions and Events* (New York: Oxford University Press, 1980). Also works by Richard M. Hare, *Essays in Ethical Theory* (Oxford: Clarendon Press, 1989); Gary Watson, ed., *Free Will* (New York: Oxford University Press, 1982); N. M. L. Nathan, *Will and World: A Study in Metaphysics* (Oxford: Clarendon Press, 1992); Bernard Berofsky, ed., *Free Will and Determinism* (New York:

Harper and Row, 1966); Keith Lehrer, ed., *Freedom and Determinism* (New York: Random House, 1966); A. I. Melden, *Free Action* (London: Routledge and Kegan Paul; New York: Humanities Press, 1961); Morton White, *Free Will: A Holistic View* (Princeton: Princeton University Press, 1993); Susan Wolf, *Freedom within Reason* (New York: Oxford University Press, 1990); and Ted Honderich, *How Free Are You? The Determinism Problem* (New York: Oxford University Press, 1993). From the hermeneutic tradition: Paul Ricoeur, *Freedom and Nature: The Voluntary and the Involuntary,* trans. Erazim V. Kohak (Evanston, Ill: Northwestern University Press, 1966). Despite the divergence in vocabularies, a case could be made that discussions of the will are the site of a rapprochement between the continental and Anglo-American traditions (e.g., the interest in dialectics on the one hand and the discussions of "compatibililst" vs. "incompatibilist" positions on the other).

5. Patrick Riley, *Will and Political Legitimacy: A Critical Exposition of Social Contract Theory in Hobbes, Locke, Rousseau, Kant, and Hegel* (Cambridge: Harvard University Press, 1982), 20f. My argument parallels Riley's in many ways but deals with the will beyond discussions of social contract theory.

6. This is, as we shall see, Heidegger's fundamental question (which he answers negatively) and it continues to the present day as a thread in some of Derrida's work and studies influenced by poststructuralism.

7. Ryle, *The Concept of the Mind* (London and New York: Hutchinson, 1949). See Oberdiek, *An Encyclopedia of Philosophy,* 481–82 for a good critical summary of Ryle's argument.

8. This perception, in large measure well grounded, could account for the conspicuous absence of feminist discussions of the will, despite the number of works that reconceptualize other concepts of Western political and ethical philosophy. Judith Butler, from her phenomenological perspective, offers the most explicit attempt to think through an alternative model of volition, which my dialectical model could supplement. *Gender Trouble: Feminism and the Subversion of Identity* (New York: Routledge, 1990), e.g., 8, and *Bodies That Matter: On the Discursive Limits of "Sex"* (New York: Routledge, 1993), e.g., 25–28. See below where I use a dialectical model of the will to help clarify issues in feminist theories of agency.

9. A quick look at the number of references listed in Eisler's encyclopedia article in *Wörterbuch der philosophischen Begriffe* gives some sense of the popularity and centrality of the concept of the will around 1900. It permeated every aspect of thought. Riley points out (*Will and Political Legitimacy,* 19f) that Freudianism extends the notion of desire and its repercussions so far that the will virtually disappears. I would point out that the will was still a central category of analysis for the early Freud and thus in fact informed his work throughout his life, even if implicitly.

10. I do not want to unroll a discussion on the differences between modern and postmodern here. Although I wish to make a distinction, I have no stake in it conceptually. I am comfortable with listing all the thinkers of this study under the general heading "modern." I also see the benefits of placing at least Kant and Nietzsche under the category "modern" while the others respond to

them and their enterprise in a "postmodern" way that would disrupt "modern" unities. Finally, there are "postmodern" elements in all these thinkers, namely the way they all undermine metaphysical notions of a self-identical subject. As we shall see presently, the very concept of the will makes these distinctions difficult to maintain in any more than a popular sense since the will has *always* been "modern" *and* "postmodern" since its contradictory determinations apply to both modernism and postmodernism. Of the many arguments addressing this distinction, I like Bernd Magnus's article, "Nietzsche and Postmodern Criticism," in *Nietzsche-Studien* 18 (1989): 301–16.

11. I use aporia in its concrete sense: the impossibility of solving a philosophical problem because contradictions are present (either in the matter itself or in the concepts used to discuss it), contradictions that have not been adequately taken into account. Aporias (as dialecticians from Plato to Hegel have shown) are damaging to a thinker's actual argument but fruitful in the long run if they lead to a new account that incorporates the contradictory determinations.

12. See Martin Schwab's introduction to the English translation of Manfred Frank's *What Is Neostructuralism?* (Minneapolis: University of Minnesota Press, 1988).

13. Such, for example, is Bloch's analysis of Hegelian dialectic in *Subjekt-Objekt: Erläuterungen zu Hegel* (Frankfurt a.M.: Surhrkamp, 1971). Other, more recent Hegelian and non-Hegelian attempts to argue for the identity between a dialectical logos and dialectical being are Manfred Wentzel's *Dialektik als Ontologie auf der Basis selbstreflexiver Erkenntniskritik* (Freiburg: Alber, 1986); Gustav E. Mueller's *The Interplay of Opposites: A Dialectical Ontology* (New York: Bookman Associates, 1956); and Leslie Armour's *Logic and Reality: An Investigation into the Idea of a Dialectical System* (Assen: Van Gorcum, 1972).

14. In this I am following a more Wittgensteinian and Rortyan approach, although it is unlikely they would place much emphasis on the concepts will or dialectic. But Rorty, in "Deconstruction and Circumvention" (*Critical Inquiry* 11, no. 1 [1984]: 1–24), did make the case for not being afraid to use metaphysical concepts pragmatically if they are useful. I would see them as tools. And the will, like a hammer, is best viewed as a "dialectical" tool; it can be used for two opposing things (taking nails out and hammering them in).

15. See Rüdiger Dubner, "Dialog und Dialektik oder Plato und Hegel," in *Zur Sache der Dialektik* (Stuttgart: Reclam, 1980), esp. 124. See also Hans-Georg Gadamer's hermeneutic studies tying dialectic back to its dialogical roots. For example, "Hegel und die antike Dialektik" in *Gesammelte Werke*, vol. 3, *Neuere Philosophie I* (Tübingen: J. C. B. Mohr [Paul Siebeck], 1987), 3–28).

16. The following simple "provisional definition" is useful: "The Greek term 'dialectic,' derived from 'dialogue' between equal partners, is used here to mean a unity of opposites. Its Latin equivalent is 'discourse.' In a dialectical relation each of the opposed 'poles' is incomplete without its own 'other,' and degenerates if it is abstractly isolated. Since there are many 'sets' of opposites, one may also speak of 'dialectics' in the plural." Mueller, *Dialectic: A Way into and within Philosophy* (New York: Bookman Associates, 1953), 17.

Panajotis Kondylis, whose work on the historical origins of Idealist dialectics (*Die Entstehung der Dialektik: Eine Analyse der geistigen Entwicklung von*

Hölderlin, Schelling und Hegel bis 1802 [Stuttgart: Klett-Cotta, 1979]) and on the Enlightenment (*Die Aufklärung im Rahmen des neuzeitlichen Rationalismus* [Stuttgart: Klett-Cotta, 1981]), argues for a positive evaluation of the "polemical" nature of the Enlightenment for many of the same reasons that I pursue dialectics (see *Die Aufklärung*, 20, 24).

17. From Hegel's lectures on the *History of Philosophy* as cited in my *The Spirit and Its Letter: Traces of Rhetoric in Hegel's Philosophy of Bildung* (Ithaca: Cornell University Press, 1988), 272ff.

18. On exploring the relationship between postmodern theories and rhetoric (esp. pre-Socratics), see David Marshall, "Dialogue and *Ecriture*," in *Dialogue and Deconstruction: The Gadamer-Derrida Encounter*, ed. Diane P. Michelfelder and Richard Palmer (Albany: State University of New York Press, 1989), 209 and note 7.

19. See Rüdiger Bubner in *Aktualität der Frühromantik*, eds. Ernst Behler and Jochen Hörisch (Paderborn: Ferdinand Schoningh, 1987). See also Mark William Roche, *Tragedy and Comedy: A Systematic Study and a Critique of Hegel* (Albany: State University of New York Press, 1998), who uses Hegel to discuss drama and thereby also illuminates the ironic features of dialectic.

20. Georg Friedrich Wilhelm Hegel, *Phänomenologie des Geistes. Theorie Werkausgabe*, vol. 3 (Frankfurt a.M.: Surhrkamp, 1977), 57–61.

21. See Allen Wood, *Hegel's Ethical Thought* (New York: Cambridge University Press, 1990), who rejects the "thesis-antithesis-synthesis" summary as non-Hegelian. His introductory discussion of Hegel's dialectical logic is highly illuminating (1–4). On the notion of recollection, see Donald Phillip Verene, *Hegel's Recolection: A Study of Images in the "Phenomenology of Spirit"* (Albany: State University of New York Press, 1985). Slavoj Žižek has also been arguing for an approach to Hegel's dialectic that recognizes its power to open up rather than impose closure on thought, most recently in *Tarrying with the Negative: Kant, Hegel, and the Critique of Ideology* (Durham: Duke University Press, 1993).

22. F. W. J. Schelling, *Philosophische Untersuchungen über das Wesen der menschlichen Freiheit und die damit zusammenhängenden Gegenstände* (Frankfurt a.M.: Surhrkamp, 1988), 39; *Philosophical Inquiries into the Nature of Human Freedom*, trans. James Gutmann (La Salle, Ill: Open Court, 1992 [1936]).

23. One hears in Schelling's formulation the echo of Kant's famous definition of Enlightenment as the "stepping out from self-imposed immaturity" ("der Austritt aus der selbstverschuldeten Unmündigkeit"). We thereby see how the Idealists transformed the Enlightenment project, implicitly defining enlightenment as the ability to think dialectically.

24. Schelling, *Philosophische Untersuchungen*, 14/38.

25. See Julius Stenzel, *Studien zur Entwicklung der platonischen Dialektik von Sokrates zu Aristoteles* (Darmstadt: Wissenschaftliche Buchgesellschaft, 1961 [1917, 1931]), 188f.

26. Hans-Georg Gadamer, *The Idea of the Good in Platonic-Aristotelian Philosophy*, trans. P. Christopher Smith (New Haven: Yale University Press, 1986), 109.

27. If dialectic is often associated with metaphysics, we see again an interesting connection to the concept of the will. It is not without irony that Schopenhauer, whose philosophy of the will is most deeply metaphysical, was not awarded the prize for his 1840 essay, *Über die Freiheit des menschlichen Willens* in *Werke in zehn Bänden* (Zurich: Diogenes Verlag, 1977), because the committee felt he did not deal sufficiently with the "nexus" between an ethics of the will and metaphysics (vol. 6, 8–15).

   Here I differ with Nathan, who also deals with the will in terms of "want and belief *conflicts*" (my emphasis), but who turns to a metaphysical conception of dialectics. Nathan, *Will and World,* 157–61, esp. 159f.

28. For this reason, Stephen Houlgate argues that Hegel's dialectical method, not Nietzsche's antidialectics, provides the stronger critique of metaphysics. *Hegel, Nietzsche and the Criticism of Metaphysics* (New York: Cambridge University Press, 1986).

29. See also Manfred Frank's summary of Dieter Henrich's interpretation of Hegelian negativity in his lectures, *Was ist Neostrukturalismus?* (Frankfurt a.M.: Suhrkamp, 1983).

30. Hannah Arendt, *The Life of the Mind.* Vol. 2, *Willing* (New York: Harcourt Brace Jovanovich, 1978), 42–47.

31. Emmanuel Levinas, *Totality and Infinity: An Essay on Exteriority,* trans. Alphonso Lingis (Pittsburgh: Duquesne University Press, 1969), likely under the influence of Franz Rosenzweig, would not want to limit the activity of the will that guarantees its freedom to negativity (40–42). It is, simultaneously, an overflowing of desire and thought and a postponing or forestalling of nonfreedom (death) into the future (237). Thus, although Levinas eschews the word dialectic and attempts to redefine metaphysics in a powerful yet idiosyncratic way that I will not follow, his arguments on the will and his mode of thinking are influential for my approach.

32. See my essay, "Of Spirit(s) and Will(s)," in *Hegel after Derrida,* ed. Stuart Barnett (New York: Routledge, 1998), 64–90, in which I read much of Derrida's oeuvre as a missed opportunity; i.e., where he is primarily focused on a deconstruction of *Geist,* he tends to pull both dialectic and will into the realm of the metaphysics to be deconstructed instead of seeing them as "alternatives."

33. Michael Theunissen, in the introduction to *Der Andere: Studien zur Sozialontologie der Gegenwart* (Berlin and New York: Walter de Gruyter, 1977) makes a somewhat different set of associations between the argumentative and experiential aspects of dialectic. In Hegel, he says, dialectic occurs because partial determinations of a concept are brought into conflict, leading to a "totalizing" concept that includes the partial contradictions. This is linked, then, to the process of recognition, in which two powers (individual or otherwise) confront each other with incompatible and falsely universalizing claims of domination (*Herrschaftsansprüche*); their failed interaction (communication) leads to the necessity of the recognition of the other if each is to survive. See *Der Andere,* x–xii. We can further relate this to the will if we consider these two opposing forces *Eigenwillen* that give way to a more genuinely inclusive *volonté général.*

34. Riley makes a point (*Will and Political Legitimacy,* 18f) not unlike mine about

186 ● *Notes to Introduction*

the turn to historical accounts of the will, but with a shift in emphasis: He says that social contract theories of the seventeenth and eighteenth centuries needed a better account of the will and we could turn to the scholastics (even though they have a weaker notion of society). That is, differences between theories (social contract theories or postmodernisms) could be adjudicated, explained, and supplemented by turning to older accounts of the will. Likewise, he argues, contemporary contractarians (Walzer, Grice, Rawls) also assume a notion of will but do not provide even the kind of deductions one finds in the Enlightenment figures.

35. Hegel applies this conception of life to the Spirit as follows: "Even our own sense of the mind's (*Geist*'s) *living* unity naturally protests against any attempt to break it up into different faculties, forces, or what comes to the same thing, activities, conceived as independent of each other. But the craving for a *comprehension* (*begreifen*) of the unity is still further stimulated, as we soon come across distinctions between mental freedom and mental determinism, antitheses between free psychic agency and the corporeity that lies external to it, whilst we equally note the intimate interdependence of the one upon the other" (§379, *Enzyklopädie der philosophischen Wissenschaften,* part 3, *Philosophie des Geistes*). Note how he focuses here precisely on the aspects of the *will*—mental vs. corporeal, free vs. determined, split vs. unified—in order to characterize the dialectic inherent in *Spirit.*

36. Concerning evolution: I cannot look at a complex biosystem and say that even if I had all the facts about it, I would know what forms would evolve. I might know what forms could thrive more, but they may never develop and the complexity of the system is such that even if a mutant were introduced as predicted, its relation to other unpredictable developments make its development uncertain. Looking backward, however, we can explain with "necessity" how a given form evolved given only the physical variables.

37. Chaos theory shows this mathematically. And even the most rudimentary life forms, given their *self*-differentiation and *self*-unification, can be said to be inherently self-reflexive. Note that I am not determining clearly whether or not willing is uniquely human. I would say that it appears that some aspects are not, since they are indeed shared with all living organisms. But some are shared, if at all, only with higher organisms.

38. Hans Jonas, *Macht oder Ohnmancht der Subjektivität: Das Leib-Seele-Problem im Vorfeld des Prinzips Verantwortung* (Frankfurt a.M.: Suhrkamp, 1987).

39. The notion of the will as "ethical energy" and the category of the infinitesimal may be derived from Hermann Cohen. His mathematically and scientifically oriented neo-Kantianism in the early twentieth century formulated a conception of willing in terms of "ethical energy." Because the reality of energy is defined through the notion of the "infinitesimal"—it is, in his terms, a "category" like movement—one can speak of its having constancy and conservation without having to fix it as a substance. Likewise, then, our actions presume a constant subject or ethical energy, but the "bearer" of those actions need not be hypostatized into a substance. Moreover, just as physical categories can be formulated in terms of laws (of motion, etc.), the consistency of the ethical will is formalizable

without being reduced to the status of a fixed or determined thing. See Cohen's *System der Philosophie, erster Teil: Logik der reinen Erkenntnis* (1914; reprint, Berlin: Bruno Cassirer Verlag, 1922), 296–302.

40. Jonas, *Macht oder Ohnmancht der Subjektivität*, 79f.

41. Ibid., 77f.

42. For example, Lehrer associates passivity and determinism. *Freedom and Determinism*, 4.

43. Melden, *Free Action*, 5f, 8.

44. Schopenhauer, *Über die Freiheit des menschlichen Willens, Werke*, vol. 6, 47f.

45. Descartes saw perception as passive and volition as active, a view that influenced many. See John G. Cottingham, "The Intellect, the Will, and the Passions: Spinoza's Critique of Descartes," *Journal of the History of Philosophy* 26, no. 2 (Apr. 1988): 239–57, 239f. This was a widespread distinction in the seventeenth and eighteenth centuries, whereby the active/passive distinction overlaps with views of the will and reason. For a good summary of early modern views, see R. F. Stalley, "The Will in Hume's Treatise," *Journal of the History of Philosophy* 24, no. 1 (Jan. 1986): 41–53. For example, those who tended toward a view that saw the entire world (including human action) as rationally explainable by causality linked the will to the "passive" faculties; those who exempted the will from chains of causation saw it as active (see Clarke against Leibniz, in Stalley, "The Will in Hume's Treatise," 45; also consider Berkeley's position of the will as active and the understanding as passive, Stalley, "The Will in Hume's Treatise," 52f). For Malebranche, the will is both active and passive. I have the ability to will or not will any finite good. However, the will toward the universal good is irresistible and implanted by God. Moreover, because any will is only the "occasion" of God's willing to move something, it is not a direct cause (but also a necessary intermediary and partially active, partially passive). See Frederick Copleston, S. J., *A History of Philosophy*, vol. 3 (London: Burns, Oates and Washbourne Ltd., 1950), 193.

46. Eisler, *Wörterbuch der philosophischen Begriffe*, 552.

47. I glean these from Stalley's discussion, "The Will in Hume's Treatise," He writes: "An agency theory leads naturally to a two-stage account of the cause of action. Since we seem to have little control over our desires, appetites and feelings, they are naturally regarded as passive. They must therefore be distinguished from the will because in willing we are active. Thus, when we act our desires must be followed by an act of will which is in turn followed by a movement of the body. By contrast, a philosopher who does not regard the active-passive distinction as basic may identify the will either with the appetites and desires in general or with some particular species of appetite or desire."

48. See, e.g., the entry on "Volonté" from Diderot's *Encyclopédie*: "It is the effect of an object's impression on our senses or powers of reflection, the consequence of which is to move us toward the object as toward a good that we recognize and that excites our appetite (desire) away from the object as away from some ill that we recognize and that excites our fear or aversion." The will is here both a cause and an effect. Cassirer (*The Philosophy of the Enlightenment*, trans. Fritz C. A. Koelin and James P. Pettegrove [Boston: Beacon Press, 1955) also stresses

188 ● Notes to Chapter 1

the role of affects and passions in Enlightenment thought, even as *ethical* action has an active part of the soul (will) triumph over the passive (105).

49. These possibilities can be diagrammed:

passions ⟶ will ⟶ action

passions ⟶ action vs. will ⟶ action

The Kantian model looks like:

will (Lacanian *vel*) ⟶ desire ⟶ will / law ⟶ action

50. These positions have roots extending as far back as Augustine (and we shall see below how Foucault traces some features of a historical development of the will and/as drives). According to Augustine, after the fall sexuality can no longer be fully controlled and so man is exposed to sexual affections. And yet, man must *assent* to them for them to be sinful. Furthermore, it is impossible for us to deny them completely because of the presence of a "perverted will" (*mala voluntas*). At every turn, the will seems to be both active and passive. See Albrecht Dihle, *The Theory of Will in Classical Antiquity* (Berkeley: University of California Press, 1982) on Augustine and sexuality (128).

51. James Baldwin, *Dictionary of Philosophy and Psychology*, vol. 3 (New York: Macmillan, 1905–11), 816.

52. For a different version of this dynamic, consider the "reconstruction" of Hellenistic thought by Hosenfelder. He argues in *Philosophie der Antike 3* ([Munich: Beck, 1985], 32–35) that Hellenistic ethics (323 B.C.–30 B.C.) defines happiness as the *consciousness* of fulfillment of will. It is an inner state of mind and hence, vis-à-vis the outside world, is utterly passive. Thus, the starting point of an active, self-positing will leads to self-reducing passivity.

53. Levinas, *Totality and Infinity*, 238.

54. Bill Readings, *The University in Ruins* (Cambridge: Harvard University Press, 1996), 84f.

55. That willing is thus not controlled by me. If this sounds like the unconscious in Freud, there are indeed both historical and conceptual links. He even began with a theory of hysteria as a form of "counter-willing" within the subject. However, to avoid the notion that the subject consists of multiple agencies (ego, id, superego as little agents in the subject) I would rather stress willing as process.

CHAPTER I

1. Riley (*Will and Political Legitimacy*, 1–10) provides one of the most succinct histories.

2. Because I am concerned with the reception of the concept of the will in various debates, I am not attempting new readings of the positions outlined below. Rather, the strength of my argument rests on the consistency with which the will is associated with opposing sides of central issues in Western thought.

One might argue that the transition from Greek to Latin via Cicero led to the peculiar richness (or vagueness) inherent in the concept of will. Dihle summarizes the effect of this transition: "Cicero . . . used the word *voluntas* not only *proairesis* or *boulesis* in Greek. Sometimes, even in philosophical texts, *voluntas* means desire or spontaneous wish rather than deliberate intention, and in other passages the impulse itself (horme), which comes from deliberation or from conscious moral attitude, is called *voluntas*. The large semantic area that is apparently attached to the word in Cicero's vocabulary corresponds to the general usage of his time. So he does not seem to have seen any difficulty in the identification of 'intellectualistic' boulesis and 'voluntaristic' *voluntas,* since he presupposed their identity even outside philosophical discussions" (*Theory of Will,* 134).

3. Indeed, we shall see that the reduction or rejection of the will is one of the positions in these historical debates.

4. This image is implied in Honderich's discussion of the "compatibilist" position that would see freedom and determination as two qualities that could apply to the will the way "round" and "green" apply to a set of bodies (*How Free Are You?,* 5).

5. Or, as Levinas argues, it is inappropriate to conceive of a free being as one "divided into one part endowed with a causality of its own and one part subject to exterior causes" (*Totality and Infinity,* 223).

6. Riley, *Will and Political Legitimacy,* 211.

7. Given the close association between our modern view of the will and the Enlightenment, it should not come as a surprise that my interest in a dialectic of willing overlaps with recent studies that uncover a genuine "dialectic" within the Enlightenment, i.e., that argue against a one-sided reading of Enlightenment-as-pure-reason versus the anti-Enlightenment-irrationalisms. And it moreover should not come as a surprise that many of those studies often contain implicit references to the concept of the will. One example will suffice: Willi Oelmüller, "Aufklärung als Prozeß von Traditionskritik und Traditionsbewahrung," in *Erforschung der deutschen Aufklärung,* ed. Peter Pütz (Verlagsgruppe Athenäum, Hain, Scriptor, Hanstein: Königstein/Ts., 1980), 59–80. Referring to the interest in reason as a "court of appeals," he writes that Lessing, Kant, and Hegel reject a concept of enlightenment and reason that remains caught in static alternatives like "autonomy and heteronomy, progress and tradition, revolution and restoration" (60). Note how this actually puts the process of Enlightenment close to the will.

8. Eisler, *Wörterbuch der philosophischen Begriffe,* 551.

9. Manfred Frank makes this point in general about theories of consciousness: "It is unclear how an isolated act of consciousness, which has a relation only to itself (and not to an I) can also become conscious of itself as belonging to a continuum of such acts." *Selbstbewußtsein und Selbsterkenntnis: Essays zur analytischen Philosophie der Subjektivität* (Stuttgart: Reclam, 1991), 27.

10. These are just some of the oppositions that are worked out in the *Letters on the Aesthetic Education of Man* (*Briefe über die ästhetische Erziehung des Menschen*) from 1794.

11. Andreas Graeser, *Die Philosophie der Antike 2. Sophistik und Sokratik, Plato und Aristoteles.* Vol. 2, *Geschichte der Philosophie,* ed. Wolfgang Röd (Munich:

Beck, 1983): "For what makes the ethical man (spoudatos or agathos) stand out is the fact that he is not led astray by pleasure or displeasure (V 5, 1030b 17ff) and can thus distinguish between the truly and the only apparently good (III 6, 1113a 15ff). His actions are different from those of others because he performs them following a clear decision for their own sake and acts out of a firm, unchanging disposition (II 4, 1105a 30ff)" (236).

12. Eisler, *Wörterbuch der philosophischen Begriffe,* 552f: "Whereas boulesis can have something impossible as an object, proairesis is directed to the possible (*Nicomachean Ethics,* III 4, 1111b 21)." This is different from Plato, according to whom "one part of our soul searches for truth and loves wisdom; it stands in sharp contrast with our appetitive nature, which can desire almost any object imaginable" (Oberdiek, *An Encyclopedia of Philosophy,* 464).

13. As an indication of the confusing dialectics involved here, it is interesting to note that there is a different way of setting these concepts in relation to each other. See Graeser on Aristotle, *Die Philosophie der Antike 2,* 238f, and Malte Hosenfelder on Hellenistic philosophy, *Die Philosophie der Antike 3. Stoa, Epikureismus und Skepsis,* in *Geschichte der Philosophie,* ed. Wolfgang Röd (Munich: Beck, 1985), 49. See Johannes Hirschberger on Christian thought, *Geschichte der Philosophie,* vol. 1, *Altertum und Mittlealter* (Freiburg im Breisgau: Herder, 1976), 341. Consider also Schopenhauer, *Welt als Wille und Vorstellung* (*Werke,* vol. 1, 367) where the will's status of being outside of time leads to the paradoxical linking of its freedom (even arbitrariness) and necessity as its *unchangeable* character.

14. Eisler, *Wörterbuch der philosophischen Begriffe,* 597.

15. This connection goes back to the origins of our tradition. Dihle (*Theory of Will,* 146) points out that *boulesis, thelo, voluntas* are used for "divine" and human will (esp. in the rational cosmological order), as well as for the "process of arbitrarily giving names."

16. Fichte in Eisler, *Wörterbuch der philosophischen Begriffe,* 559.

17. The French phrase, *vouloir dire,* conveys still the association between meaning and willing and will be dealt with in chapter 3. See also Oberdiek: Our creation and use of symbols is "a feat accomplished by the intellect working through the will" (*An Encyclopedia of Philosophy,* 463).

18. Hans-Georg Gadamer, *Wahrheit und Methode: Grundzüge einer philosophischen Hermeneutik,* 2d ed. (Tübingen: J. C. B. Mohr, 1965). See also Gadamer, "Destruktion and Deconstruction," in *Dialogue and Deconstruction: The Gadamer-Derrida Encounter,* ed. Diane P. Michelfelder and Richard E. Palmer (Albany: State University of New York Press, 1989), 111.

19. As Suabedissen says: "Willing, considered as movement, is the activity of mental life through which it gets its active *direction*" (Eisler, *Wörterbuch der philosophischen Begriffe,* 557; my emphasis). Or, as Eisler summarizes Stammler, the will is "not a force but a direction of consciousness" (560). Moreover, William James's influential analysis of the will in his *Psychology* makes the ability to focus or direct *attention* the essential feature of willing. It is a prior condition of conscious meaning, since unless we attend to something it has no significance for us. Thus, willing and meaning are fundamentally linked in the process of directing consciousness.

20. Ricoeur offers the following formulation of a dialectical relationship: "Now the event of choice stands in a peculiar relation to the process which precedes it: it *completes* it and at the same time *breaks it off*. A living dialectic constantly brings us back from one aspect of choice to the other: choice as the *peak* of previous growth and as the surge of novelty" (*Freedom and Nature*, 164). Levinas sees the will as a kind of "interval" that undermines historical time, a rupture linked to the act of *creation* (*Totality and Infinity*, 58). See also his connection between the primacy of the ethical relation to the Other (which is the condition of novelty) and the irreducibility of the will (218f).

21. One way to appreciate the tensions involved is to consider White's discussion of Moore (*Free Will*, 35–37). He gives an "epistemic" analysis of the notion of freedom: "I am free to do x if no one knows for certain if, in the coming second, I will do x." This raises questions, of course, about my own *self-knowledge*. Am I therefore not free precisely in the situation when I "know what I'm doing"?

22. As Dihle points out, "the Greeks had no word . . . to denote will or intention as such" (*Theory of Will*, 20). "One word in the earliest vocabulary of Greek, however, contradicts the traditional intellectualism. Whenever the Homeric heroes display extraordinary activities, whenever their exploits surpass all expectation, it is due to their menos" (34). It is given to them by the gods; has no real "place" in the human faculties or body. "It is something numinous which only appears where the gods unpredictably interfere with human affairs, thus disturbing the calculable sequence of events" (34f). But this concept drops out with the rationalist reduction of Greek psychology.

23. Stenzel (*Studien zur Entwicklung der platonischen Dialektik von Sokrates zu Aristoteles* [Darmstadt: Wissenschaftliche Buchgesellschaft, 1961 (1917, 1931)] characterizes this intellectualism as follows: "the idea that I might know and recognize the good yet not act accordingly, i.e., knowingly act wrongly, evilly, is accepted by neither Plato nor Socrates" (184). For other versions of "rational determinism," see below.

24. The terms involved in discussions of ethics and action are: *boulesis*, often translated as willing, which was a striving for some perceived good; *ethymia*, or the desire for things; *proairesis*, or choice; and *hekousion* and *akousion*, as adjectives for voluntary or involuntary actions. See Schopenhauer, *Über die Freiheit des menschlichen Willens, Werke*, vol. 6, 103.

25. See especially *Protagoras*, 322b. Dihle summarizes: "non-intentionality is interpreted as ignorance of the better"; "intention (proairesis) . . . entirely and solely depends on intellectual activity (phronein)" (*Theory of Will*, 32). See also Hirschberger: "Ethical situations are conceived of parallel to technical situations. Whoever has learned and understands architecture is an architect and builds buildings; and whoever has learned and understands virtue—so runs the analogy—is virtuous and exercises virtue" (*Geschichte der Philosophie*, 65–66).

26. Dihle analyzes this origin of a form of Greek askesis (*Theory of Will*, 38–42).

27. Susan Wolf provides a strong case for a modern version of this position in her "reason view" of the freedom/determinism question. Wolf, *Freedom within Reason*.

28. Although Aristotle did not represent such a strong "intellectualism" and doubted

that knowledge of the good alone would lead one to good behavior, he nonetheless did not have an apparatus for dealing with actions that go against "better judgment." This is why he was interested in the phenomenon of *akrasia* (generally translated as "weakness of the will"). In the *Nicomachean Ethics* (VII 3, 1145b 25–26), he criticizes Plato's and Socrates' intellectualism for not dealing sufficiently with *akrasia* (see Graeser, *Die Philosophie der Antike 2,* 94). This issue has generated considerable debate over the past twenty years. There are two main problems. First, if I know/believe/judge x to be better, does it make sense to say, if I do y, that I did it intentionally/voluntarily? And second, if I know someone's wants by his/her judgments and actions, what if they diverge? This is not the place to unroll the entire debate or offer a solution. But it is relevant to point out that the existence of this issue is only possible given a tension between knowing and willing.

29. Here he is clearly Aristotelian since Aristotle saw the focus of ethical behavior in "rational desire." See Hirschberger: Aquinas "shares the view with Aristotle that reason is the highest human faculty and grants the intellect primacy over the will" (*Geschichte der Philosophie,* 511). Consider also the extensive discussions by Frederick Copleston, S. J., *A History of Philosophy,* vol. 2, *Medieval Philosophy. Augustine to Scotus* (London: Burns, Oates and Washbourne Ltd., 1950). He argues that although for Aquinas man is in a sense always willing God, his ability to do this depends on our conscious judgment, which may be clear or indistinct. Aquinas thus comes close to interpreting free will in terms of the faculty of judgment when he writes: "*Liberum arbitrium* is thus the power by which man is able to judge freely" (*De Veritate* 24, 4 and 6; cited in Copleston, 382).

30. *Summa Theologica,* I, qu.82, a.4; in Arendt, *Life of the Mind,* vol. 2, 121.

31. Kondylis (*Die Aufklärung* 63) also sees in Aquinas's "intellectualism" a deeper ambiguity, whereby the will and senses do get their due thanks to the driving force of *appetitus.* These ambiguities have consequences for the Western tradition, as he even implies (328) that for Locke these part/whole distinctions become confused because of the willing *Triebkraft* behind *both Geist* and *Wille.*

32. Hirschberger on Augustine: "the ethical is for him a matter of will, or as he says, love. Will makes up the whole human being: 'Will is always present, indeed all movements of the soul (*motus*) are nothing else but will' (De Civ. Dei XIV, 6)" (*Geschichte der Philosophie,* 369). Also Dihle: "Augustine separated willing from both potential and achieved cognition" (*Theory of Will,* 125).

33. Copleston: "In some respects of his thought Scotus did indeed carry on the Augustian-Fransiscan tradition: in his doctrine of the superiority of will to intellect, for example" (*History of Philosophy,* vol. 3, 482). On Scotus and his works: *Duns Scotus on the Will and Morality,* selected and trans. with an introduction by Allan B. Wolter, O. F. M. (Washington D.C.: The Catholic University of America Press, 1986).

34. *Opus Oxoniese,* 4, 49, quaestio ex latere, nos. 16 and 18; cited in Copleston, *History of Philosophy,* vol. 3, 40. Arendt quotes Scotus in opposition to Aquinas: "To put the opposing arguments in a nutshell: If Thomas had argued that the Will is an executive organ, necessary to execute the insights of the

Intellect, a merely 'subservient faculty,' Duns Scotus holds that 'Intellectus . . . est causa subserviens voluntatis' " (*Life of the Mind,* vol. 2, 126). See also Eisler, *Wörterbuch der philosophischen Begriffe,* 574, on Aquinas vs. Duns Scotus. It is an interesting fact that Heidegger's first book (*Habilitation*) was on Duns Scotus. Although it deals with his theory of categories and language, it remains to be investigated whether or not Duns Scotus's voluntarism entered into Heidegger's thought.

Given the fact that many of the debates among the scholastics are not the focus of contemporary interest, it is not surprising that Descartes is considered by some to be the first to give primacy to the will, also in intellectual judgments. See Anthony Kenny, "Descartes on the Will," in *Cartesian Studies* (Oxford: Blackwell, 1972); and John G. Cottingham, "The Intellect, the Will, and the Passions: Spinoza's Critique of Descartes," *Journal of the History of Philosophy* 26:2 (Apr. 1988): 239–57, here 241.

35. The Enlightenment is by no means as uniformly, i.e., unambiguously rationalist as its reputation leads most to believe. Recent arguments highlighting the "anti-intellectual rationalism," the rehabilitation of the senses, and the disruptive "performativity" within the Enlightenment reveal it to be an age grappling intensely with the very contradictoriness of the will as *appetitus rationalis.* See, e.g., Panajotis Kondylis, *Die Aufklärung im Rahmen des neuzeitlichen Rationalismus,* (Stuttgart: Klett-Cotta, 1981); John A. McCarthy, *Crossing Boundaries: A Theory and History of Essay Writing in German 1680–1815* (Philadelphia, 1989); and Harry Chinaman and Heat de Vries, eds., *Enlightenments: Encounters between Critical Theory and Contemporary French Thought* (Dampen, Netherlands: KKK Pharos Publishing House, 1993), e.g., 8f. Thymuses and Christies, for example, for all their rationalism, promote a strong version of voluntaries. See Kondylis, 551, 556–58. The roots for this dichotomy could lie in the ambivalent possibilities inherent in Cartesian dualism: On the one hand, it can lead to theories of the all-powerful intellect (e.g., Wolf, *Freedom within Reason*), while on the other, it also opens up the possibility of a sphere of willing (associated with the bodily desires) beyond knowledge.

36. Frederick Neuhouser, *Fichte's Theory of Subjectivity* (New York: Cambridge University Press, 1990), 3.

37. On the roots of this interpretation in Spinoza, see also Cottingham ("The Intellect, the Will, and the Passions," 242–45, 248), who claims that Spinoza stresses the identity of intellect and will to remove the apparent freedom that Descartes attributed to the latter (as if there were a will outside of our perceptions, choosing whether or not to believe or assent). See also E. M. Curley, "Descartes, Spinoza and the Ethics of Belief," in *Spinoza: Essays in Interpretation,* ed. E. Freeman and M. Mandelbaum (LaSalle, Ill.: Open Court, 1975).

38. Levinas argues that Idealism ultimately does reduce the will to reason (*Totality and Infinity,* 217). In challenging that reduction, he, of course, also offers a radically alternative conception of will.

39. R. Z. Friedman, "Hypocrisy and the Highest Good: Hegel on Kant's Transition from Morality to Religion," *Journal of the History of Philosophy* 24, no. 4

(Oct. 1986): 503–22, summarizes this ambiguity as a state where moral action (willing) can do neither with nor without reason: "The moral view is the best that man, who can abandon neither reason nor action, can do. It is a view that expresses both but couches them in the modesty of belief rather than in a subjectivism that does not care or in an arrogance that claims to know all" (522).

This ambiguity is formulated a century earlier by Pascal in the concept of the "heart" (*le coeur*), which Copleston summarizes thus: "Sometimes it appears to be used as synonymous with 'the will.' And when it is used in this sense it does not designate a kind of knowledge or an immediate instrument of knowing, but rather the movement of desire and interest which directs the attention of the intellect to some object. . . . At other times le coeur designates a kind of knowledge or an instrument of knowing. . . . 'We know truth not only by the reason but also by the heart. It is in this second way that we know first principles.' " (*History of Philosophy*, vol. 4, 164; see *Pensées*, 2, 99, 375; 4, 282, 459).

40. Manfred Frank, *Materialien zu Schellings philosophischen Anfängen* (Frankfurt a.M.: Suhrkamp, 1975), Andrew Bowie, and Slavoj Žižek have attempted to bring Schelling back into the present scene.

41. For this reason Schopenhauer will not be one of the main thinkers in the following text. Although it is true that he is one of the first names to come to mind in association with philosophies of the will, from the perspective of both his origins (clear and admitted Kantian) and his consequences (surpassed by Nietzsche for postmodernity), other thinkers are more important.

42. Schopenhauer on the will as beyond all knowledge: "The will as thing in itself is completely different from its appearance and completely free from all forms of appearance. It interacts with these forms only insofar as it takes on appearance. Thus, they affect only its objectivity and are otherwise foreign to it. . . . The will as thing in itself thus lies outside of the sphere of the law of sufficient reason and is thus groundless" (*Welt als Wille und Vorstellung, Werke*, vol. 1, 158–59). On the other hand, Schopenhauer stresses the link between the will and the meaning (*Bedeutung*) of the world as appearance, a meaning that is "immediately known or familiar to each individual" (142–43).

   In his 1840 essay on the essence of the free will, he sees the will both as *before* consciousness and as *the* object of self-consciousness (VI, 50f). He argues that self-consciousness only recognizes my freedom to *do* what I want but it cannot get at the freedom of my wanting itself. Thus, he shows beautifully the duality of our perception: We know our willing most intimately, yet our willing lies outside the sphere of our self-consciousness. See 55–57. He explicitly claims to have pushed freedom (of the will) to a place that is harder to reach by our faculties of cognition (139).

43. Arendt, *Life of the Mind*, vol. 2, 49.

44. Diverse strands of modern philosophy work with these same tensions, often creating unexpected parallels. A very different thinker, Max Planck, argues likewise for the "freedom of the will" vis-à-vis knowledge based on temporal concerns and on the difference between macro- and microscopic analysis. Looking backwards in time, he says, we can (indeed, in order to be rational,

must) come up with an unbroken chain of explainable and explained causes or motivations. But the closer we move to the present, the more difficult it becomes to establish determinations, so that the sphere of the will, operating at the microscopic level of the radical *now* of my need to act, remains separate, and the future open. Max Planck, "Kausalgesetz und Willensfreiheit," and "Vom Wesen der Willensfreiheit," in *Vom Wesen der Willensfreiheit und andere Vorträge* (Frankfurt a.M.: Fischer Taschenbuch Verlag, 1990), 102, 108, 112, 161, 163. Precisely the *lack of knowledge* therefore grants us freedom of the will. Note, however, that this does not commit one to a strictly speaking irrationalist position in other spheres of ethics, metaphysics, or epistemology. On the other hand, it can. See Ricoeur on Bergson's irrationalism (*Freedom and Nature*, 160–63).

This is also the only way in which Spinoza would grant (the illusion of) freedom of will: "If men clearly understood the whole of nature, they would find everything just as necessary as the things treated of in mathematics; but since this is beyond human understanding, we regard certain things as contingent" (*Cogitationes Metaphysicae IX*, ii [G 1:266; C 332]; cited in Cottingham, "The Intellect, the Will, and the Passions," 249).

Recall as well Cohen's use of scientific categories in order to deal with this fundamental opposition between knowing and willing. He sees "*die Bewegung als Verbindung von Denken und Wollen*" ("movement as the connection between thinking and willing"; *Logik der reinen Erkenntnis* 425).

45. See Höffe's *Lexikon der Ethik* (München: Beck, 1997) and the article on "Determination." The Anglo-American discussions in recent years focus on this opposition and the question of "compatibilism."

46. Levinas rejects this entire approach: "The notion of independence must be grasped elsewhere than in causality" (*Totality and Infinity*, 223).

47. Recall the model of the Venn diagram. In this case, if we assign the left circle the realm of the "body" and the right whatever transcends it, then we see that the full rejection of the right circle eclipses the middle section as well. We are left, as we saw above, with an incomplete circle.

48. See Melden's fine summary of these developments in *Free Action*, 5f.

49. Quoted extensively in Schopenhauer, vol. 6, 115f.

50. Oberdiek, *An Encyclopedia of Philosophy*, 471. See also Schopenhauer, vol. 6, 118–20, with the relation to Priestley's account. Hobbes's argument is also summarized in Riley, *Will and Political Legitimacy*.

51. See Emilio Vailati, "Leibniz on Locke on Weakness of Will," *Journal of the History of Philosophy* 28, no. 2 (Apr. 1990): 213–28. He calls this view of the will "externalism" since the individual's "internal" evaluation has no effect on his/her willing (215f).

52. Again, see Oberdiek, *An Encyclopedia of Philosophy*, 474. According to Stalley, this view has also led philosophers to neglect Hume's theory of the will since they assume that he reduces it to the passions as the cause of actions. Hume's definition, which most critics pass over, mistakenly so, according to Stalley, is: "the internal impression we feel and are conscious of, when we knowingly give

rise to any new motion of our body, or new perception of our mind" (cited in Stalley, "The Will in Hume's Treatise," 41).

Cassirer in his *Philosophy of the Enlightenment* argues that Condillac attempts to take Locke's position and reinterpret it in the direction of radical voluntarism (103).

53. See William L. Rowe, "Causality and Free Will in the Controversy between Collins and Clarke," *Journal of the History of Philosophy* 25, no. 1 (Jan. 1987): 51–67. He says: Locke directed "attention to the question whether we are free to *do* what we will, while pushing into the background the more fundamental question of whether we are free to *will* what we will" (51). In this way Locke seems to unite both determination of the will and freedom. *An Essay Concerning Human Understanding,* book 2, sec. 33.

    The *Handbuch philosophischer Grundbegriffe* article on "Wille" by Schöpf, gives a good critical summary of the interpretation of this empiricist reduction by behaviorism (1703–5).

    Riley argues convincingly throughout *Will and Political Legitimacy* (see, e.g., 15) that the social contract theorists like Hobbes and Locke are caught in a contradiction, since their political theories rely on a theory of will that they otherwise discount. I see this kind of contradiction as typical.

54. Needless to say, my word choice here (they were "determined") is ironic, indicating that extreme determinism is engaged in a performative contradiction.

55. Mach in Eisler, *Wörterbuch der philosophischen Begriffe,* 569.

56. In terms of the Venn diagram, here we have the opposite eclipsing, with the same results—a point that Adorno and Horkheimer, e.g., will stress.

57. See Oberdiek, *An Encyclopedia of Philosophy,* 474.

58. Kant, *Critique of Practical Reason,* 25. See also the *Grundlegung* (A VIII), where he argues that a moral law must have absolute necessity. See Heiz Röttges, *Nietzsche und die Dialektik der Aufklärung* (Berlin, New York: Walter de Gruyter, 1972), 177.

    For Levinas's critique: "The idealist intelligible constitutes a system of coherent ideal relations whose presentation before the subject is equivalent to the entry of the subject into this order and its absorption into those ideal relations. The subject has no resource in itself that does not dry up under the intelligible sun" (*Totality and Infinity,* 216).

59. For this reason Hirschberger sees Aristotle introducing for the first time a special notion of the will into Greek thought that goes beyond the rational determinism of the Socratics. Aristotle opposes general acts of will (*echourion*), which animals and children also perform, to action of free will (*proairesis*). See Hirschberger, *Geschichte der Philosophie,* 234–35.

60. Eisler's condensed history (*Wörterbuch der philosophischen Begriffe,* 574f) is informative.

61. Hirschberger: "Human beings can choose between the sensual-earthly and the transcendental-spiritual world. . . . This is why human beings are free (*ante-chourios*) and possess self-determination. . . . That freedom can be misused for the sake of evil is explained by Origin, and following him Gregory of Nysa, in terms of human's essence as created beings. Whereas God has being out

of Himself, and is therefore unchanging and necessary, created beings have a beginning and are thus mutable" (*Geschichte der Philosophie,* 340–41).

62. This is another reason, besides his epigonal status, why Schopenhauer, *the* philosopher of the will, is, ironically, one of the least useful for the dialectical models presented in this book.

63. Schopenhauer, *Welt als Wille und Vorstellung, Werke,* vol. 1, 142.

64. The German for metaphor is, in fact, *Übertragung.* And Schopenhauer raises this method to the height of philosophical knowledge. He writes: "Erkenntniß des Identischen in verschiedenen Erscheinungen und des Verschiedenen in ähnlichen ist eben, wie Plato so oft bemerkt, Bedingung zur Philosophie" ("Knowledge of what is the same in different phenomena and of what is different in similar ones, is precisely, as Plato often remarks, the condition of philosophy"; *Welt als Wille und Vorstellung, Werke,* vol. 1, 155). This is also Aristotle's definition of metaphor.

65. It is interesting that on this same page (193) he appeals to the Scholastics, who would have likewise maintained a distinction between *forma substantialis* and *forma accidentalis,* albeit not always calling the former "will," as we have seen.

66. Eisler, *Wörterbuch der philosophischen Begriffe,* 574f. Schelling deals with this in the *Philosophische Untersuchungen über das Wesen der menschlichen Freiheit,* 75. See also Schopenhauer, *Über die Freiheit des menschlichen Willens,* vol. 6, 117. Also Cottingham ("The Intellect, the Will, and the Passions," 253f), who shows that precisely around their interpretation of this dilemma Descartes and Spinoza approach each other. Descartes's apparent radical indeterminism/indifference saves the man in such a situation, but reduces this kind of "free will" compared to that of "necessarily assenting" to a clear truth. Thus, Descartes writes, "the indifference which I feel when I am not swayed by any reason to one side rather than the other is the lowest grade of liberty and reveals a lack of knowledge rather than a perfection of will" (*Meditations,* 4; cited in Copleston, *History of Philosophy,* vol. 4, 141). Spinoza has the man faced with an "indifferent" choice perish, but then questions whether a being with such indistinct reasoning (that would not compel him to a choice) is even human. In other words, Descartes preserves some notion of radically free choice but prefers the rational necessitation of Spinoza.

67. Schelling, *Philosophische Untersuchungen über das Wesen der menschlichen Freiheit,* 29.

68. Schöpf, in *Handbuch philosophischer Grundbegriffe,* 1712. He also writes: "Arbitrary willfulness (*Willkür*) appears as the flipside of necessity" (1708). Locke, for example, for all his empirical determinism, also represents a view of the will as a separate "power to bear or forebear, continue or end several actions of our minds and motions of our bodies, barely by a thought or preference of the mind, ordering or, as it were commanding, the doing or not doing of such and such a particular action." *Essay Concerning Human Understanding,* book 2, xxi, 5.

See also Riley (*Will and Political Legitimacy* 202 and note 11, referring to Aarsleff): Locke did try to revise this reductive and determinist position.

See Vailati on Locke's "voluntarist" stance: "even with all the uneasiness [of passions] in place, as it were, whether the agent will decide to act is still undetermined" ("Leibniz on Locke on Weakness of Will," 224f).

69. The main religious thinkers were Augustine (in his debates with the Plegians) and later, Luther.

70. Spinoza says: "In the nature of things nothing is contingent, but all things are determined from the necessity of divine nature to a certain mode of action and existence" (*Ethics,* I, 29). See Richard V. Mason, "Spinoza on the Causality of Individuals," *Journal of the History of Philosophy* 24, no. 2 (Apr. 1986): 197–210. He looks at the serious problems that arise in Spinoza's system from the gap between the endless chain of causally connected finite events and the infinite (God, "infinite modes"). Spinoza: "There is by necessity for each and every existing thing some definite cause on account of which it exists" (*Ethics,* I, 8, Scholium 2); or: "For everything whatsoever a cause or reason must be ascribed, either for its existence or for its non-existence" (*Ethics,* I, 11, Demonstration 2). See Mason, "Spinoza on the Causality of Individuals," 207.

71. Eisler, *Wörterbuch der philosophischen Begriffe,* 575f. One of Schopenhauer's favorite lines comes from Spinoza, who claimed that a stone falling with the inevitability of physical laws would, if it were conscious, believe itself to be free.

72. See Cassirer, *Philosophy of the Enlightenment,* 122, on the inner dynamism of this doctrine of "immanence" that leads to a form of voluntarism.

73. *Theodicy,* sec. 336. See Vailati, "Leibniz on Locke on Weakness of Will," 217n.16.

74. Vailati: "In Leibniz' system, the issue of freedom occupies a prominent position. Moreover, since for him freedom does not only involve absence of external impediments, but also, among other things, the power to will as one should, it directly conflicts with weakness of will" ("Leibniz on Locke on Weakness of Will," 213).

75. The *Pantheismusstreit* at the end of the eighteenth century shows how the religious and the secular came together. What sounds like a conflict over strictly religious concerns (the nature of God in the world) became identified via the main object of dispute, Spinoza, with the legitimate extent of systematizing in philosophy. That is, the sense that pantheism (God is in everything equally) must be fought by traditional Christian thought was parallel to the attacks on systems of philosophy that would see reason and order in everything.

76. He writes: "at the ground of things is always disorder [*das Regellose*], as if it could break through to the surface; and nowhere does it seem that order and form are at the origin but rather that a primal disorder has been brought to order. This is the incomprehensible basis of the reality of things, the indivisible remainder, the problem that even the greatest effort of the understanding cannot solve. It will remain forever ungrounded [*im Grunde*]" (*Philosophiche Untersuchungen über das Wesen der menschlichen Freiheit* 54).

77. Riley, in *The General Will before Rousseau: The Transformation of the Divine into the Civic,* Studies in Moral, Political and Legal Philosophy (Princeton: Princeton University Press, 1986), has traced the use of the concept of "general will" from the seventeenth century to Rousseau. Thanks to Malebranche, he

writes, a "ready-made notion of non-particular, non-willful will was available to Rousseau, who completed [Bayle's secular conversion and] Montesquieu's conversion of the general will of God into the general will of the citizen" (250).

Consider also Judith N. Shklar's article "General Will" in *Dictionary of the History of Ideas,* vol. 2, ed. Philip D. Wiener (New York: Charles Scribner's Sons, 1973), 275ff; and Alberto Postigliola, "De Malebranche à Rousseau: Les Apories de las Volonté Générale et la Revanche du 'Raissonneur Violent,' " *Annales de la Société Jean-Jacques Rousseau,* vol. 39 (Geneva: Chez A. Jullien, 1980), 134ff.

78. Cassirer, *Philosophy of the Enlightenment,* 260f.

79. This notion of "particularism" was inherited from Malebranche. See W. T. Jones, "Rousseau's General Will and the Problem of Consent," *Journal of the History of Philosophy* 25, no. 1 (Jan. 1987): 105–30, for a strong argument in favor of Rousseau's notion. He interprets the "general will" in non-supraindividual terms: "The general will does not differ from the will of all in being a group will; it is no more a supraindividual will than is the will of all. Like the will of all, the general will is the aggregated expression of a number of distinct, individual decisions" (112). The difference is that in the case of the general will these individual decisions take the general interest into account and are reached by following consensus-making rules established by the "sovereign."

Koselleck's view is much bleaker in *Kritik und Krise: Eine Studie zur Pathogenese der bürgerlichen Welt* (Frankfurt a.M.: Suhrkamp, 1976). Rousseau's decisive step, he writes, is to take the sovereign will, detach it from the monarch, and turn it into the general will: "This will as sovereign cannot be delegated or represented; it becomes invisible. . . . The result is the totalitarian state" (136).

80. The main arguments against the individual will as the ground of ethics and politics appear in the chapter on moral reason in Hegel's *Phänomenologie des Geistes* and the second section of the *Philosophie des Rechts.*

Hösle points out that precisely at this point there is a contradiction in Hegel because he does not develop the individual *and* intersubjective features of will. See especially his *Hegels System. Der Idealismus der Subjektivität und das Problem der Intersubjektivität,* 2 vols. (Hamburg: Meiner, 1987).

Although Riley does indicate the ambivalence that persists in both Rousseau and Hegel (*The General Will Before Rousseau,* 15f), he also stresses the movement that would increasingly subsume the individual under the universal.

81. See Sally Sedgwick, "Hegel's Critique of the Subjective Idealism of Kant's Ethics," *Journal of the History of Philosophy* 26, no. 1 (Jan. 1988): 89–105. According to Hegel, she writes: "The 'formalism' of the Critical philosophy could produce no better than the inevitable corruption of the categorical imperative into a license for subjective arbitrariness—reducing ethics to the 'special theory of life held by the individual . . . and his private conviction' " (90). See Hegel, *Philosophie des Rechts,* §§ 140 and 137.

82. Habermas attempts to mediate this tension by means of communicative reason: "In communicative processes of education, the identity of the individual and that of the collective are formed and maintained simultaneously (gleichursprünglich)" (*Erläuterungen zur Diskursethik* [Frankfurt a.M.: Suhrkamp,

1991], 15). This formation of identity he commonly calls "Willensbildung," and it is here that he could use a more developed theory of the will.

83. Riley, *The General Will*, 167.

84. Consider Žižek's powerful formulation of a dialectic in his sense between the individual and universal will in *Tarrying with the Negative: Kant, Hegel, and the Critique of Ideology* (Durham: Duke University Press, 1993). Recall that according to Žižek's reading of Hegel, the negative "passage" from one dialectical extreme to another arises out of an internal negation, i.e., from the negation inhering within the one extreme and emerging precisely as it would try to negate its own lack. He offers the more "concrete" example from the domain of politics: "The 'unity' of universal and particular Will does not consist in their codependence, but in the dialectical reversal of the universal Will into its opposite: insofar as the universal Will is opposed to the multitude of particular Wills, it turns into the utmost particular Will of those who pretend to embody it (since it *excludes* the wealth of particular Wills)" (123).

CHAPTER 2

1. See Höffe's article on the will: Man is not merely an animal because his language makes the fulfillment of his needs more than causal stimuli-reaction. I would then argue: That gap between needs and the law, made possible by language and the opening of desire, is the site of the will. Otfried Höffe, ed., *Lexikon der Ethik* (München: Beck, 1997). See Derrida and Butler on the law.

2. See Jürgen Habermas, "Treffen Hegels Einwände gegen Kant auch auf die Diskursethik zu?" in *Erläuterungen zur Diskursethik* (Frankfurt a.M.: Suhrkamp, 1991).

3. Generally I shall speak of Adorno although there are times when I must refer to Adorno/Horkheimer as coauthors of the *Dialektik der Aufklärung: Philosophische Fragmente* (1944; reprint, Frankfurt a.M.: Fischer, 1989).

4. The connections between Adorno and Lacan have received little attention. Slavoj Žižek has provided the most illuminating analyses in *Enjoy Your Symptom! Jacques Lacan in Hollywood and Out* (New York: Routledge, 1992); *For they know not what they do: Enjoyment as a Political Factor* (New York: Verso, 1991); *The Sublime Object of Ideology* (London: Verso, 1989); and *Tarrying with the Negative* (Durham: Duke University Press, 1993). I am grateful Bruce Fink for his assistance in working out many of these ideas.

5. As Lacan points out, Sade's *Philosophie dans le boudoir* (1796) appeared just eight years after Kant's *Kritik der praktischen Vernunft*. "So as to produce the kind of shock or eye-opening effect that seems to me necessary if we are to make progress, I simply want to draw your attention to this: if *The Critique of Practical Reason* appeared in 1788, seven years after the first edition of *The Critique of Pure Reason*, there is another work which came out six years after *The Critique of Practical Reason*, a little after Thermidor in 1795, and which is called *Philosophy in the Boudoir*" (*Seminar VII*, 78).

6. Kant deals with the "schematism of pure understanding" in book 2 of the *Kritik*

der reinen Vernunft on the faculty of judgment. The schematism helps that faculty subsume the particular under the general.

7. Žižek comes back time and again to the Hegelian notion of an "infinite judgement" that can bridge the gap between the most abstract and most concrete, although misinterpretations typically reduce such judgments to the one aspect or the other. In Hegel's infamous example, the infinite judgment asserting the reality of Spirit is reduced by phrenology to the claim that my thoughts can be read in my skull's morphology. (Or the male's sexual organ's dual function gets reduced to urination.) In this case, we perhaps could see Adorno performing the same reduction on Kant's transcendental argument.

8. Adorno/Horkheimer do see an ambiguity in Kant's definition and recognize in "das transzendentale überindividuelle Ich" also a *utopian* moment (see *DA,* 90, 92), where they say that science must deny this other side of Kant. But that other side is not brought out in this "fragment"; we shall see it emerge later, however, in *Negative Dialektik.*

9. This bind is typical of the Enlightenment, as we saw, given the shifting function of natural law vis-à-vis divine determination and free (human) will.

10. See the excellent notes by the translator, James Swenson.

11. Consider Habermas's formulation of Hegel's critique of Kant: "Because the Categorical Imperative separates the pure demands of practical reason from processes of formative education and historical concretizations of Spirit, it justifies for the guardians of morality a politics that would see the realization of reason as the goal at any price (even immoral actions)" (*Erläuterungen zur Diskursethik,* 10–11). Habermas proposes one argument to save both Kant and his own form of *Diskursethik* from this charge. But we can see Lacan's attempt to tie pleasure and that which is "beyond the pleasure principle" to the psychical development of the individual in a social order as another such attempt.

12. Lacan formulates the distinction in the *Seminar VII* as follows: The Kantian term *Wohl* "has to do with the comfort of the subject insofar as, whenever he refers to *das Ding* as his horizon, it is the pleasure principle that functions for him. . . . On the horizon, beyond the pleasure principle, there rises up the *Gut, das Ding,* thus introducing at the level of the unconscious something that ought to oblige us to ask once again the Kantian question of the *causa noumenon*" (72f).

13. See Foucault's *L'usage des plaisirs* (Paris: Gallimard, 1984); *The Use of Pleasure. Volume 2, The History of Sexuality* (New York: Vintage, 1986).

14. Hegel's earliest critiques of Kant formulated many versions of this inversion, leading him from the oppositional mode of Critical Idealism to his own dialectics. Hegel, however, has also been recently criticized and revised in order to better take into account the role of intersubjectivity. See Roche, *Tragedy and Comedy* and Hösle, *Hegels System.*

15. Again consider Habermas on Hegel's critique of Kant: "Hegel's objection to the formalism of Kantian ethics: Because the Categorical Imperative insists on abstracting from all particular content of maxims of actions and duties, the application of this moral principle must lead to tautological judgments" (*Erläuterungen zur Diskursethik* 9).

16. Lacan quotes: "Long live Poland, for if there were no Poland, there would be no Poles" (*KS*, 57).

17. See Susan Wolf's arguments in *Freedom within Reason* and in chapter 1 of this book.

18. One way of seeing the direction of my argument is as follows: The originally planned (1770) subtitle that Kant was to give the *Kritik der reinen Vernunft* was "Die Grenzen der Sinnlichkeit und der Vernunft." The limits and borders which it is "critique's" job to draw, however, took the form of disjunctions between these two spheres. Adorno and Lacan reveal the limits of such a disjunctive model, thereby leading us to the need to reconceptualize their interrelationship, to redraw the borders and limits of the spheres of interpenetration between sensuality and reason.

19. Here Adorno and Horkheimer make an interesting association between women and Jews.

20. This is a crucial point for Adorno. Hamlet is an early example of modern, Western, bourgeois subjectivity "at the point where the self-liberating modern subject begins to engage in self-reflection" (*ND*, 227). This allows Adorno to tie Kant's problems, i.e., his dangerous conceptual splitting of the spheres of nature and reason, desire and law, drive and freedom, to an origin in the history of thought. See *ND*, 217: "Reflection on the question of the free will does not put the question to rest but rather gives it a turn toward the history of philosophy: why did the theses 'the will is free' and 'the will is unfree' become antinomies?"

21. One could connect Adorno's notion of *das Hinzutretende* here to more recent discussions by translating it as "the abject." See Butler, *Gender Trouble* and *Bodies That Matter.*

22. Schelling, as we have seen, opens his *Philosophical Enquiries into the Nature of Human Freedom* with examples of typical reductions of dialectical sentences to meaningless and absurd identities.

23. Adorno points out here that this view is undoubtedly motivated by a "progressive" politics in Kant, i.e., individual autonomy against "the violence done [to the individual] by a hierarchical society" (*ND*, 237).

24. Adorno gives the contradiction a form that echoes Lacan's interrelation between the "brute subject" (S) and the Other of the symbolic order: "The dawning consciousness of freedom nourishes itself on the archaic impulses that are not yet directed by the Ego. The more the Ego controls them, the more that earlier freedom appears to it as mere chaos. Without recollection (*Anamnesis*) of the untamed, pre-Ego impulses, which are later banned to the zone of unfree nature, there could be no understanding of freedom, which in turn ends by strengthening the Ego. In the philosophical concept of spontaneity, which rouses acts of freedom beyond empirical existence, we hear the echo of that which the Ego would have destroyed to maintain its own form of freedom" (*ND*, 221). We will encounter a similar line of reasoning in Habermas's discussion of "the interests of reason" (*Vernunftsinteressen*) in chapter 3.

25. Schelling, *Philosophical Enquiries into the Nature of Human Freedom*, 46: "wanting is primal being (Ursein) and as such takes on the same predicates: groundlessness, eternity, temporal independence, and self-affirmation."

26. Adorno describes a development that echoes the argument in *Dialektik der Aufklärung*. In the first stage, "the irrationality of the will is repressed and branded false as a result of Reason's bad conscience." But then it returns as "bourgeois evil . . . as the afterlife of the older repressed yet not completely subjected will." The problem is that once it gets separated from rationality, this "will, whose triumph the National Socialists celebrated at their party rallies, is open to commit any crime" (*ND*, 240).

27. Adorno: "separating out the constituting transcendental subject from the constituted empirical subject does not remove the contradiction, since the transcendental exists only as the individuated unity of consciousness, as a moment of the empirical" (*ND*, 239).

28. Adorno stresses the difficulty of portraying our nature as becoming in "a language that bears the stigmata of being" (*ND*, 292f).

29. Adorno is discussing the problem with Kant's "Gedankenexperimente," in which Kant tries to show the free will in action by *isolating* particular choices. Precisely that act, according to Adorno, betrays the will's power and leads it into a debilitating double bind.

30. Recall Lacan's definition: a signifier represents a subject to another signifier; he thereby breaks with the communicative model according to which two subjects exchange signifiers between them in a reciprocal manner.

31. See Manfred Frank, *Das individuelle Allgemeine: Textstrukturierung und Text interpretation nach Schleiermacher* (Frankfurt a.M.: Suhrkamp, 1977) for a similar reading of Lacan. Here I tie the dialectic he unfolds there in terms of Schleiermacher to the will.

32. I refer here to Hegel's dialectical sentence that forces us to interpret backwards from predicate to subject. This is also the movement of the reversed arrow in the first nodule of the graph of desire (see note 59 to this chapter).

33. The fact that the subject, in order to gain definition, also must be in some sense killed off, i.e., give up a part of itself, is related to the example of "your money or your life" that will play a role later.

34. See Lacan's discussion of *das Ding* in Freud's early *Entwurf einer Psychoanalyse:* "it is to the extent that the signifying structure interposes itself between perception and consciousness that the unconscious intervenes, that the pleasure principle intervenes. . . . And it is at this point that that reality intervenes, which has the most intimate relationship to the subject, the *Nebenmensch.* . . . The *Ding* is the element that is initially isolated by the subject in his experience of the *Nebenmensch* as being by its very nature alien, *Fremde.* . . . It is then in relation to the original *Ding* that the first orientation, the first choice, the first seat of subjective orientation takes place" (*Seminar VII*, 51–54).

35. The term "perversion," which in Lacan echoes punningly the neologism "père-version," is not intended to be judgmental but to indicate a particular kind of "turn" (or vicissitude) in the Oedipal configuration. Lacan writes in Seminar VII: "I have outlined then two cases that Kant doesn't envisage, two forms of transgression beyond the limits normally assigned to the pleasure principle in opposition to the reality principle given as a criterion, namely, excessive object sublimation and what is commonly known as perversion" (109).

36. The role of identification in sadomasochism clearly goes back to Freud's analysis, e.g,. in "Ein Kind wird geschlagen."

37. Žižek's gloss is illuminating: "Desire is constituted by 'symbolic castration,' the original loss of the *Thing;* the void of this loss is filled out by *objet petit a,* the fantasy-object; this loss occurs on account of our being 'embedded' in the symbolic universe which derails the 'natural' circuit of our needs; etc., etc." (*Sublime Object of Ideology,* 3). And further, from *Tarrying with the Negative*: Desire is "what in demand is irreducible to need" (121). It produces a new object which replaces the lost-sublated object of need—*objet petit a,* the object-cause of desire. This paradoxical object "gives body" to the dimension because of which demand cannot be reduced to need: it is as if the surplus of the demand over its (literal) object—over what the demand immediately-literally demands—again embodies itself in an object. "*Objet a* is a kind of 'positivization,' filling out, of the void we encounter every time we are struck by the experience of 'This in not that!' In it, the very inadequacy, deficiency, of every positive object assumes positive existence, i.e. becomes an object" (121f).

38. I see no reason, however, why this list needs to be limited in this clearly Freudian fashion. Our skin itself, for example, forms such an intermediary zone, as could hair, tears, etc.

39. Lacan writes: "Whoever has read us this far knows that desire, more exactly, is supported by a fantasy which has at least one foot in the Other, and precisely the one that counts, even and particularly if it happens to limp" (KS, 67). This playful and dense formulation brings a number of points together. Desire is only possible because of fantasy, which, as $\mathcal{S} \lozenge a$ occurs at the interlocking of the spheres. The one foot in the Other limps because it is the Oedipal foot, the cut being the effect of castration.

40. Lacan notes in the Seminar VII: "[S]ince it is a matter of finding it again, we might just as well characterize this object as a lost object. But although it is essentially a question of finding it again, the object indeed has never been lost" (58).

41. The sadist is always "getting at" something in the tortured's body, some other substance, the "cause" in the "object of desire." Žižek analyzes this in the *Sublime Object of Ideology* when he discusses the "second death" (and the wonderful example of video games). Also, recall Adorno on the dialectic of the strong and the weak: The pleasure of the strong over the weak is particularly impossible since in "getting off" on eradicating the weak it needs the weak and is thus reminded of its own repressed weakness.

42. I think the first and second mention of "will" in Lacan's quote are thus different.

43. Lacan writes in the Seminar VII: "*Das Ding* is that which I will call the beyond-or-the-signified. It is as a function of this beyond-of-the-signified and of an emotional (*pathetique*) relationship to it that the subject keeps its distance and is constituted in a kind of relationship characterized by primary affect, prior to any repression" (54).

44. The phrase "rejects the pain of existing into another" is ambivalent. I would read it in the following two ways: (1) "Existing" for a subject means coming into (contact with) an Other, which is a painful process (castration); the Sadist

subject rejects this painful existence. (2) The Sadist takes the pain of his or her own existence and pro-(re-)jects it into the Other.

45. For a gloss on this term, see Anthony Wilden's commentary in *The Language of the Self: The Function of Language in Psychoanalysis* (Baltimore: Johns Hopkins University Press, 1968).

46. This abstract sounding process gets played out all too concretely in Sade. His characters can be interpreted as striving to gain an autonomy by literally filling, and having filled, every bodily orifice (hence the acrobatics of multiple bodies in the effort to leave none open). But what is done in the name of an absolute will to master desire in fact would lead to an end of both willing and desire, which depend on the self's splitness and openness toward the other (and vice versa).

47. There seems to be a major ambiguity in Kant's reference to *Ding an sich*. These things in themselves are generally understood to be the things "behind" appearances, as if behind the world we experience there were another world of things in themselves, like Ideal Forms, that we cannot experience. (Hence, Schopenhauer saw Kant as a basic Platonist.) But Kant also refers to basic ideas (freedom, God, immortality of the soul) as the *Dinge an sich*. These "things" indeed must be defined differently than objects in the world of experience.

48. Hence, although the first *Kritik* precedes the second by seven years, the needs of the second, the arguments guaranteeing freedom, were probably the pressing ones all along. Kant's main goal was less epistemological than ethical/moral, namely to preserve the sphere of freedom over and against the domination of causal knowing.

49. Actually we shall see as the argument progresses that Kant's thought shifted in regards to the will. The concept began more as an intermediary agency between nature and reason, but by the time of the *Metaphysik der Sitten* (1797) he identified will with practical reason itself. It becomes the transcendental condition behind *Willkür*, which now takes over the role of the actual agency that humans use to choose, decide, and realize their ideas (*Vorstellungen*). Perhaps this "idealization" of will vis-à-vis *Willkür* is responsible for the decline of the latter concept into the modern meaning of arbitrary.

50. Adorno stresses this link negatively in the section "Intelligibles und Bewußtseins-einheit" in *Negative Dialektik*.

51. The ambivalence contained in this notion of *Nötigung* is thus linked to the ambivalence contained in the notion of wanting.

52. "Wir werden also die Möglichkeit eines kategorischen Imperativs gänzlich a priori zu untersuchen haben, da uns hier der Vorteil nicht zustatten kommt, daß die Wirklichkeit desselben in der Erfahrung gegeben und also die Möglichkeit nicht zur Festsetzung, sondern bloß zur Erklärung nötig wäre" ("We will have to investigate the possibility of a categorical imperative solely a priori since we do not have the advantage of finding the reality of such an imperative in our experience or of being able merely to explain rather than establish it"; *GzMdS*, 41).

53. Thus we see how close he is to Sade: Both point to the radical gap in human existence and would (brutally) close it.

54. Note how this formulation has us acting out of freedom and in recognition of our splitness and yet also, as its fantasmatic result ("as if"), turns us into the objects of natural law. This is exactly what we saw above in Lacan's reading of Sade and the flipping over of the interlocking circles to give the sense of wholeness.

55. See Lacan's "God and the Jouissance of The Woman," in *Feminine Sexuality* (New York: Norton, 1985), 142.

56. See also the footnote, *GzMdS,* 41.

57. By analytic he means that the attainment of happiness would be necessarily contained in the concept of virtue, and vice versa.

58. See Lacan on desire and metonymic chain, e.g., "The Agency of the Letter in the Unconscious," in *Ecrits: A Selection,* trans. Alan Sheridan (New York: Norton, 1977).

59. We can make this Kantian argument appropriately dynamic by varying another of Lacan's diagrams, namely the "arc" of desire from "The Subversion of the Subject and the Dialectic of Desire in the Freudian Unconscious" (Ecrits: A Selection, 292–325). (I am grateful to Ken Reinhard for pointing this out.) Take the model for the drive and add the circle of the Other. The drive leaves the body (through and by carving out "rims"), enters into the Other, and hollows out a space/*objet petit a* that belongs to both.

60. This notion of the will "at the crossroads" is historically and conceptually rich. It echoes the example from Buridan of the ass (= will) that would die of thirst, unable to choose "at the crossroads" between two equally distant wells unless some motivation did not impel it to motion. Moreover, we can recall the conceptual model mentioned in chapter 1 of the differential: The will "at the crossroads" is the infinitesimally small gap (as between two asymptotically approaching lines or the top of a parabolic function). It takes an infinitesimal amount of motivation (from the physical or noumenal side of our being) to move us from this point, to overcome the gap, but the point must be left open if we are not to be determined by either nature or the law.

61. Swenson points out these linguistic possibilities without providing an interpretation in his final note.

62. Žižek formulates this dialectic in a way that unites Adorno and Lacan: "the ultimate proof of the constitutive character of the dependence on the Other is precisely so-called 'totalitarianism': in its philosophical foundation, 'totalitarianism' designates an attempt on the part of the subject to surmount this dependence by taking upon himself the performative act of grace. Yet the price to be paid for it is the subject's perverse self-objectivization, i.e., his transmutation into the object-instrument of the Other's inscrutable Will" (*Tarrying with the Negative,* 272n. 10).

63. Žižek's summary: "This is what Kant's theory of metaphysics ultimately is about: metaphysics endeavors to heal the wound of the 'primordial repression' (the inaccessibility of the 'Thing which thinks') by allocating to the subject a place in the 'great chain of being.' What metaphysics fails to notice is the price to be paid for this allocation: the loss of the very capacity it wanted to account for, i.e., human freedom. Kant himself commits an error when, in his *Critique of Practical Reason,* he conceives of freedom (the postulate of practical

reason) as a noumenal Thing; what gets obfuscated thereby is his fundamental insight according to which I retain my capacity of a spontaneous-autonomous agent precisely and only insofar as I am not accessible to myself as a Thing" (*Tarrying with the Negative*, 15).

64. See the end of *GzMdS*.

CHAPTER 3

1. It might furthermore be claimed that Nietzsche is not interested, ultimately, in "concepts" and that he does not want to replace bad concepts in older philosophies with his newer, better ones. But if we have an appropriately dialectical understanding of what a concept is, and certainly a "concept of the will" would have to be complexly dialectical given the nature of willing, then I see no problem in referring to Nietzsche's "concept of the will (to power)," even as we accept that it is fluid, fluctuating, becoming, self-overcoming, continuous, and strains against the very borders of linguistic and conceptual definition.

2. See Habermas, "Philosophie als Platzhalter und Interpret," in *Moralbewußtsein und kommunikatives Handeln* (Frankfurt a.M.: Suhrkamp, 1983), 9–28, for an account of his conception of philosophy not as "queen" of the disciplines (standing above and outside of them), but as the site *within* the disciplines where theoretical reflection occurs.

3. What comes in between these two treatments is, of course, the theory of communicative action (*Theorie des kommunikativen Handelns* [Frankfurt a.M.: Suhrkamp, 1981]). Although Nietzsche is not dealt with explicitly there, some basic formulations of that theory should be kept in mind for what follows. First, picking up on a parallelism between Kant's three critiques and Weber's three worlds, Habermas argues against the movement of modern Western thought to divorce aesthetics, epistemology, and ethics. Second, the political ramifications of the splitting of thought into components between which it is impossible to choose, i.e., the connections between nihilism and (proto)fascism, are clearer. And third, the solution to the first two problematic developments is offered in the form not of a new metaphysics or *Fundamentalontologie* but of a theory of intersubjective agency. It is most fruitful, especially if we want to build bridges to Foucault, to see this solution as coming *from* Nietzsche (his theory of the will) rather than as *opposed* to him (his theory of power).

4. Here we could use the diagram of interlocking circles again, with one representing, say, creativity or "life" and the other knowledge or power.

5. See Manfred Frank, *Der kommende Gott: Vorlesungen über die neue Mythologie* (Frankfurt a.M.: Suhrkamp, 1982).

6. This argument by association between Foucault and Heidegger runs throughout the section, e.g., *PDM*, 313. But even if a structural parallel exists between the hermeneutic prereflexive concepts that constitute meaning for a structure even though they are not directly accessible from within the system, and Foucault's "historical a priori," they need not be dismissed as religious or mystical. In the next chapter, I connect hermeneutics indirectly to Foucault via the notion of a "will to interpretation."

7. Thus, the following statement occurs apparently as a critique of Foucault, whereas even for Habermas it could and should point towards the strength of Foucault's effort: "Like Heidegger, Foucault undertakes a fusion of opposed meanings" (*PDM* 300).
8. Habermas writes: "In making the transition to a theory of power, Foucault isolates the will to power from its context in the history of metaphysics and allows it to be absorbed completely by the category of power" (*PDM*, 317).
9. Ironically, Jonathan Arac in "The Function of Foucault at the Present Time," *Humanities and Society* 3, no. 1 (Winter 1980): 73–86 turns this same argument around against Habermas—thereby at least implicitly limiting the plausibility of the biographical approach in general (see especially 80f).
10. See also the interviews "On Power" and "Power and Sex" in *PPC* and the interview in Hubert L. Dreyfus and Paul Rabinow, *Michel Foucault: Beyond Structuralism and Hermeneutics* (Chicago: University of Chicago Press, 1983).
11. Alan Sheridan, *Michel Foucault: The Will to Truth* (London and New York: Routledge, 1980); Dreyfus and Rabinow, *Michel Foucault: Beyond Structuralism and Hermeneutics*; Michael Mahon, *Foucault's Nietzschean Genealogy: Truth, Power, and the Subject* (Albany: State University of New York Press, 1992); Allan Megill, "Foucault, Structuralism, and the Ends of History," *Journal of Modern History* 51 (Sept. 1979): 451–503; and John Rajchman, "Nietzsche, Foucault, and the Anarchism of Power," *Semiotext(e)* 3 (1978): 96–107.
12. One of the most recent positive uses of Foucault's later turn to the self is Elsbeth Probyn's chapter, "Technologizing the Self: Foucault and 'le souci du soi,' " in her *Sexing the Self: Gendered Positions in Cultural Studies* (New York: Routledge, 1993), 108–37. Also Lois McNay, *Foucault and Feminism: Power, Gender and the Self* (Boston: Northeastern University Press, 1992).
13. Charles C. Lemert and Garth Gillan in *Michel Foucault: Social Theory and Transgression* (New York: Columbia University Press, 1982) also imply that the division between power and the will to power is central to Foucault's project. "The answer to power," they write, "is thus a transformed will to power" (90). The will to power need not be "subjected to power" or "in love with power" (their reformulation of Foucault's gloss on fascism; 90). The will to power, with intentional yet nonsubjective transgression as its motor, can transgress even the desire for power. They thus imply that the gap between power and the will to power is the same gap between different kinds of history (history-as-continuity contains the historian's hidden desire for power whereas history-as-event is motivated by the historian's willingness to thwart control) or between different kinds of political strategy (rationally unified or dispersed).
14. Note how this already links up with Habermas: The radical self-critique contained according to Habermas in the concept of the Enlightenment is not abandoned here but *aufgehoben* in the concept of the will to knowledge. Foucault also says in an interview from 1977 that "beneath" his interest in power and sexuality lies a concern with a different kind of will: "But my problem has always been on the side of another term: truth. How did the power exerted in insanity produce psychiatry's 'true' discourse? The same applies to sexuality: *to revive the will to know* the source of the power exerted upon sex" (*PPC*,

112; my emphasis). The concept of the "will to know" allows him to pursue his critical project *against* specific regimes (of power, truth). Knowledge is by no means abandoned but, rather, reunited with its broader "interests."

15. Although "rationality" can be linked with the will and thus removed from its more limiting determination.

16. Recall also Adorno's critique of reason reduced to self-preservation.

17. Foucault in fact defines power in relational terms but this is not all he is interested in since shifts in relations require the introduction of other principles or forces. Dissymmetries between elements create a tension between the system's technology of maintaining itself and a "will" to change, resistance, augmentation. "Power," as he defines it, "has its principle not so much in a person as in a certain concerted distribution of bodies, surfaces, lights, gazes; in an arrangement whose internal mechanisms produce the relation in which individuals are caught up" (*DP*, 202). But Foucault's questioning goes beyond the apparent stasis of this structural approach by examining how the "multiplicity of often minor processes . . . converge and gradually produce the blueprint of a general method" (*DP*, 138). That unifying "blueprint" or strategy, analyzed via genealogy, is not itself power but the will to power.

18. Another term he uses is "matrices of transformation" (*HS*, 99), less well chosen perhaps but at least echoing etymologically a dynamic, generative force.

19. John Rajchman, *Michel Foucault: The Freedom of Philosophy* (New York: Columbia University Press, 1985), 121.

20. As he says in the afterword to Dreyfus and Rabinow, it is not power, but the subject, which is the general theme of his later research (*Michel Foucault*, 208).

21. Foucault's later interest in issues of "self-mastery" also fit into this examination of aspects of the will's dialectical determinations, like active/passive, desire/ the law.

22. Recall the passage near the conclusion of "Kant with Sade": "That the Sadian fantasy situates itself better in the bearers of Christian ethics than elsewhere is what our structural landmarks allow us to grasp" (74).

23. Recall Dihle on Augustine: "It is mainly through this entirely new concept of his own self that St. Augustine superseded the conceptual system of Greco-Roman culture" (*Theory of Will*, 127). See also Arendt, *The Life of the Mind*, vol. 2, who highlights Augustine's role as the "first philosopher of the will."

24. Another place where we see echoes of a dialectic of the will—in this case, the interplay of individual and supraindividual forces at the sociopolitical level— would be the argument Foucault developed in his last years concerning the relationship between ancient and modern politics. On the one hand, the Greeks played the "city-citizen game," one that involved totalization, whereby the individual is subsumed under institutions; on the other, modern (Christian) societies play a "shepherd-flock game" of "pastorship," where the goal is a kind of self-identity. See "Politics and Reason" in *PPC*, 71. Also his afterword to Dreyfus and Rabinow (*Michel Foucault*, 213).

25. An additional point of departure could be his essay on "The Dangerous Individual" in which he shows how a new conception of the "responsible agent" arose in modern forensic discourse. We have here a working out of the dialectic

of will and law, as well as an investigation of the relationship between will and representations. See *PPC,* 132, 137f, 141f, 149.

26. See my introduction.

27. The general thrust of my reading overlaps with Michael Mahon's *Foucault's Nietzschean Genealogy.* Although my focus on the will is markedly different, he does point out its centrality: "Genealogy focuses upon the specific quality of the will at the origin of values. For example, Nietzsche would reinterpret a statement such as 'Truth is a value' or 'Truth deserves reverence' into the more accurate statement, 'I will truth instead of error.' Genealogy, then, is the study of the way in which the will wills. Is it a weak or strong will? Is it a noble or a servant will? Is it creative-active or revengeful-reactive? Is it a life-affirming or a life-denying will?" (83). And yet the analysis of the concept of will is absent from his discussions of both Nietzsche and Foucault. I suspect the reason is that Mahon would associate the will with either "metaphysical baggage," or "psychologically" oriented interpretations, or "quasi-transcendentals such as human instincts or human nature" (3).

28. The title of his 1936 lectures was "Wille zur Macht als Kunst." On Heidegger's reading, see chapter 4.

29. Most references in the body of my text will be to the three-volume edition of Nietzsche's *Werke,* ed. Karl Schlechta (Frankfurt a.M.: Ullstein, 1969). On the whole I would characterize myself in the words of Bernd Nagel as a "lumper," i.e., I shall quote liberally from Nietzsche's unpublished writings, the *Nachlaß* (in vol. III of the *Werke*). I shall try to take care, however, to see that the formulations of the *Nachlaß* support rather than contradict or go far beyond formulations in Nietzsche's published works. See Magnus's essay, "Nietzsche and Postmodern Criticism" in *Nietzsche-Studien* 18 (1989). Heidegger also deals with these passages (*N,* I, 72).

30. For a parallel discussion without reference to Darwin, see the aphorism, "Warum die Schwachen siegen" (*Nachlaß, Werke* III, 707–9). For a strong materialist reading of Nietzsche, see Eric Blondel, *Nietzsche: The Body and Culture. Philosophy as a Philological Genealogy,* trans. Sean Hand (Stanford: Stanford University Press, 1991).

31. See *Die fröhliche Wissenschaft* (*Werke* II, 215, aphorism 349) for a similar argument against Darwinism as a limitation of will, which is by nature expansive, not preserving. The fact that Nietzsche may be reducing Darwin's position here does not affect my point. I am interested in the conceptual opposition that Nietzsche is setting up, regardless of whether the actual opponent is a straw man.

32. This connection between the will and interpretation will be central to the following chapter. See *Nachlaß, Werke* III, 455, 704–5, where Nietzsche rejects the interpretation of *Kraft* in physics for an inner process of will to power.

33. Some readers might argue here that Nietzsche intended to break with that tradition and that I do his radical thought a disservice by interpreting him in its light. But my response would be that it is "radical enough" to see his thought as a brilliant reformulation of the dialectics of willing. Indeed, it undermines any attempt at argumentation to claim that Nietzsche's radicality lies in his critique of the conceptual language of traditional philosophy as such.

34. On Heidegger's notion of nihilism as a "psychological" and "ontological" condition, see the next chapter.

35. Here is where the caveat mentioned above needs reiterating: Nietzsche's "concept" of the will clearly strains the limits of traditional notions of a "concept."

36. See Walter Kaufmann, *Nietzsche: Philosopher, Psychologist, Antichrist* (Princeton: Princeton University Press, 1950). But I also do not see the benefit of reading Nietzsche as non- or antidialectical, since I fear that leads to an ultimately reductive interpretation. See Gilles Deleuze, *Nietzsche and Philosophy,* trans. Hugh Tomlinson (1962; reprint, New York: Columbia University Press, 1983).

37. The associations of will to power with desire are complicated, but I think can be understood in terms of (1) Nietzsche's recognition of the primacy of these responses in human relations with the world and (2) his rejection of any reduction of will to power to *Lustgefühl*. At a minimum he wants the nonunitary will to be comprised of both *Lust* and *Unlust*. That is, the danger of viewing the will merely in terms of pleasure is that this view quickly devolves into mechanism.

38. Here we see how the will to power is linked to the notion of the "eternal return of the same"—namely via the concept of *Werden* as totality. A full exploration of this connection goes beyond the bounds of this book, but it is important to see that the notion of the totality of becoming opens up a theory of temporality that embraces the present. Nietzsche formulates this "theory" numerous times in *Also sprach Zarathustra*. For example, in the section, "Von der Erlösung" (*Werke* II, 394–95), he speaks of turning the weight of the unchangeble past, "Es war," into an acceptance of the present by saying: "So wollte ich das!" In this way, the world of being is changed into a world of will, and the "causality" of the past is changed into the willing acceptance of the present. This implicit temporal theory that embraces the present could be seen as the basis of the concept of the "eternal return of the same." Moreover, this conceptualization is present-oriented even as it avoids the aporia Habermas referred to as "presentism" (the presence of the will avoids "crypto-normativism").

39. In a chapter of his book, *Ideology* (New York: Verso, 1991), dealing with conceptual developments "from Schopenhauer to Sorel," Terry Eagleton cites Albert O. Hirschman (*The Passions and the Interests*) in a way that shows this dialectic at work: "There is, in fact, a distinction between passions and interests, which Albert Hirschman has usefully examined. For seventeenth- and eighteenth-century thought, to follow one's interests was on the whole positive, whereas to follow one's passions was not. 'Interests' suggested a degree of rational calculation, as opposed to being driven on by blind desire; it acts as a kind of intermediary category between the passions, which are generally base, and the reason, which is generally ineffectual. In the idea of 'interests,' so Hirschman argues, the passions are upgraded by reason, while reason is lent force and direction by passion. Once the sordid passion of greed can be transmuted to the social interest of making money, it can suddenly be acclaimed as a noble goal. There was always of course the risk that this opposition could be deconstructed—that 'promoting one's interest' just meant counterposing one set of passions to another; but 'interest' had the sense of a *rational* self-love about it, and was seen as conveniently predictable, whereas desire was not. 'As

the physical world is ruled by the laws of movement,' proclaimed Helvetius, 'so is the moral universe ruled by laws of interest'; and we shall see that it is only a short step from this classic bourgeois doctrine to the assumptions of postmodernism" (160).

40. This concept of *Willensbildung* is used at least six times in this lecture from *Der philosophische Diskurs der Moderne* and plays a central role in his essay on "Volkssouveränität als Verfahren. Ein normativer Begriff der Öffentlichkeit" in *Die Moderne—ein unvollendetes Projekt: Philosophisch-politische Aufsätze 1977–1992* (Leipzig: Reclam, 1992), 180–212. In that essay he appeals to conceptions of the political public sphere from the French Revolution and nineteenth century (esp. Julius Fröbel) that try to develop a "procedure for the formation of public opinion and will which would establish when a political will that is not identical with reason nonetheless can have rational support" ("Prozedur der Meinungs- und Willensbildung, die festlegt, wann ein politischer Wille, der mit Vernunft nicht identisch ist, die Vermutung der Vernunft für sich hat"; 194f). Habermas here links up with the tradition of theorizing the political will between the universal/general and individual, the rational and irrational, which we explored in chapter 1.

41. This is also an explicit point of overlap with Foucault, who, in a late interview, characterizes the specific task of the intellectual as "to participate in the formation of a political will (in which he has his role as citizen to play)" ("The Concern for Truth," in *PPC*, 265).

CHAPTER 4

1. First documented in Philippe Forget, ed., *Text und Interpretation: Deutschfranzösische Debatte* (Munich: Wilhelm Fink, 1984). In English, with different responses, Diane P. Michelfelder and Richard E. Palmer, eds., *Dialogue and Deconstruction: The Gadamer-Derrida Encounter* (Albany: State University of New York Press, 1989). Also Ernst Behler, *Derrida-Nietzsche/Nietzsche-Derrida* (Munich: Ferdinand Schöningh, 1988), and Behler, "Deconstruction vs. Hermeneutics: Derrida and Gadamer on Text and Interpretation," *Southern Humanities Review* 21, no. 3 (1987): 201–30.

2. Here Derrida places himself in the same tradition as Adorno and Lacan, although the association between the Kantian will and its inherent force/power remains unexplored in Derrida's exchange with Gadamer. His lectures on "Justice" (esp. the comments on the "enforceability of the law") could be used to illuminate his approach to this question (*Force de Soi: Le Fondement mystique de l'autorité* [Paris: Galilee, 1994]).

3. On Derrida's "avoidance" of the concept of the will, also in the face of his analysis (in *Of Spirit*) of Heidegger's "avoidance" of *Geist,* see my "Of Spirit(s) and Will(s)" in *Hegel after Derrida,* ed. Stuart Barnett (New York: Routledge, 1998), 64–90.

4. Consider Gadamer's focus on the *Sache,* a concept he gets from Hegel and is thereby associated with the *Geist.* In this way he also follows a form of forensic interpretation from Roman law that would strive to find the *voluntas* behind the *verba.* See Dihle, *Theory of Will.*

5. Hence the focus on the *gramme* of grammatology. My study of Hegel (see note above) tries to mediate these positions vis-à-vis Hegel.

6. See Michelfelder and Palmer, ed., *Dialogue and Deconstruction* for some of these different evaluations of Derrida's response.

7. The reference here is unclear. "Beide" means, obviously, both "Gesprächspartner" although the antecedent would be grammatically the two kinds of conversation—which makes no sense. Translations are generally my own or modified from *DD* since the editors seemed to have worked with a slightly different original text.

8. In this sense, Gadamer's textual hermeneutic is close to religion as "re-ligio" or that which binds a community by always being reread (to combine the literal and a more questionable etymology). See Werner Hamacher's "pleroma—zu Genesis und Struktur einer dialektischen Hermeneutik bei Hegel," in Hegel, *Der Geist des Christentums: Schriften, 1796–1800* (Berlin: Ullstein, 1978), who develops this definition from Quintilian. Also, what Gadamer says is highly relevant for any conception of a sacred text as that to which a community appeals to reestablish a harmony of understanding. Gadamer says: "Every recourse to the text, whether it be a written one or merely the repetition of an oral utterance, presumes an underlying message (Urkunde) that guarantees unity of meaning (*sinnhaft Identisches*)" (*TI*, 39; *DD*, 35).

9. There is an important issue of translation here. The German version reads: "Wie könnte man nicht versucht sein, die machtvolle Evidenz dieses Axioms zu *unterschreiben?*" (my emphasis). The English translation in *DD* is: "How could anyone not be tempted to *acknowledge* how extremely evident this axiom is?" (52; my emphasis). Something is lost in using the term "acknowledge," namely the aspect of writing and signing. We will have to return to the *form* of this question and its appeal to the issue of "signing" when we consider Derrida's written response, "Die Unterschriften interpretieren" ("Interpreting Signatures"). For now we can note that even the counterfactual "Evidenz" of this (or any axiom) still needs to be "signed" by the subject. This will raise the issue of interpreting *écriture* but also the subject in a way Derrida might not fully intend.

10. The connection to Kant is interesting on another level as well: Gadamer's hermeneutic argument is not without its ethical component. See the paragraph in *TI*, 39, where Gadamer uses the term "soll" once and "Aufgabe" (why not hear in this the echo of Kantian duty or "Pflicht"?) twice, and then, not by chance, uses the example of the speech act of the command (*Befehl*).

11. It is telling and not quite clear why the translators of Derrida's response decided to drop the first part of the title as the short piece appeared in both French and English, namely "Bonnes Volontés de Puissance" ("Guter Wille zur Macht," "Good Will to Power"), leaving only the subtitle from the German: "Three Questions to Hans-Georg Gadamer" ("Drei Fragen an Hans-Georg Gadamer"). In so doing, they downplay what I would see as the central concept, the will.

12. For example, he avoids the Kantian implications of his own position by interpreting the good will in terms of Plato. See Gadamer's essay "Arguments(s)" for a critique of Gadamer's "arguments" in *DD*, 129–49.

13. Gadamer, *Gesammelte Werke. Hermeneutik II. Wahrheit und Methode. Ergän-zungen* (Tübingen: J. C. B. Mohr, 1965), 207–15.

14. This point is argued in a very different context by Judith Butler in "Burning Acts: Injurious Speech," in *Deconstruction is/in America: A New Sense of the Political,* ed. Anselm Haverkamp (New York: New York University Press, 1995), 149–53. I would argue that Bulter's argument also would benefit from a dialectical concept of the will.

15. It appeared in *Text und Interpretation* with the title supplied by the editor, Philippe Forget, "Und dennoch: Macht des Guten Willens" and in the volume *Die Aktualität der Frühromantik.* Translated with the title "Reply to Jacques Derrida" in *DD* (55–57).

16. This is the basis of his rejection (based on Frank) of Derrida's starting point in a critique of Husserl. That is, Gadamer would agree fully with Derrida's deconstruction of the notion that meaning is located in the self-presence of the word within the subject. But the difference between Derrida and Gadamer here is that that deconstruction makes no difference to Gadamer and a constructive theory of meaning, since he saw that starting point as limited anyway.

17. Frank's criticism appears for the first time in *Das individuelle Allgemeine* (1977). Gadamer responds briefly to Frank's charge in "*Destruktion* and Decon-struction" (in *DD,* 111). See also my "The 'Transcendance' of the Individual," *Diacritics* 19, no. 2 (1989): 80–98.

18. Also in *DD* as "*Destruktion* and Deconstruction" (102–13).

19. Two points need to be made that link this formulation to Heidegger. First, this notion of "willig-unwillig," i.e., of the possibility/necessity of the will to will its own unwilling, is central to Heidegger's thought on *Gelassenheit* (see also below where we encounter a quote from Heidegger that parallels this formulation). But also, it is remarkable that Gadamer uses similar terms to characterize his own relation to Heidegger. He writes in a "Letter to Dallmayr" that he was the "williges Opfer" of Heidegger's interpretations (*DD,* 93). Moreover, there is a remarkable point of overlap here with Lacan's central formulation about *das Ding:* "It is a register where there is both good and bad will, that volens nolens, which is the true meaning of the ambivalence one fails to grasp, when one approaches it on the level of love and hate" (*Seminar VII,* 104). One could add to the last quote: which one fails to grasp if one does not see the will as both subjective and objective, active and passive.

20. In his discussion of Schleiermacher, for example: "Wir gehen von dem Satz aus: Verstehen heißt zunächst, sich miteinander verstehen. Verständnis ist zunächst Einverständnis. So verstehen einander die Menschen zumeist unmittelbar, bzw. sie verständigen sich bis zur Erzielung des Einverständnisses. Verständigung ist also immer: Verständigung über etwas. Sich verstehen ist Sichverstehen in etwas" ("We begin with the proposition: Understanding means first of all to get along with others. Understanding means agreement. Most people understand each other immediately or they work on understanding until they achieve an agreement. Understanding means always to reach an understanding about something. And to get along means to share in the understanding of something"; *WM,* 168).

21. The good will might be associated, as "attitude," with Pierre Bourdieu's notion of "disposition." See, for example, *Outline of a Theory of Practice,* trans. Richard Nice (Cambridge: Cambridge University Press, 1977).

22. In the preface to the second edition of *Wahrheit und Methode* he sides with Heidegger in seeing hermeneutics as an act of resistance against the technocratic will (xxvf). "Understanding," therefore, "is to be thought of not so much as an act of a subjectivity as the insertion into a process of transmission (*Einrücken in ein Überlieferungsgeschehen*)" (275). Likewise, the unfolding of a conversation (*Gespräch*) "does not reside in the will of the one or the other partner" (361). On the other hand, appealing specifically to Nietzsche, he stresses that the (hermeneutic) experience of the other only works insofar as the "will to power" of the other (even the slave in the master-slave relation) is recognized (342). Given this duality, it is understandable that "the true site of hermeneutics lies in this in-between (*Zwischen*)" (279).

23. This is clearly not to say that Gadamer did not try to work out a dialectic for understanding in general. The last third of *Wahrheit und Methode,* as he reminds us also in "*Destruktion* and Deconstruction" (*DD,* 111), is an attempt to work through Hegel's dialectic of experience and transfer it to the experience of interpretation. But it is significant that although the will plays a key role in that experience, its inherently dialectical structure is underilluminated.

24. Hegel, *Phänomenologie des Geistes,* 155–57, esp. 162f.

25. See *Dialogue and Deconstruction* for the various responses to Derrida. For example, Madison and Rappaport tend to see an (ironic) "logic" in Derrida's misunderstanding. Marshall, to the contrary, opens with an obvious and sharp criticism.

26. In this Gadamer is very much a Kantian and this also parallels Habermas. The good will is a task or duty of interpretation but does not guarantee factual success.

27. One can get to this counterfactually. What if after the talk a person approached Derrida and said: "You made a great point in your response and really showed the convergence of deconstruction and hermeneutics! You really understood Gadamer and agree with him on the universality of understanding!" Would Derrida not respond: "I'm afraid you misunderstood me. I understood full well what Gadamer wanted to say about understanding and if you understood me you would see that I made statements that have to be construed as *not* agreeing with him."

28. I am almost tempted to introduce an ungrammatical passive voice here: Derrida can show that the text of Gadamer's talk "can be wanted to say something else."

29. *Of Spirit: Heidegger and the Question,* trans. Geoffrey Bennington and Rachel Bowlby (Chicago: University of Chicago Press, 1991; originally published as *De l'esprit,* 1987); "Interpreting Signatures (Nietzsche/Heidegger): Two Questions" in *DD,* 58–71; and "Otobiographies: The Teaching of Nietzsche and the Politics of the Proper Name," trans. Avital Ronell, in *The Ear of the Other: Otobiography, Transference, Translation,* ed. Christie McDonald (Lincoln: University of Nebraska Press, 1988).

30. The brief second part of the essay addresses the issue of totality (*Ganzheit*), which is closely related.
31. The introduction of gender into these arguments occurs in Derrida's *Spurs/ Esperons: Nietzsche's Styles,* trans. Barbara Harlow (Chicago: University of Chicago Press, 1979) and in "Geschlecht" in *Heidegger et la Question* (Paris: Flammarion, 1990).
32. Recall the conclusion of chapter 3 on the conceptual relationship between interests and will.
33. This is not unlike Manfred Frank's criticism of the way traditional structuralist interpretation often imputes subjective, self-reflexive characteristics to structures. See especially his *Was ist Neostrukturalismus?*
34. Consider the critique of Heidegger: "When he is pretending to rescue Nietzsche from this or that distortion—that of the Nazis, for example—he does so with categories that can themselves serve to distort" (*DD,* 65). It is interesting and valuable to point out these places, but they in no way reduce the value of someone's interpretive effort, since none of us can avoid using categories that are open to distortion even as we struggle *against* distortion (and vice versa, for Derrida: none of us can avoid struggling against distortion even as we accept the use of categories that are [intentionally or not] open to distortion).
35. In many ways this argument echoes Rorty's and Fish's pragmatic approach to deconstruction, namely: Deconstruction is right that the traditional oppositions of Western thought can be deconstructed, but precisely because it is right it loses the right to criticize someone for having texts that can be deconstructed. My argument does try to go a step further, however, by turning to the concept of the will that helps to account for the inherent contradictions of understanding and its necessity.
36. This preamble is not contained in the English reedition, to which I will otherwise be referring. The following quote is thus my translation from the German edition, which included this preamble from the 1976 version of the lecture.
37. For example: Recalling the dialectic between the individual and the supraindividual will, we can see that this opening on the "state" treats it, in fact, like a will. That is, Derrida is working here with a traditional association between these two levels.
38. The fact that Derrida makes a pronouncement (*OTO,* 19) that such a negation is "beyond" dialectic does not change the fact that the way it unfolds in Derrida's text nonetheless allows us to identify it with a richly negative dialectic. That is, certainly this *dynamis* is not a dialectic in some simplistic sense of a synthesizing *Aufhebung* without negativity, but, rather, the radical negativity inhering within and always overcoming any positing. Rather than reject this dialectic, I would enhance its productively negative character. Here I am in agreement with Žižek (e.g., *Tarrying with the Negative*).
39. Derrida's analysis of the passages on Nietzsche as *décadent* would be enriched by an interpretation of the will. He is a *décadent* because he is living out the doubleness of the will that his *décadent* age is experiencing. Also, consider the basic link in this essay between the notion of *autos,* the independent self, and the *otos,* the "ear" of the other that must receive the text destined to it so that

the sender can constitute him/herself. This means that neither do the self and its message make up a self-constituting *vouloir dire,* nor does the other impose itself on a blank slate of the self. Rather, the self's and other's ears are "willing" in the sense of being "actively open." True autonomy would thus consist in being open (having an open ear) to the Other. Such, we saw through the reading of Kant with Lacan, is the nature of all wanting. This view is similar to Gadamer and we will encounter it below in Heidegger.

40. Nietzsche often associates this "nonplace" with the "Mittag des Lebens" or "der große Mittag" ("midday of life" or "the high noon"), where "man stands at the midpoint of his transition between animal and overman" ("da der Mensch auf der Mitte siener Bahn steht Zwischen Tier und Übermensch"), and this "midday" in turn with "unser letzter Wille" ("our last will"). See, e.g., *Zarathustra, Werke* II, 340. At the core of the self is a punctuating act of willfull affirmation, the Kantian "leerer Platz," or crossroads, of wanting.

41. This is, of course, Derrida's right to select the object of his analysis for his own reasons. I am saying that in doing so, he misses what I see as an opportunity to develop a concept in a nonpolemical way. See my "Of Spirit(s) and Will(s)" for a more thorough reading of Derrida's "avoidance" of the concept of will in general. Also David Wood, ed., *Of Derrida, Heidegger, and Spirit* (Evanston, Ill: Northwestern University Press, 1993), esp. Gilian Rose's "Of Derrida's Spirit," where Derrida is criticized for falsely reducing rich concepts to abstract voluntarism or "metaphysics of subjectivity" (which applies mostly to Hegelian concepts, whereby Hegel sees such "reductions" not as the goal but a product of a certain "Spirit" of modernity that needs to be overcome dialectically).

42. Especially important in this regard are the 1936 and 1941 lectures on Schelling, which have not received full attention and are only briefly alluded to by Derrida in ways that could in fact disrupt his own readings. For in Schelling we find a dialectical conception of willing, as we saw in my introduction.

43. See Derrida, *OS,* 93. "all these assertions [by Schelling on God, evil, desire], which Heidegger analyzed in his lectures, left a trace in his reading of Trakl."

44. Derrida, pointing out that Heidegger's essay on Trakl has linguistic echoes from Schelling, asks: "Why might such a continuity seem both natural and disconcerting?"

45. I shall *not* take up his concept of the "*Seinsgeschichte* of metaphysics" as such. My point is that Heidegger's views of a "history of Being" and the role of "metaphysics" in it are in many ways absurd, although when writing about him it is difficult to avoid his reifying language. In spite of that reification of *Seinsgeschichte,* the mechanisms of the dialectic of will that Heidegger works out are powerful. We will see how Heidegger's dialectic points the way to both a Gadamerian and Derridean reduction of the will to one of its partial determinations.

46. Here I pursue a modified version of Arendt's interpretation of the *Kehre* as a turn away from the centrality (of the dialectic) of the will.

47. I hope that the parallel to the arguments in chapters 2 and 3 is clear, since there, too, a thinker—Kant and Nietzsche, respectively—both opened up a powerful dialectic of willing and pointed the way to one-sided, "metaphysical" readings.

48. Heidegger argues that seeing the nature of beings in terms of effective reality ("Seiendheit als Wirklichkeit") reveals the connection between subjective effecting ("Wirken and Erwirken"), empowerment ("Ermächtigen zur Macht") and will to power, and hence the connection between being as subjectivity and being as will to power (*N* II, 236f).

49. Heidegger sees the connection between *energeia* and will to power as deeper and more complex ("verborgener und reicher") than the mere association of physical energy and power" (*N* II, 238).

50. Heidegger expresses this same image in the dialogue, *Gelassenheit,* as follows: "The horizon is thus only the side of a surrounding openness that faces us and that is filled with our view of what appears to our minds as an object" ("Das Horizonthafte ist somit nur die uns zugekehrte Seite eines uns umgebenden Offenen, das erfüllt ist mit Aussicht ins Aussehen dessen, was unserem Vorstellen als Gegenstand erscheint"; *N* II, 37). Since we saw above the way *ideia* and *Vorstellen* are linked to will (to power), this "filling" of a space with our activity can be considered the limited sphere of our representing and willing.

51. Heidegger argues that man is the measure of all things ("das Anwesende") because the sphere of his perceptions unfolds within a wider sphere that "unconceals it" ("Das Vernehmen des Anwesenden gründet auf dessen Verweilen innerhalb des Bezirks der Unverborgenheit"; *N* II, 137).

52. That is, the original sense of the "subiectum" is that which is presumed to be the ground of things ("schon vor-und so für anderes zum Grunde liegt und dergestalt Grund ist"; *N* II, 142).

53. An idea like Nietzsche's on nihilism ("Nietzsche's Gedanken des Nihilismus") is, Heidegger argues, neither the individual thinker's opinion nor the expression of a particular time but "the echo of the not yet recognized history of Being that is contained in the word that the historical individual speaks as if it were 'his language' " ("Der Widerklang der noch nicht erkannten Geschichte des Seins in dem Wort, das der geschichtliche Mensch als seine 'Sprache' spricht"; *N* II, 43f).

54. Although Heidegger never says so, in terms of intellectual history this flip into nihilism could be seen as a direct consequence of Feuerbach's reading of the essence of Christianity.

55. To keep the connection to the will to interpretation in mind, I recall that both Nietzsche and Heidegger argue for the interchangeability of "Wert" and "Sinn" in this regard and so the tensions we see inherent in nihilism and metaphysics are also present in hermeneutics as such.

56. Consider also *N* II, 67, 89.

57. "Affect: the blindly inciting attack. Passion: the clear-sighted gathering extension into being" ("Affekt: der blindlings aufregende Anfall. Leidenschaft: der hellsichtig sammelnde Ausgriff in das Seiende"; *N* I, 59).

58. Heidegger refers to the paradox of the "Beständigung des Bestandlosen."

59. Given the historical context of Heidegger's interpretation, it is, of course, significant that he masks the powerful analysis of the disastrous and yet self-overcoming acts of human willing in a reified rhetoric of *Seinsgeschichte.* In this way he covers his own responsibility as a human agent for the disastrous acts

of Nazi willing and the necessary acts of overcoming (resistance) that needed to be performed.

60. I would read this as Heidegger's version of the dialectical determination between reason/intellect and will that we saw in chapter 1.

61. Note the phrase that Gadamer paraphrases; since the will is involved here we feel justified in seeing it in Gadamer as well.

62. On the role of names, see *G*, 45–48. Here we see the opposition that Derrida so often makes central to his deconstructions, namely the pure thought beyond all experience on the one hand and the name on the other.

63. We see the same fundamental ambivalence in the following exchange:

> R[esearcher]: Accordingly, *Gelassenheit* lies—to the extent that one can speak here of lying—beyond the distinction between activity and passivity. . . .
>
> S[cholar]: . . . because *Gelassenheit* does not belong to the sphere of the will.
>
> F[orscher]: Demnach liegt die Gelassenheit, falls man hier von einem Liegen sprechen darf, außerhalb der Unterscheidung von Aktivität und Passivität . . .
>
> G[elehrter]: weil die Gelassenheit nicht in den Bereich des Willens gehört. (*G*, 33)

And yet as we have seen, perhaps the best way to conceive of the will is to see it precisely as beyond—and both—active and passive.

64. Recall Lacan's formulation of the radically ambivalent "will" of desire, the nolens volens.

CONCLUSION

1. See Eve Kosofsky Sedgwick, *Epistemology of the Closet* (Berkeley: University of California Press, 1990) and her working paper on the will and addiction.

2. Note that in the binaries and hierarchies just listed, the stresses often contradict each other. But such contradictions are often encountered and reveal the need for a richer conceptualization.

3. Søren Kierkegaard, *The Sickness unto Death: A Christian Psychological Exposition for Upbuilding and Awakening,* trans. Howard V. Hong and Edna H. Hong (Princeton: Princeton University Press, 1980), 13f.

4. Allison M. Jaggar, "Feminist Ethics: Some Issues for the Nineties," in *Feminism, Vol II. Schools of Thought in Politics,* ed. Susan Moller Okin and Jane Mansbridge (Brookfield, Vt.: Edward Elgar Publishing, 1994), 366–67, originally in *Journal of Social Philosophy* 20, nos. 1–2 (Spring/Fall 1989): 91–107.

5. Jean Grimshaw, "Autonomy and Identity in Feminist Thinking," in *Feminist Perspectives in Philosophy,* ed. Morwenna Griffiths and Margaret Whitford (Bloomington: Indiana University Press, 1988), 106. See also her *Feminist Philosophers: Women's Perspectives on Philosophical Traditions* (Sussex: Wheatsheaf Books Ltd., 1986).

6. Here I am casting a "wider net" because a broad enough understanding of willing could help account for the paradoxes inherent *within* psychoanalysis (not the other way around). Indeed, it could be argued that much of psychoanalytic theory emerges from a reformulation (and reduction) of understandings of willing in terms of desire.

7. Mary Jeanne Larrabee, ed., *An Ethic of Care: Feminist and Interdisciplinary Perspectives* (New York: Routledge, 1993). She provides a good overview of the different positions that have been adopted in the debate.

8. Consider Butler's *Gender Trouble.* She quotes Haar on Nietzsche (21); see also her discussion of Foucault (124). In her more recent work, *The Psychic Life of Power: Theories in Subjection* (Stanford: Stanford University Press, 1997), she does recognize in Nietzsche's analysis of will a more complex phenomenon: "the formative and fabricating dimension of psychic life, which travels under the name of 'will,' and which is usually associated with a restrictively aesthetic domain, proves central to refashioning the normative shackles that no subject can do without, but which no subject is condemned to repeat in exactly the same way" (64f).

9. Paul Benson, "Feminist Second Thoughts about Free Agency," *Hypathia* 5, no. 3 (Fall 1990): 47–64.

10. See also my "Queering the Will," *Symploke* 3, no. 1 (1995): 7–28, for a discussion of a radical ambivalence associated with the will in modern discourses concerning (homo)sexuality.

11. Drucilla Cornell, *Beyond Accommodation: Ethical Feminism, Deconstruction, and the Law* (New York: Routledge, 1985), 199.

12. Luce Irigaray, *An Ethics of Sexual Difference,* trans. Carolyn Burke and Gillian C. Gill (Ithaca: Cornell University Press, 1993), 93.

13. Other places in ethics and the law where a conception of the will is necessary would be the issues of rape, pornography, and sexual harassment.

14. Rosi Braidotti, *Nomadic Subjects: Embodiment and Sexual Difference in Contemporary Feminist Theory* (New York: Columbia University Press, 1994), 113.

15. Consider Brownmiller on rape in *Against Our Will: Men, Women, and Rape* (New York: Simon and Schuster, 1975).

16. Simone de Beauvoir, *The Second Sex,* trans. H. M. Parshley (1949; reprint, New York: Vintage, 1974), 665f.

17. See Hannah Arendt on the temporality of willing.

18. Michael Warner, ed. *Fear of a Queer Planet: Queer Politics and Social Theory* (Minneapolis: University of Minnesota Press, 1993), xviiif.

19. See my "Queering the Will." For a more historical perspective, see my essay: "Abulia: Sexuality and Diseases of the Will in the Late Nineteenth Century," *Genders,* no. 6 (Fall 1989): 102–24.

20. Gayle Rubin, "From Perversity to Diversity." Paper delivered at the University of California, Irvine, February, 1995.

21. For a more extended argument, see my essay: "Nietzsche's 'Will to Power': Politics beyond (Hegelian) Recognition," *New German Critique* (Summer 1998): 133–63.

22. Other key words are "character" and "identity," each with roots as well in conceptualizations of will. A recent example is the way Etienne Balibar uses the term in the course of his summary of the situation in Algeria: "that independent Algeria made assimilating the 'Bebers' to 'Arbnes' the key test of the nation's will in its struggle with the multicultural heritage of colonization" (53). Etienne

Balibar and Immanuel Wallerstein, *Race, Nation, Class: Ambiguous Identities,* trans. Chris Turner (London: Verso, 1992).

23. A third voice in this conversation would have to be Marx. Where Hegel sees the social developing like self-consciousness and Nietzsche focuses on the affects, Marx stresses *praxis* and *production* as the model for willed human activity.

24. See Mark Warrren's *Nietzsche and Political Thought* (Cambridge: MIT Press, 1988), for a discussion of Nietzsche in relation to postmodern politics. The concept of the will, however, plays little role there.

25. I refer here to his and Immanuel Wallerstein's essay, "Citizen Subject," in *Who Comes after the Subject?* ed. Eduardo Cadava et al. (New York: Routledge, 1991), 33–57.

26. This argument would allow us to interpret Gramsci fruitfully. See esp. Antonio Gramsci, "The Study of Philosophy" from *Selections from the Prison Notebooks,* ed. and trans. Quintin Hoare and Geoffrey Nowell Smith (New York: International Publishers, 1971), 333–37.

Bibliography

Adorno, Theodor. *Negative Dialektik.* 1966. Reprint. Frankfurt a.M.: Suhrkamp, 1982.

———, and Max Horkheimer. 1944. Reprint. *Dialektik der Aufklärung: Philosophische Fragmente.* Frankfurt a.M.: Fischer, 1989.

Arac, Jonathan. "The Function of Foucault at the Present Time." *Humanities and Society* 3, no. 1 (Winter 1980): 73–86.

Arendt, Hannah. *The Life of the Mind.* Vol. 2, *Willing.* New York: Harcourt Brace Jovanovich, 1978

Armour, Leslie. *Logic and Reality: An Investigation into the Idea of a Dialectical System.* Assen: Van Gorcum, 1972.

Baldwin, James. *Dictionary of Philosophy and Psychology.* 3 vols. New York: Macmillan, 1905–11.

Balibar, Etienne, and Immanuel Wallerstein. "Citizen Subject." In *Who Comes after the Subject?* edited by Eduardo Cadava et al. New York: Routledge, 1991.

———. *Race, Nation, Class: Ambiguous Identities.* Translated by Chris Turner. London: Verso, 1992.

Beauvoir, Simone de. *The Second Sex.* Translated by H. M. Parshley. 1949. Reprint. New York: Vintage, 1974.

Behler, Ernst. "Deconstruction vs. Hermeneutics: Derrida and Gadamer on Text and Interpretation." *Southern Humanities Review* 21, no. 3 (1987): 201–30.

———. *Derrida-Nietzsche/Nietzsche-Derrida.* Munich: Ferdinand Schöningh, 1988.

———, and Jochen Hörisch, eds. *Aktualität der Frühromantik.* Paderborn: Ferdinand Schöningh, 1987.

Benson, Paul. "Feminist Second Thoughts about Free Agency." *Hypathia* 5, no. 3 (Fall 1990): 47–64.

Berofsky, Bernard, ed. *Free Will and Determinism.* New York: Harper and Row, 1966.

Bloch, Ernst. *Subjekt-Objekt: Erläuterungen zu Hegel.* Frankfurt a.M: Suhrkamp, 1971.

Blondel, Eric. *Nietzsche: The Body and Culture. Philosophy as a Philological Genealogy.* Translated by Sean Hand. Stanford: Stanford University Press, 1991.

Bourdieu, Pierre. *Outline of a Theory of Practice.* Translated by Richard Nice. Cambridge: Cambridge University Press, 1977.

Bowie, Andrew. *Schelling and Modern European Philosophy: An Introduction.* New York: Routledge, 1993.

Braidotti, Rosi. *Nomadic Subjects: Embodiment and Sexual Difference in Contemporary Feminist Theory.* New York: Columbia University Press, 1994.

Brownmiller, Susan. *Against Our Will: Men, Women, and Rape.* New York: Simon and Schuster, 1975.

Bubner, Rüdiger. "Dialog und Dialektik oder Plato und Hegel." In *Zur Sache der Dialektik.* Stuttgart: Reclam, 1980.

Butler, Judith. *Bodies That Matter: On the Discursive Limits of "Sex."* New York: Routledge, 1993.

―――. "Burning Acts: Injurious Speech." In *Deconstruction is/in America: A New Sense of the Political,* edited by Anselm Haverkamp. New York: New York University Press, 1995.

―――. *Gender Trouble: Feminism and the Subversion of Identity.* New York: Routledge, 1990.

―――. *The Psychic Life of Power: Theories in Subjection.* Stanford: Stanford University Press, 1997.

Cassirer,Ernst. *The Philosophy of the Enlightenment.* Translated by Fritz C. A. Koelin and James P. Pettegrove. Boston: Beacon Press, 1955.

Cohen, Hermann. *System der Philosophie, erster Teil: Logik der reinen Erkenntnis.* 1914. Reprint. Berlin: Bruno Cassirer Verlag, 1922.

Copleston, Frederick, S. J. *A History of Philosophy.* 9 vols. Westminster, Md.: Newman Bookshop, 1946–75.

Cornell, Drucilla. *Beyond Accommodation: Ethical Feminism, Deconstruction, and the Law.* New York: Routledge, 1985.

Cottingham, John G. "The Intellect, the Will, and the Passions: Spinoza's Critique of Descartes." *Journal of the History of Philosophy* 26, no. 2 (Apr. 1988): 239–57.

Curley, E. M. "Descartes, Spinoza and the Ethics of Belief." In *Spinoza: Essays in Interpretation,* edited by E. Freeman and M. Mandelbaum. LaSalle, Ill.: Open Court, 1975.

Davidson, Donald. *Essays on Actions and Events.* New York: Oxford University Press, 1980.

―――, and Patrick Suppes. *Decision Making: An Experimental Approach.* Westport, Conn.: Greenwood Press, 1977.

Deleuze, Gilles. *Nietzsche and Philosophy.* Translated by Hugh Tomlinson. 1962. Reprint. New York: Columbia University Press, 1983.

Derrida, Jacques. *Force de Loi: Le Fondement mystique de l'autorité.* Paris: Galilee, 1994.

―――. *Of Spirit: Heidegger and the Question.* Translated by Geoffrey Bennington and Rachel Bowlby. Chicago: University of Chicago Press, 1991.

―――. "Otobiographies: The Teaching of Nietzsche and the Politics of the Proper Name." In *The Ear of the Other: Otobiography, Transference, Translation,* edited by Christie McDonald and translated by Avital Ronell. Lincoln: University of Nebraska Press, 1988.

————. "Interpreting Signatures (Nietzsche/Heidegger): Two Questions." In *Dialogue and Deconstruction: The Gadamer-Derrida Encounter,* edited by Diane P. Michelfelder and Richard E. Palmer. Albany: State University of New York Press, 1989.

————. *Spurs/Eperons: Nietzsche's Styles.* Translated by Barbara Harlow. Chicago: University of Chicago Press, 1979.

————. *Heidegger et la Question* (including "Geschlecht"). Paris: Flammarion, 1990.

Diderot, et al. *Encyclopédie: Selections.* Translated by Nelly S. Hoyt and Thomas Cassirer. Indianapolis: Bobbs-Merrill, 1965.

Dihle, Albrecht. *The Theory of Will in Classical Antiquity.* Berkeley: University of California Press, 1982.

Dreyfus, Hubert L., and Paul Rabinow. *Michel Foucault: Beyond Structuralism and Hermeneutics.* Chicago: University of Chicago Press, 1983.

Duns Scotus. *Duns Scotus on the Will and Morality.* Selected, translated, and introduced by Allan B. Wolter, O. F. M. Washington, D.C.: The Catholic University of America Press, 1986.

Eagleton, Terry. *Ideology.* New York: Verso, 1991.

Eisler, Rudolf. *Wörterbuch der philosophischen Begriffe.* 4th ed. Berlin: Mittler und Sohn, 1930.

Forget, Philippe, ed. *Text und Interpretation: Deutsch-französische Debatte.* Munich: Wilhelm Fink, 1984.

Foucault, Michel. *The Archaelogy of Knowledge and the Discourse on Language.* Pantheon: New York, 1972.

————. *Discipline and Punish: The Birth of the Prison.* New York: Vintage, 1979.

————. *The History of Sexuality.* Vol. 1, *An Introduction.* Vintage: New York, 1980.

————. *Language, Counter-Memory, Practice. Selected Essays and Interviews.* Edited by Donald F. Bouchard. Ithaca: Cornell University Press, 1977.

————. *Politics, Philosophy, Culture. Interviews and Other Writings, 1977–1984.* Edited by Lawrence D. Kritzman. New York: Routledge, 1988.

————. *Power/Knowledge. Selected Interviews and Other Writings, 1972–1977.* Edited by Colin Gordon. New York: Pantheon, 1980.

————. *The Use of Pleasure* Vol. 2, *The History of Sexuality.* New York: Vintage, 1986.

Frank, Manfred. *Das individuelle Allgemeine: Textstrukturierung und Textinterpretation nach Schleiermacher.* Frankfurt a.M.: Suhrkamp, 1977.

————. *Der kommende Gott: Vorlesungen über die neue Mythologie.* Frankfurt a.M.: Suhrkamp, 1982.

————. *Selbstbewußtsein und Selbsterkenntnis: Essays zur analytischen Philosophie der Subjektivität.* Stuttgart: Reclam, 1991.

————, and Gerhard Kurz, eds. *Materialien zu Schellings philosophischen Anfängen.* Frankfurt a.M.: Suhrkamp, 1975.

————. *Was ist Neostrukturalismus?* Frankfurt a.M: Suhrkamp, 1983.

Friedman, R. Z. "Hypocrisy and the Highest Good: Hegel on Kant's Transition from Morality to Religion." *Journal of the History of Philosophy* 24, no. 4 (Oct. 1986): 503–22.

Gadamer, Hans-Georg. *"Destruktion* and Deconstruction."* In *Dialogue and Deconstruction: The Gadamer-Derrida Encounter,* edited by Diane P. Michelfelder and Richard E. Palmer. Albany: State University of New York Press, 1989.

———. *Gesammelte Werke. Hermeneutik II. Wahrheit und Methode. Ergänzungen.* Tübingen: J. C. B. Mohr, 1985.

———. "Hegel und die antike Dialektik." In *Gesammelte Werke.* Vol. 3, *Neuere Philosophie I.* Tübingen: J. C. B. Mohr, 1987.

———. *The Idea of the Good in Platonic-Aristotelian Philosophy.* Translated by P. Christopher Smith. New Haven: Yale University Press, 1986.

———. *Wahrheit und Methode: Grundzüge einer philosophischen Hermeneutik,* 2d ed. Tübingen: J. C. B. Mohr, 1965.

Graeser, Andreas. *Die Philosophie der Antike 2. Sophistik und Sokratik, Plato und Aristoteles.* Vol. 2, *Geschichte der Philosophie.* Edited by Wolfgang Röd. Munich: Beck, 1983.

Gramsci, Antonio. "The Study of Philosophy." In *Selections from the Prison Notebooks,* edited and translated by Quintin Hoare and Geoffrey Nowell Smith. New York: International Publishers, 1971.

Grimshaw, Jean. "Autonomy and Identity in Feminist Thinking." In *Feminist Perspectives in Philosophy,* edited by Morwenna Griffiths and Margaret Whitford. Bloomington: Indiana University Press, 1988.

———. *Feminist Philosophers: Women's Perspectives on Philosophical Traditions.* Sussex: Wheatsheaf Books Ltd., 1986.

Habermas, Jürgen. *Erkenntnis und Interesse.* Frankfurt a.M.: Suhrkamp, 1988.

———. "Philosophie als Platzhalter und Interpret." In *Moralbewußtsein und kommunikatives Handeln.* Frankfurt a.M.: Suhrkamp, 1983.

———. *Der philosophische Diskurs der Moderne.* Frankfurt a.M.: Suhrkamp, 1989.

———. *Theorie des kommunikativen Handelns.* Frankfurt a.M.: Suhrkamp, 1981.

———. "Treffen Hegels Einwände gegen Kant auch auf die Diskursethik zu?" In *Erläuterungen zur Diskursethik.* Frankfurt a.M.: Suhrkamp, 1991.

———. "Volkssouveränität als Verfahren. Ein normativer Begriff der Öffentlichkeit." In *Die Moderne—ein unvollendetes Projekt: Philosophisch-politische Aufsätze 1977–1992.* Leipzig: Reclam, 1992.

Hamacher, Werner. "Pleroma—zu Genesis und Struktur einer dialektischen Hermeneutik bei Hegel." In Hegel, *Der Geist des Christentums: Schriften, 1796–1800.* Berlin: Ullstein, 1978.

Hare, Richard M. *Essays in Ethical Theory.* Oxford: Clarendon Press, 1989.

———. *Freedom and Reason.* Oxford: Clarendon Press, 1963.

Hegel, Georg Friedrich Wilhelm. *Phänomenologie des Geistes.* Vol. 3, Theorie Werkausgabe. Frankfurt a.M.: Suhrkamp, 1977.

———. *Enzyklopädie der philosophischen Wissenschaften im Grundrisse,* Theorie Werkausgabe, vols. 8, 9, 10. Frankfurt a.M.: Suhrkamp, 1970.

———. *Grundlinien der Philosophie des Rechts oder Naturrecht und Staatswissenschaft im Grundrisse.* Theorie Werkausgabe, vol. 7. Frankfurt a.M.: Suhrkamp, 1970.

Heidegger, Martin. *Gelassenheit.* Pfullingen: Neske, 1959.

———. *Nietzsche.* Vols. I and II. Pfullingen: Neske, 1961.

Hirschberger, Johannes. *Geschichte der Philosophie*. Vol. 1, *Altertum und Mittlealter.* Freiburg im Breisgau: Herder, 1976.

Hösle, Vittorio. *Hegels System. Der Idealismus der Subjektivität und das Problem der Intersubjektivität.* 2 vols. Hamburg: Meiner, 1987.

Höffe, Otfried, ed. "Determination." In *Lexikon der Ethik.* München: Beck, 1997.

Honderich, Ted. *How Free Are You? The Determinism Problem.* New York: Oxford University Press, 1993.

Hosenfelder, Malte. *Die Philosophie der Antike 3. Stoa, Epikurismus und Skepsis.* In *Geschichte der Philosophie,* edited by Wolfgang Röd. Munich: Beck, 1985.

Houlgate, Stephen. *Hegel, Nietzsche and the Criticism of Metaphysics.* New York: Cambridge University Press, 1986.

Hume, David. *Enquiries Concerning Human Understanding and Concerning the Principles of Morals.* Oxford: Clarendon Press, 1975.

Irigaray, Luce. *An Ethics of Sexual Difference.* Translated by Carolyn Burke and Gillian C. Gill. Ithaca: Cornell University Press, 1993.

Jaggar, Allison M "Feminist Ethics: Some Issues for the Nineties." In *Feminism.* Vol. 2, *Schools of Thought in Politics,* edited by Susan Moller Okin and Jane Mansbridge. Brookfield, Vt.: Edward Elgar Publishing, 1994. Originally in *Journal of Social Philosophy* 20, nos. 1–2 (Spring/Fall 1989): 91–107.

Jonas, Hans. *Macht oder Ohnmancht der Subjektivität: Das Leib-Seele-Problem im Vorfeld des Prinzips Verantwortung.* Frankfurt a.M.: Suhrkamp, 1987.

Jones, W. T. "Rousseau's General Will and the Problem of Consent." *Journal of the History of Philosophy* 25, no. 1 (Jan. 1987): 105–30.

Kant, Immanuel. *Grundlegung zur Metaphysik der Sitten,* edited by Karl Vorländer. Hamburg: Felix Meiner, 1965.

———. *Kritik der praktischen Vernunft.* Vol. 5, Akademie-Textausgabe. Berlin: Walter de Gruyter, 1968.

———. *Kritik der reinen Vernunft* (Nach der ersten und zweiten Original-Ausgabe). Hamburg: Felix Meiner, 1956.

———. *"Was ist Aufklärung?" Aufsätze zur Geschichte und Philosophie.* Edited by Jürgen Zehbe. Göttingen: Vandenhoeck und Ruprecht, 1985.

Kaufmann, Walter. *Nietzsche: Philosopher, Psychologist, Antichrist.* Princeton: Princeton University Press, 1950.

Kenny, Anthony. "Descartes on the Will." In *Cartesian Studies.* Oxford: Blackwell, 1972.

Kierkegaard, Søren. *The Sickness unto Death: A Christian Psychological Exposition for Upbuilding and Awakening.* Translated by Howard V. Hong and Edna H. Hong. Princeton: Princeton University Press, 1980.

Kondylis, Panajotis. *Die Aufklärung im Rahmen des neuzeitlichen Rationalismus.* Stuttgart: Klett-Cotta, 1981.

———. *Die Entstehung der Dialektik: Eine Analyse der geistigen Entwicklung von Hölderlin, Schelling und Hegel bis 1802.* Stuttgart: Klett-Cotta, 1979.

Koselleck, Rainer. *Kritik und Krise: Eine Studie zur Pathogenese der burgerlichen Welt.* Frankfurt a.M.: Suhrkamp, 1976.

Krings, Hermann, Hans Michael Baumgartner, and Christoph Wild, eds. *Handbuch philosophischer Grundbegriffe.* Munich: Kösel-Verlag, 1974.

Kunneman, Harry, and Hent de Vries, eds. *Enlightenments: Encounters between Critical Theory and Contemporary French Thought.* Kampen, Netherlands: Kok Pharos, 1993.

Lacan, Jacques. "The Agency of the Letter in the Unconscious." In *Ecrits: A Selection.* Translated by Alan Sheridan. New York: Norton, 1977.

——. *The Four Fundamental Concepts of Psycho-Analysis.* Edited by Jacques-Alain Miller. Translated by Alan Sheridan. New York: W. W. Norton, 1978.

——. "God and the Jouissance of The Woman." In *Feminine Sexuality.* New York: Norton, 1985.

——. "Kant with Sade." Translated by James B. Swenson, Jr. *October* 51 (Winter 1989): 55–104. Originally published as "Kant avec Sade" in *Ecrits II*, Paris: Editions du Seuil, 1971.

——. *The Seminar of Jacques Lacan: Book VII. The Ethics of Psychoanalysis 1959–1960.* Edited by Jacques-Alain Miller. Translated by Dennis Porter. New York: Norton, 1992.

Larrabee, Mary Jeanne, ed. *An Ethic of Care: Feminist and Interdisciplinary Perspectives.* New York: Routledge, 1993.

Lehrer, Keith, ed. *Freedom and Determinism.* New York: Random House, 1966.

Lemert, Charles C., and Garth Gillan. *Michel Foucault: Social Theory and Transgression.* New York: Columbia University Press, 1982.

Levinas, Emmanuel. *Totality and Infinity: An Essay on Exteriority.* Translated by Alphonso Lingis. Pittsburgh: Duquesne University Press, 1969.

Locke, John. *An Essay Concerning Human Understanding.* Oxford: Clarendon Press, 1979.

Magnus, Bernd. "Nietzsche and Postmodern Criticism." *Nietzsche-Studien* 18 (1989): 301–16.

Mahon, Michael. *Foucault's Nietzschean Genealogy: Truth, Power, and the Subject.* Albany: State University of New York Press, 1992.

Mason, Richard V. "Spinoza on the Causality of Individuals," *Journal of the History of Philosophy* 24, no. 2 (Apr. 1986): 197–210.

McCarthy, John A. *Crossing Boundaries: A Theory and History of Essay Writing in German 1680–1815.* Philadelphia: University of Pennsylvania Press, 1989.

McNay, Lois. *Foucault and Feminism: Power, Gender and the Self.* Boston: Northeastern University Press, 1992.

Megill, Allan. "Foucault, Structuralism, and the Ends of History." *Journal of Modern History* 51 (Sept. 1979): 451–503.

Melden, A. I. *Free Action.* London: Routledge and Kegan Paul; New York: Humanities Press, 1961.

Michelfelder, Diane P., and Richard E. Palmer, eds. *Dialogue and Deconstruction: The Gadamer-Derrida Encounter.* Albany: State University of New York Press, 1989.

Mueller, Gustav E. *Dialectic: A Way into and within Philosophy.* New York: Bookman Associates, 1953.

——. *The Interplay of Opposites: A Dialectical Ontology.* New York: Bookman Associates, 1956.

Nathan, N. M. L. *Will and World: A Study in Metaphysics.* Oxford: Clarendon Press, 1992.

Neuhouser, Frederick. *Fichte's Theory of Subjectivity.* New York: Cambridge University Press, 1990.

Nietzsche, Friedrich. *Werke.* Edited by Karl Schlechta. 3 vols. Frankfurt a.M.: Ullstein, 1969.

———. *Kritische Studienausgabe.* Edited by Giorgio Colli and Mazzino Montinari. Berlin: Deutscher Taschenbuch Verlag/de Gruyter, 1988.

Oberdiek, Hans. "Der Wille." In *An Encyclopedia of Philosophy,* edited by G. H. R. Parkinson. London: Routledge, 1988.

Oelmüller, Willi. "Aufklärung als Prozeß von Traditionskritik und Traditionsbewahrung." In *Erforschung der deutschen Aufklärung,* edited by Peter Pütz. Verlagsgruppe Athenäum, Hain, Scriptor, Hanstein: Königstein/Ts., 1980.

Planck, Max. "Kausalgesetz und Willensfreiheit," and "Vom Wesen der Willensfreiheit." In *Vom Wesen der Willensfreiheit und andere Vorträge.* Frankfurt a.M.: Fischer Taschenbuch Verlag, 1990.

Postigliola, Alberto. "De Malebranche à Rousseau: Les Apories de la Volonté Générale et la Revanche du 'Raissonneur Violent.'" *Annales de la Société Jean-Jacques Rousseau.* Vol. 39. Geneva: Chez A. Jullien, 1980.

Probyn, Elsbeth. *Sexing the Self. Gendered Positions in Cultural Studies.* New York: Routledge, 1993.

Rajchman, John. *Michel Foucault: The Freedom of Philosophy.* New York: Columbia University Press, 1985.

———. "Nietzsche, Foucault, and the Anarchism of Power." *Semiotext(e)* 3 (1978): 96–107.

Readings, Bill. *The University in Ruins.* Cambridge: Harvard University Press, 1996.

Ricoeur, Paul. *Freedom and Nature: The Voluntary and the Involuntary.* Translated by Erazim V. Kohak. Evanston, Ill.: Northwestern University Press, 1966.

Riley, Patrick. *The General Will before Rousseau. The Transformation of the Divine into the Civic.* Studies in Moral, Political and Legal Philosophy. Princeton: Princeton University Press, 1986.

———. *Will and Political Legitimacy: A Critical Exposition of Social Contract Theory in Hobbes, Locke, Rousseau, Kant, and Hegel.* Cambridge: Harvard University Press, 1982.

Roche, Mark William. *Tragedy and Comedy: A Systematic Study and a Critique of Hegel.* Albany: State University of New York Press, 1998.

Rorty, Richard. "Deconstruction and Circumvention." *Critical Inquiry* 11, no. 1 (1984): 1–24.

Röttges, Heinz. *Nietzsche und die Dialektik der Aufklärung.* Berlin, New York: Walter de Gruyter, 1972.

Rowe, William L. "Causality and Free Will in the Controversy between Collins and Clarke." *Journal of the History of Philosophy* 25, no. 1 (Jan. 1987): 51–67.

Rubin, Gayle. "From Perversity to Diversity." Paper delivered at the University of California, Irvine, February 1995.

———. "Thinking Sex: Notes for a Radical Theory of the Politics of Sexuality." In *Pleasure and Danger,* edited by Carole S. Vance. New York: Routledge, 1984.

Ryle, Gilbert. *The Concept of the Mind.* London and New York: Hutchinson, 1949.

Sade, Marquis de. *Justine, Philosophy in the Bedroom, and Other Writings.* Edited and translated by Richard Seaver and Austryn Wainhouse. New York: Grove Weidenfeld, 1965.

Schelling, F. W. J. *Philosophische Untersuchungen über das Wesen der menschlichen Freiheit und die damit zusammenhängenden Gegenstände.* Frankfurt a.M.: Suhrkamp, 1988. Translated by James Gutmann and published as *Philosophical Inquiries into the Nature of Human Freedom.* La Salle, Ill.: Open Court, 1992.

Schöpf, Alfred. "Wille." In *Handbuch philosophischer Grundbegriffe,* edited by Hermann Krings, Hans Michael Baumgartner, and Christoph Wild. Munich: Kösel-Verlag, 1973–74.

Schopenhauer, Arthur. *Zürcher Ausgabe: Werke in zehn Bänden.* 10 vols. Zurich: Diogenes Verlag, 1977.

Schwab, Martin. Introduction to the English translation. In Manfred Frank, *What is Neostructuralism?* Minneapolis: University of Minnesota Press, 1988.

Sedgwick, Eve Kosofsky. "Addictions of the Will." Working paper of the Princeton Women's Studies Group.

———. *Epistemology of the Closet.* Berkeley: University of California Press, 1990.

———. "Gender Criticism." In *Redrawing the Boundaries: The Transformation of English and American Literary Studies,* edited by Stephen Greenblatt and Giles Gunn. New York: The Modern Language Association of America, 1992.

Sedgwick, Sally. "Hegel's Critique of the Subjective Idealism of Kant's Ethics." *Journal of the History of Philosophy* 26, no. 1 (Jan. 1988): 89–105.

Sheridan, Alan. *Michel Foucault: The Will to Truth.* London and New York: Routledge, 1980.

Shklar, Judith N. "General Will." In *Dictionary of the History of Ideas,* edited by Philip D. Wiener. New York: Charles Scribner's Sons, 1973.

Smith, John H. "Abulia: Sexuality and the Diseases of the Will in the Late Nineteenth Century." *Genders,* no. 6 (Fall 1989): 102–24.

———. "Nietzsche's 'Will to Power': Politics beyond (Hegelian) Recognition." *New German Critique* (Summer 1998): 133–63.

———. "Queering the Will." *Symploke* 3, no. 1 (1995): 7–28.

———. *The Spirit and Its Letter: Traces of Rhetoric in Hegel's Philosophy of Bildung.* Ithaca: Cornell University Press, 1988.

———. "Of Spirit(s) and Will(s)." In *Hegel after Derrida,* edited by Stuart Barnett. New York: Routledge, 1998.

———. "The 'Transcendance' of the Individual." *Diacritics* 19, no. 2 (1989): 80–98.

Spinoza, Baruch. *The Ethics and Selected Letters.* Translated by Samuel Shirley. Indianapolis: Hacket, 1982.

Stalley, R. F. "The Will in Hume's Treatise." *Journal of the History of Philosophy* 24, no. 1 (Jan. 1986): 41–53.

Stenzel, Julius. *Studien zur Entwicklung der platonischen Dialektik von Sokrates zu Aristoteles.* Darmstadt: Wissenschaftliche Buchgesellschaft, 1961.

Theunissen, Michael. *Der Andere: Studien zur Sozialontologie der Gegenwart.* Berlin and New York: Walter de Gruyter, 1977.

Vailati, Emilio. "Leibniz on Locke on Weakness of Will." *Journal of the History of Philosophy* 28, no. 2 (Apr. 1990): 213–28.

Verene, Donald Phillip. *Hegel's Recolection: A Study of Images in the "Phenomenology of Spirit."* Albany: State University of New York Press, 1985.

Warren, Mark. *Nietzsche and Political Thought.* Cambridge: MIT Press, 1988.

Warner, Michael, ed. *Fear of a Queer Planet: Queer Politics and Social Theory.* Minneapolis: University of Minnesota Press, 1993.

Watson, Gary, ed. *Free Will.* New York: Oxford University Press, 1982.

Wentzel, Manfred. *Dialektik als Ontolgie auf der Basis selbstreflexiver Erkenntniskritik: Neue Grundlegung einer "Wissenschaft der Erfahrung des Bewußtseins" und Prolegomena zu einer Dialektik in systematischer Absicht.* Freiburg: Alber, 1986.

White, Morton. *Free Will: A Holistic View.* Princeton: Princeton University Press, 1993.

Wilden, Anthony. *The Language of the Self: The Function of Language in Psychoanalysis.* Baltimore: Johns Hopkins University Press, 1968.

Williams, B. A. O. "Freedom and the Will." In D. F. Pears, *Freedom and the Will.* London: MacMillan, 1965.

Wolf, Susan. *Freedom within Reason.* New York: Oxford University Press, 1990.

Wood, Allen. *Hegel's Ethical Thought.* New York: Cambridge University Press, 1990.

Wood, David, ed. *Of Derrida, Heidegger, and Spirit.* Evanston, Ill.: Northwestern University Press, 1993.

Žižek, Slavoj. *Enjoy Your Symptom! Jacques Lacan in Hollywood and Out.* New York: Routledge, 1992.

———. *For they know not what they do: Enjoyment as a Political Factor.* New York: Verso, 1991.

———. *The Indivisible Remainder: An Essay on Schelling and Related Matters.* New York: Verso, 1996.

———. *The Sublime Object of Ideology.* London: Verso, 1989.

———. *Tarrying with the Negative: Kant, Hegel, and the Critique of Ideology.* Durham: Duke University Press, 1993.

Index

Adorno, 12; dialectical determination of will, 65–67; dialectic of reason and nature, 59–61; on freedom of will, 61–67; limited reading of Kant, 52–54; on Sade, 52, 54, 59–61
aestheticism: Habermas's reductive reading of Nietzsche, 96, 123; and Nietzsche, 110, 120
agency, 92; in Foucault, 105, 106–7, 109; in interpretation, 125; modern theories of, 169
akrasia (weakness of will), 22, 191–92n. 28
alienation, 71, 74
aporia, 12, 13, 21, 35, 37, 50, 52, 91, 97–98, 111, 113, 119, 121, 135, 138, 139, 141, 147, 183n. 11; of theories of power, 100–101, 115, 169
appetites, 38, 40, 41
Aquinas, 38
Arac, Jonathan, 208n. 9
Arendt: on Duns Scotus, 192–93n. 34; on Hegel, 39; and negation, 17
Aristotle, 35, 37, 41, 191–92n. 28; Heidegger on, 150
atomism: Nietzsche's criticism of, 113, 116–17
Augustine, 188n. 50

Baldwin, James: *Dictionary of Philosophy and Psychology,* 23

Balibar, Etienne, 177–78, 220n. 22
barred subject (*sujet barré*). *See* splitting of subject
Beauvoir, Simone de, 174–75
Benson, Paul, 172
binarisms: discourses about sexuality, 167–68; in Heidegger 141, 143, 146
boulesis (willing), 35, 189n. 1, 190n. 15, 191n. 24
Braidotti, Rosi, 173–74
Buridan: image of donkey, 42
Butler, Judith, 25–27, 171–72, 182n. 8, 214n. 14, 220n. 8

Cassian: Foucault on, 108
Cassirer, Ernst, 45; on Condillac, 196n. 52
categorical imperative, 69, 81, 82–83, 205n. 52
cause, 189n. 5, 61; as *causa sui,* 113–14; of desire, 68–69, 74, 87, 89, 168; and effect, 112; of freedom, 85–87, 122; in Kant, 83, 85–87; lost, 75, 79; and will, 40, 83. *See also* das Ding, objet petit a
Cicero, 188n. 2
Cohen, Hermann, 186–87n. 39, 195n. 44
Copleston, Frederick: on Aquinas,

233

Copleston (*cont.*)
  192n. 29; on Duns Scotus, 192n.
  33; on Pascal, 194n. 39
Cornell, Drucilla, 172–73
Cottingham, John: on Descartes and
  Spinoza, 197n. 66; on Spinoza,
  193n. 37
critique: Kantian notion of, 59, 202n. 18

Darwin: Nietzsche's reading of, 110,
  210n. 31
decadence: in Nietzsche, 110, 216n. 39
Declaration of Independence: Derrida
  on, 142
deconstruction: and hermeneutics,
  125–27, 141
Derrida, 12, 185n. 32; on borderline,
  143; encounter with Gadamer,
  125–26; on Heidegger, 138–41,
  145–47; on machine, 144–45;
  misunderstanding of Gadamer,
  135–36; on name, 138, 140; on
  Nietzsche, 141–45; reductive
  reading of will as fragmenting,
  144–45; willing in, 140–41
Descartes, 193n. 34, 197n. 66
desire: diagram of arc, 206n. 59; Kant's
  analysis of, 87–88; and law, 61,
  67–68, 79; Nietzsche's analysis of,
  211n. 37
determinism, 30–31, 39–43; and
  mechanistic explanations, 112–13;
  Nietzsche's critique of, 112
dialectic: and argumentation, 14, 17–18;
  definition of, 183n. 16; and dialog,
  14, 183n. 15; of nature and law in
  Lacan, 70; opposed to metaphysics,
  14, 16–17, 185n. 28; origins of, 14;
  of totalitarianism, 206n. 62
Diderot: on *volonté*, 187n. 48
differential. *See* infinitesimal
Dihle, Albrecht: on Augustine, 192n.
  32, 209n. 22; on Cicero, 188–89n.
  1; on Greek and Latin terms for

will, 190n. 15, 191n. 22; on Plato,
  191n. 25
das Ding, 68–69, 74, 203n. 34, 204n. 43
Duns Scotus, 38

Eagleton, Terry, 211n. 39
Einheit. See unity
Eisler, Rudolf: *Wörterbuch der
  philosophischen Begriffe*, 22, 34,
  35–36, 182n. 9, 190nn. 12, 19
empiricism, 11, 22, 31, 40
energeia and will, 150
Enlightenment, 52, 189n. 7, 193n.
  35, 201n. 9; dialectic of, 59–61;
  Habermas on, 95–96

fantasy, 74–75, 77–78, 204n. 39
feminism: and ethics, 171–73; and law,
  172–73; rejection of autonomous
  self, 171–72; theories of agency,
  170–75
Fichte, G., 38–39
Fichte, I. H., 36
formation of common will
  (*Willensbildung*), 123–24,
  212nn. 40, 41
Foucault, 12; agency in, 105, 106–
  7; ambivalence according to
  Habermas, 99; archeology,
  limitations of, 104; genealogy, 103;
  knowledge-power as will, 105–6;
  morphology of will to knowledge,
  102–3; power in, 98, 100–101,
  104, 209n. 17; reductionist reading
  of will as power, 92, 101; stages
  of work, 102, 107; techniques of
  power, 105; truth-power as will,
  105–6; will in, 102–9, 209n. 24;
  will to knowledge/truth, 99, 102–4,
  208–9n. 14
Frank, Manfred, 189n. 9, 216n. 33; on
  Nietzsche and Dionysos, 96
freedom, 27, 51, 56, 70; Adorno on,
  61–67, 202n. 24; Heidegger,
  152–53; Kant on, 80–81, 85–87,

89; Lacan, 75, 77; Nietzsche on, 114–16; of will, 39

free will, 194–95n. 44; and Christianity, 181n. 381; and the Good in Kant, 87; and interplay of forces, 21; and Kantian ought (*Sollen*) and Lacan, 75; Nietzsche's rejection of, 113–14; and "unfree" will, 112–16. *See also* freedom

French Revolution: Lacan on, 55

Freud, 56, 182n. 9, 188n. 55

Friedman, R. Z.: on Hegel and Kant, 193–94n. 39

Gadamer, 12; Aristotle on choice, 16; and dialectic, 183n. 15; encounter with Derrida, 125–26; and Hegel, 215n. 23; on meaning, 36–37, 127–29, 131–32, 134; on oral conversation, 128–31, 133–35; overemphasis of unity, 135; on Plato, 126, 133; on text, 128–29, 213n. 8

gap in subject, and cause of willing, 83, 86–87; closing of, 85–89, 205n. 46; and infinite judgment, 201n. 7; Kant on, 81–83, 85–87, 89; as site of will, 200n. 1

Geist (spirit), 11, 17, 19, 39, 137, 186n. 35; Derrida on Heidegger, 145–48

general will. *See volonté générale*

Gillan, Garth: on power vs. will to power, 208n. 13

Gilligan, Carol, 171

good, the highest, 87

good will, 58–59, 67, 79, 85, 165; as attitude, 130–31, 134; Derrida's interpretation of, 126, 130; and feminism, 173; in Gadamer, 126, 127–35; guarantees identity of meaning, 129; in Heidegger, 163

Graeser, Andreas, 189–90n. 11

Grimshaw, Jean, 171

Habermas, 12; aesthetic reading of Nietzsche, 96, 110; and communicative action/reason, 121–24, 207n. 3; conception of philosophy, 207n. 2; critique of concept of power, 98–99; critique of positivism, 93–94, 121–22; on Enlightenment, 95–96; on Hegel's critique of Kant, 201nn. 11, 15; on individual and collective identity, 199n. 82; interests of reason (*Vernunftinteresse*), 121–22; on Kant, 121–22; reductionist reading of Foucault, 91, 97–102; reductionist reading of Nietzsche, 91, 93–97, 123; related to Foucault and Nietzsche, 121–24

Hamacher, Werner, 213n. 8

Hegel, 39; concept of life, 19; concept of *Sittlichkeit*, 45; critique of individual will, 45; critique of Kant, 201n. 14; critique of voluntarism, 42; and dialectic, 15; dialectical sentence, 15, 203n. 32; *Philosophie des Rechts*, 177; on Spirit, 186n. 35; unhappy consciousness, 135

Heidegger, 13; analysis of willing, 156–59; dialectic of *Einheit* and *Unterschied*, 148, 160–61; *Entschlossenheit*, 164; *Gegnet*, 163; *Gelassenheit*, 161–65, 219n. 63; history of Being as willing, 154–55; history of metaphysics (*Seinsgeschichte*), 138, 148; horizon, 218n. 50; inherent dialectic of will, 147–48, 156–59; *Kehre* and will, 155–56, 217n. 46; on nihilism, 153–54, 159–61; nonwilling, 162–65; overcoming of nihilism, 160–61; on Protagoras, 151–52; on Schelling, 217n. 42; unity in, 139–40; on will and value, 149–50; willing vs. Being, 149; willing vs. Thinking, 162–65

hermeneutics: art of, 132; and
deconstruction, 125–27, 141;
theory of meaning, 36–37, 127–35
Hirschberger, Johannes: on Aristotle,
196n. 59; on Augustine, 192n.
32; on Christian view of free will,
196–97n. 61; on Plato, 191n. 25
Hobbes, 22, 40
Höffe, Otfried, 200n. 1
holy (*heilig*): Kant, 84
Honderich, Ted, 189n. 4
Horkheimer, Max, 200n. 3
Hosenfelder, Malte: on Hellenistic
ethics, 188n. 52
Hösle, Vittorio: on Hegel, 199n. 80
Houlgate, Stephen, 185n. 28
Hume, 181n. 1
Hurley, Robert, 106

Idealism, 35, 38–39
identity: Derrida on Nietzsche's,
143–44; of meaning, 128–32, 138;
politics, 175–76; reductive in Kant,
63, 89; of willing, 30
in-between (*Inzwischen*): and Adorno,
67; and Foucault, 107, 109; and
Gadamer, 215n. 22; and Kant,
83–84, 85; and Levinas, 23; will
as, 20, 33, 170. *See also* Derrida,
on borderline
inclination (*Neigung*), 35
infinitesimal: and ethical energy, 20,
186n. 39; and willing, 20, 206n. 60
innovation, 33; and will to power,
110–11
intellect. *See* reason
intelligible character: Adorno on, 66;
Kant on, 81
Irigaray, Luce, 173–74
irrationality: of willing, 30, 203n. 26

Jacobi, Friedrich, 38
Jaggar, Alison, 170–71
James, William, 190n. 19
Jonas, Hans, 20

Jones, W. T.: on general will, 199n. 79
jouissance: and "holy" being in Kant,
84; right to, 55, 69, 79; Sadian, 76,
78; will-to, 75, 77, 84

Kant, 13, 22; analysis of desire, 87–88;
antinomy between freedom and
necessity, 80; dialectical reading
of, 51, 79–80; *Ding an sich,* 80,
204n. 47; *gut* vs. *wohl,* 56, 57, 87,
201n. 12; *Kritik der praktischen
Vernunft,* 50, 56, 85–87; *Kritik der
reinen Vernunft,* 80; notion of "I
think," 35, 53, 81; and Sade, 60–61,
75; synthetic approach to will,
85, 87–88; theory of motivations,
81–82; two conceptions of will,
84–88
Kierkegaard, 170
Kondylis, Panajotis: on Enlightenment,
192n. 31
Koselleck, Rainer: on general will,
199n. 79

Lacan, 12; definition of signifier,
203n. 30; on Kant, 51, 54, 56–57,
67–79; relation between Self and
Other, 71–79; on Sade, 52, 67–79;
synthetic approach to will, 58, 85,
87
law, 30, 51, 55, 56; in Derrida, 142,
212n. 2; and desire, 67–68, 79;
in Foucault, 104–5; individual's
subsumption under, 56–57; and
Nietzsche, 114
Leben. See life
Leibniz, 43–44; and life, 19
Lemert, Charles C.: on power vs. will to
power, 208n. 13
Levinas, 23, 185n. 31; on causality,
189n. 5, 195n. 46; on creativity,
191n. 20; on Idealism, 193n. 38,
196n. 58
liberum arbitrium indifferentiae (free
will), 41–42, 114, 192n. 29

life: and Derrida, 141; and evolution, 19, 186n. 36; and Heidegger, 158; and Nietzsche, 111, 116–17; and willing, 19, 111
Locke, 40, 197n. 68

Mach, Ernst, 41
Mahon, Michael, 210n. 27
Mann, Thomas: *Death in Venice,* 35
Mason, Richard: on Spinoza and causality, 198n. 70
mechanism. *See* determinism
metaphysics: Heidegger on, 148–65; and Nietzsche, 110, 119; as nihilism, 154; opposed to dialectic, 14, 135, 185n. 28; opposed to positivism, 20; and Schopenhauer on will, 42; of subjectivity, 12, 147, 156, 164–65, 171–72, 217n. 41; of will, 126, 130, 135, 147, 156; Žižek on Kantian, 206–7n. 63
middle space of willing. *See* in-between model of willing, 169–70
modern: and postmodern, 12, 182–83n. 10

nation, 24; subject or will of, 176–77
nationalism: theories of, 176–78
nature: dialectic with reason, 59–61, 63–64; and law, 50–52; vs. reason in Sade, 54, 55
Nazism: and Heidegger, 156, 218n. 59
negative dialectics: will as model of in Adorno, 61–67
negativity: in argument, 18; in Derrida, 216n. 38; in Hegel, 200n. 84
Neuhouser, Frederick, 38
Nietzsche, 12, 13; ambivalence according to Habermas, 94, 97, 98; concept of becoming (*Werden*), 115–20; dialectical understanding of will, 95, 110, 113–14, 116, 119, 168–69; eternal return, 211n. 38; and life, 19; and national will, 177; rejection of dualism, 113–19

nihilism, 110; Heidegger on, 153–54; Nietzsche's response to, 94, 95, 113, 114–15

Oberdiek, 40; on Plato, 190n. 12; on will and language, 190n. 17
objet petit a: definition, 204n. 37; as middle space between self and other, 73, 74; and sadist subject, 76–78; and thing-in-itself, 89
Oelmüller, Willi: on Enlightenment, 189n. 7

pantheism (*Pantheismusstreit*), 198n. 75
perversions, 71, 175, 203n. 35
phenomenology: theory of meaning, 36–37
Planck, Max: on free will, 194–95n. 44
Plato, 37, 190n. 12; and dialectic, 15; Heidegger on, 150
political will, 44
positivism, 40, and Foucault, 110; Habermas's critique of, 93 94; and Nietzsche, 110–11; opposed to metaphysics, 20
power: nondialectical, 100–101; vs. will in Foucault, 102, 104
practical reason. *See* reason, practical
presentism: in Foucault, 101, 102
proairesis (rational choice), 16, 35, 41, 189n. 1, 191n. 24
psychopathology: will in, 22

queer theory, 175–76

Rajchman, John: on will in will-to-knowledge, 107
rationalism, 41
rationality: of willing, 30, 203n. 26
Readings, Bill, 24
reason, 13; dialectic with nature, 59–61, 63–64; Habermas on, 95; and Kant, 52; vs. nature in Sade, 54; practical, 41, 51, 52, 80–81, 84, 87–88; and will, 37–39, 95–96

Ricoeur, Paul, 191n. 20
Riley, Patrick, 182n. 5, 185–86n. 34; on general will, 198–99n. 77; on Hobbes and Locke, 196n. 53
Roche, Mark, 184n. 19
Romanticism: and Foucault, 97; and Nietzsche, 96
Rorty, 183n. 14
Rose, Gilian, 217n. 41
Rousseau, 44–45
Rowe, William: on Locke, 196n. 53
Ryle, 40

Sade, 52; Adorno on, 54, 59–61; and Kant, 60–61; and will, 54, 78–79
Sadian relationship: Adorno on, 60; Lacan on, 72–73
Schelling, 39, 42–43, 44; and Derrida, 147; and dialectic, 15–16, 46; and primal disorder, 198n. 76; will as *Ursein,* 44, 64
Schiller, 35
Schopenhauer, 39, 42, 185n. 27, 190n. 13, 194nn. 41, 42, 197nn. 62–64
Schöpf, Alfred, 43; on determinism, 197n. 68
Sedgwick, Eve Kosofsky, 167–68
Sedgwick, Sally: on Hegel, 199n. 81
Seinsvergessenheit (forgetting of Being): and will, 151–53, 159–60
self-determination, 36
self-preservation: Nietzsche opposed to, 110–11, 112
separation, 74
sexuality: and will, 175–76
Smith, John H., 185n. 32, 212n. 3, 220nn. 10, 19, 21
Socrates, 16, 37
Sophists, 14–15
Spinoza, 38–39, 43, 195n. 44, 197n. 66, 198n. 70
Spirit: and letter, 127, 137, 138. *See also* Geist
splitting of subject, 60, 64, 67, 70–71; cuts (castration), 73–74; and

dialectical determination of will, 88; Kant 84, 89; sadist denial of, 76–78, 88–89. *See also* gap in subject
Stalley, R. F., 187nn. 45, 47; on Hume, 195–96n. 52
Stenzel, Julius: on rationalism in Plato and Socrates, 191n. 23
subject, 14; formation of according to Lacan, 70–75
supplement (*das Hinzutretende*): and abject, 202n. 21; in Adorno, 62–63

Theunissen, Michael, 185n. 33
thinking (*Denken*): in Heidegger, 148–65

understanding (*Verstehen, Verständigung*), 37, 129–30, 134, 214n. 20; essentially dialectical, 161
unity: deconstruction of, 137; in Heidegger, 137–41, 148; of meaning, 128–32, 138; of will, 34–37, 126

Vailati, E.: on Leibniz, 198n. 74; on Locke, 197–98n. 68
Venn diagram, 31, 71–72, 75, 143, 195n. 47, 196n. 56
Verständigung. See understanding
Verstehen. See understanding
volo (I will), 35, 39, 53–54
volonté: in Foucault, 98; in Lacan, 74, 76–77
volonté générale, 44–45, 198–99n. 77, 199n. 79
voluntarism, 30, 37, 38
voluntas, 189n. 1, 190n. 15
vouloir dire, 131, 140

wanting: ambiguity of, 50, 51, 54, 108, 127, 133, 178, 205n. 51; and good will, 131; Kant on, 84; Schelling on, 202n. 25
Warner, Michael, 175

Werden (becoming): opposed to being (*Sein*), 117; and will in Nietzsche, 115–16, 158

White, Morton, 191n. 21

will: Adorno's dialectical model, 61–67; and affect, passion, feeling, 157–58; as becoming (*Werden*), 115–20; as cause, 52–53; and Christianity, 11, 38, 41–42, 43, 108–9; as *coincidentia oppositorum*, 33, 169; collective, 30; contradictory determinations of, 29–31, 34; as dance, 119; definition of, 45–46; dialectical understanding of, 12–13, 14, 33, 46, 65, 83, 88, 92, 107, 110, 133, 174–75; as *Ding an sich*, 64, 65–66; divine, 43; and *energeia*, 150; fragmentation of, 30, 34–37, 118–19, 137–48; and Greek thought, 11, 37–38, 108–9, 191n. 22; and Hellenistic ethics, 188n. 52; history of concept, 13, 14, 18, 29–30; and identity, 27; individual, 30–31, 43–45; as intelligible character, 66; interests of reason (*Vernunftinteresse*), 121–22; at intersection of power, knowledge, pleasure, 106, 107–8; Kant's two views, 84–88; and meaning, 36–37; as middle ground or space, 31, 32, 64–65, 79, 88 (*see also* in-between); model of, 169–70; of nation or people, 24, 177–78; as practical reason, 205n. 49; as reason, 58; sadist, 75, 76, 77–79; split in Kant, 85–89; supraindividual, 43–45; unity of, 34–37, 118–19; universal, 31; as *Ursein*, 44, 64; and value, 149–50. *See also* willing

Willensbildung. *See* formation of common will

Williams, B. O., 181n. 3

willing: activity and passivity of, 21–24, 162–63, 173, 187nn. 45, 47, 48, 188n. 60; and gap in subject, 83; and life, 19; of nonwilling, 162–65, 214n. 19; and passions, 22–23, 188n. 49; and play of forces, 21; as process, 33, 46; and Sade, 54; and self-reflexivity 19–20; as "something complicated," 118, 157; and strategy in Foucault, 105; and subject/object duality, 26. *See also* will

Willkür, 22, 35–36, 41, 114, 197n. 68, 205n. 49

will to interpretation: dialectics of, 126–27, 136–37, 141–42

will to power: in Heidegger, 148–64; opposed to mere power, 110, 119; reduced to mere power, 91–92, 96–97, 99–100; and *Werden*, 119; and Western metaphysics, 150–51

will to truth: and Foucault, 99, 102–4; and Nietzsche, 119

will to understand. *See* will to interpretation

Wittgenstein, 183n. 14

Wolf, Susan, 191n. 27

Wood, Allen, 184n. 21

Žižek, Slavoj, 184 n. 21, 200n. 84, 201n. 7, 204n. 37, 206nn. 62, 63

BOOKS IN THE KRITIK: GERMAN LITERARY THEORY
AND CULTURAL STUDIES SERIES

Walter Benjamin: An Intellectual Biography, by Bernd Witte, trans. by James Rolleston, 1991

The Violent Eye: Ernst Jünger's Visions and Revisions on the European Right, by Marcus Paul Bullock, 1991

Fatherland: Novalis, Freud, and the Discipline of Romance, by Kenneth S. Calhoon, 1992

Metaphors of Knowledge: Language and Thought in Mauthner's Critique, by Elizabeth Bredeck, 1992

Laocoon's Body and the Aesthetics of Pain: Winckelmann, Lessing, Herder, Moritz, Goethe, by Simon Richter, 1992

The Critical Turn: Studies in Kant, Herder, Wittgenstein, and Contemporary Theory, by Michael Morton, 1993

Reading After Foucault: Institutions, Disciplines, and Technologies of Self in Germany, 1750–1830. Edited by Robert S. Leventhal, 1994

Bettina Brentano-von Arnim: Gender and Politics. Edited by Elke P. Frederiksen and Katherine R. Goodman, 1995

Absent Mothers and Orphaned Fathers: Narcissism and Abjection in Lessing's Aesthetic and Dramatic Production, by Susan E. Gustafson, 1995

Identity or History? Marcus Herz and the End of the Enlightenment, by Martin L. Davies, 1995

Languages of Visuality: Crossings between Science, Art, Politics, and Literature. Edited by Beate Allert, 1996

Resisting Bodies: The Negotiation of Female Agency in Twentieth-Century Women's Fiction, by Helga Druxes, 1996

Locating the Romantic Subject: Novalis with Winnicott, by Gail M. Newman, 1997

Embodying Ambiguity: Androgyny and Aesthetics from Winckelmann to Keller, by Catriona MacLeod, 1997

The Freudian Calling: Early Viennese Psychoanalysis and the Pursuit of Cultural Science, by Louis Rose, 1998

By the Rivers of Babylon: Heinrich Heine's Late Songs and Reflections, by Roger F. Cook, 1998

Reconstituting the Body Politic: Enlightenment, Public Culture, and the Invention of Aesthetic Autonomy, by Jonathan M. Hess, 1999

The School of Days: Heinrich von Kleist and the Traumas of Education, by Nancy Nobile, 1999

Walter Benjamin and the Corpus of Autobiography, by Gerhard Richter, 2000

Dialectics of the Will: Freedom, Power, and Understanding in Modern French and German Thought, by John H. Smith, 2000